C000261752

The Empire at Home

The Empire at Home

Internal Colonies and the End of Britain

James Trafford

PLUTO PRESS

First published 2021 by Pluto Press
345 Archway Road, London N6 5AA

www.plutobooks.com

British Library Cataloguing in Publication Data
A catalogue record for this book is available from the British Library

ISBN   978 0 7453 4099 9   Hardback
ISBN   978 0 7453 4100 2   Paperback
ISBN   978 1 7868 0674 1   PDF eBook
ISBN   978 1 7868 0676 5   Kindle eBook
ISBN   978 1 7868 0675 8   EPUB eBook

Typeset by Stanford DTP Services, Northampton, England

For those who struggle under cover of darkness

Contents

Preface

This book argues that as a combination of neo-imperialism and internal colonialism, the continuation of empire has been a fundamental condition of British life, politics, and economics. As formal empire was transformed into commonwealth and neo-imperial domination, Britain attempted to establish itself as a post-colonial nation. To do so required a spatio-temporal 'cut' from empire, which disavowed the violence in the world that it had terraformed. But through this post-colonial cut, the exceptionalism of a pristine island nation would be rebuilt through the redeployment of structures that had facilitated and legitimised slavery, exploitation and extermination across empire. Shaped in this context, contemporary Britain is existentially, politically, and economically grounded in a geopolitics of exploitation, extraction, and dispossession.

In part, this book attempts to think contemporary political shifts towards regained sovereignty and securitising border regimes. It is an attempt to centre the political and social machinery that is capable of holding together the proposition that Britain can't be racist since it is the most tolerant and lovely country in Europe, with the Windrush scandal, where thousands of Caribbean migrants who had lived in Britain since they were children were illegally detained, threatened with deportation, and prevented from accessing necessary healthcare.

These tensions are explicable against a backdrop of empire and its continuing modes of capitalist accumulation and subjugation. The 2016 referendum vote to leave the European Union and the election of Conservative prime minister Boris Johnson in 2019 have sedimented *explicit* shifts towards nativist nationalism. Johnson was a figurehead for the Vote Leave campaign prior to the referendum, during which he consistently denounced migrants as benefit scroungers, and claimed they have been responsible for a strained NHS and high levels of unemployment. The campaign was fueled by anti-immigrant rhetoric, perceived weaknesses at the edges of the EU, and the demonisation of freedom of movement within the Schengen zone. A critical moment in the campaign focused on the idea that Britain would soon by flooded by Muslim people and Middle Eastern refugees with the possibility of Turkey joining the EU.

They argued that 'murderers, terrorists and kidnappers from countries like Turkey could flock to Britain if it remains in the European Union', and their posters proclaimed that 'Turkey (population 76 million) is joining the EU: Vote leave, take back control'.

As many writers have suggested, Brexit is best understood in the longer context of empire. Concerns over Brexit have been chalked up not only to anxieties over immigration controls but also to patriotism and nostalgia for an empire whose history is grounded both in amnesia and fantasy.[1] Mainstream media painted the vote as 'England's last gasp of empire' carried out by a nation 'sickened by nostalgia' and 'post-colonial melancholia' for its lost colonies. Before the referendum in 2016, a survey carried out by YouGov found most people think that British empire is something to be proud of (59 per cent) rather than ashamed of (19 per cent).[2] This nostalgic pride is founded on the pathological romanticisation of an empire of railway building and the magnanimous dissemination of civility.

However, whilst such denialist nostalgia has certainly been used to characterise and chastise those who voted to leave the European Union, eulogising empire whilst erasing its historical and contemporary realities has been a persistent condition of its perpetuation since its supposed collapse. Framed on these terms, the vote might be seen to sediment the desire for a renewed sovereignty against an 'other' whose claims upon Britain are seen as inherently rapacious and uncivil – with migrant people figured as inherently criminal, security threats, and antagonistic to so-called British values. As such 'Britain' shouldn't be understood as a given – or even as pragmatic political, social, or economic category. Rather, Britain and Britishness are explicable *only* through the colonial machinery that gives them integrity and ground.

The Conservative party has made explicit its position of nationalist protection, an increasingly cruel and revanchist approach towards immigration policy, and patriotic exceptionalism. However, current leftist arguments are also reliant on the nation as a basic political unit. The left have borrowed from right-wing discourse to support the claim that a strengthened nation-state is required to protect the interests of a fantasy xenophobic white working class. This is given succour by a widely-made argument that anti-immigrant sentiment has resulted from an inability to explain how neoliberalism and globalism are the workers' true enemy. Focusing on the latter, the central target of messaging under the Labour party since the referendum has been the crisis in global finance leading to austerity measures. These are seen as the culmination of a longer neo-liberal erosion of public services and welfare, with the mobilisation of right-wing ethnonationalism just a protective sheen masking strategies to maintain class power and capital.

But this forgets that neoliberalism and globalism are neo-imperial formations. Both have been directed towards the extraction and expropriation of value from people who have been figured as not the rightful inheritors of this earth. They have relied on extractive modes of capital that hyper-exploit, dispossess, and make expendable. As I show in this book, this violence has been justified and implemented through the redeployment of colonial strategies: of segregation; the retributive protection of property regimes; migrant-subsidised economies; the racialised stratification of labour force; the criminalisation and pathologisation of groups of people; hyper-exploitation; social control; containment; expulsion.

The state's admixture of authoritarianism and privatised responsibility in response to the spread of COVID-19 in early 2020 clarified that death is discriminatory. Since the distributions of death are far from unknown and arbitrary, official policies of 'herd immunity' encapsulated eugenic calculations. Britain prepared for lockdown amidst a discourse underpinned by militarised nationalism, nostalgic exceptionalism, and calls for hugely expanded police powers. This desire for increased policing was backed-up with police hotlines and 'snooper' forms overwhelmed by over 200,000 reports in the first few weeks they were open. Police powers under the Coronavirus Bill quickly led to increasing roadblocks, fines, checkpoints, random stops, and a seemingly arbitrary use of powers and disruption of movement that ramped-up and made-explicit the differential policing of Black and Asian people in Britain. It is indisputable that policing shaped the lockdown as crisis – fining the already poor; spurious arrests that forced people into contact; restricting access to parks, exercise, necessary services; enforcing incarceration in already overcrowded and virus-ridden prisons.

The intensification of separation across urban landscapes similarly became more focused – with wealthy Londoners leaving the city or insulated by luxury flats that became permanent panic rooms – a precarious workforce literally servicing their needs. As lockdown under COVID-19 has confirmed, the wealthy are reliant on service workers, cleaners, childminders, and Deliveroo riders, whilst those people are required to live elsewhere. As much as those in healthcare, people in insecure jobs were suddenly figured as essential workers. Forced to continue commutes and contact, this rapidly led to the highest death rates from COVID-19 in the most deprived boroughs on the outskirts of London. The differential contiguity with death discussed throughout this book has been made as unequivocally evident as the government's response has been vicious. In August 2020, Black people had been nearly four times more likely to die from the virus as white people. Britain's internal colonialism has been quite blatantly translated into vulnerability to health conditions. And, this precarity and vulnerability-to-poverty reverberated across broken contracts and unpaid labour across the world. The juridical order required to manage this viscous proximity and separation relies on the naturalisation of contingent classifications of people as other, foreigner, migrant.

Amidst this pandemic, whilst asylum seekers were on hunger strike against threat of deportation, the Home Office distributed a video showing cartoon aircraft flying from Britain in a homage to the TV comedy series *Dad's Army*. The planes representing the deportation flights that were being rushed through against legal due process. The video was released in the same week that Ugandan migrant Mercy Baguma was starved to death after the Home Office removed her right to remain. When legal appeals mercifully blocked the deportation flights, the spectre of Brexit was raised as harbinger of sovereignty as the right to expel at will – as the Home Office put it, 'soon we will no longer be bound by EU laws and can negotiate our own return arrangements'.

Whilst disparate and divided, what holds together our contemporary political moment is an emphasis on the securitisation of the British economy and its borders – internal and external. The response to COVID-19 was processed through the lens of threat, insurgency, and the invisible enemy – foregrounding the protection of citizens and national economy. But for years, the answer to our alleged crises on both sides of parliament has been the enlargement and strengthening of the nation-state. The left argues that controls over migrant workers and capital outflows would supposedly allow us to determine which relations are held in common and which are not, so making way for the restitution of nation-state sovereignty against global capital. Here, the political left and right collapse – not in a post-political centre, but labouring under the horizon of an increasingly strengthened nation-state.

Britain has long-been dependent upon the management and legitimation of violence, submerged through the ideological alibis and institutional super-structure – of law, rationality, culture, values. This book argues that accounting for this dependence requires us to look not only at historical confluence and spatiotemporal entanglements, but also at how Britain's existential and political integrity is reliant on the production, management, and negation of those people crafted as 'perpetual others'. This is particularly important as corrective against arguments that we have recently entered political crises, or that we've entered a more coercive stage of history. To produce property, capital, and law has required a violent excess as the aporetic matter upon which a juridical calculus adjudicates.

The fundamental conditions of its deadly regimes, citizenry, politics and criminal justice systems are the imperial frameworks and material infrastructures that, stretched across the empire, bring their techniques and strategies into the heart of Britain itself. This is set to continue, aggravated under the pressures of crisis: of financial collapse, austerity, public health disaster, planetary climate emergency. The intensification of this violent colonialism will be justified by the need to preserve national resources against those who would lay claim to them. What has resulted from the continuation of colonialism under the image of the post-colonial cut is a nation-state whose form increasingly tends towards extinction. I mean this literally – through the expropriation of homes and wealth; the ramping-up of criminalisation and incarceration; the massification of a pre-crime space across British dominated zones; the hyper-exploitation and extraction of and from people and places across the world, which does not just leave people to die but acts to make those worlds unliveable in the first place.

Far from being the only available unit for political thought, the nation requires active dismantling – Britain is an imperial structure that must be ended.

But let us be clear from the start. The account in this book is far from unknown for many – its stories told with unnerving recurrence, and forged through entanglements of force, resistance, and care. For this reason, its critical focus lies with Britain's whiteness, which is reproduced by and productive of, mass-scale coloniality. Necessarily then, these arguments, narratives, threads are not an attempt to unveil or to render objective. Rather, in conversation with a vocabulary that has been woven into being primarily by Black thinkers, they trace and track the vectors of power and counter-power; the circuitry of reactive and manufactured crises; the intimacies of proximities and separations.

So writing and thinking Britain's internal colonialism is to describe a set of practices and hegemonic logics that *attempt* to wholly manage and fix but that could not possibly do so. This to clarify that which might make power shudder: that at the kernel of empire lies its own impossibility – 'a splinter to the heart of the world' as Fanon wrote – because the totalising structures of colonialism are both necessary and impossible. If the hegemonizing account of imperial expansion is upset by resistance and force that is unequally distributed across the spatio-temporalities of non-European worlds, *internal* colonial operations proliferate traces, tensions, kinships. Tracing these vectors leads us away from the domain of political possibility, and towards an openness to the often quiet insurgencies in which the end of Britain is already being practiced. As Saidiya Hartman writes:

> To strike, to riot, to refuse. To love what is not loved. To be lost to the world. It is the practice of the social otherwise, the insurgent ground that enables new possibilities and new vocabularies; it is the lived experience of enclosure and segregation, assembling and huddling together. It is the directionless search for a free territory; it is a practice of making and relation that enfolds within the policed boundaries of the dark ghetto; it is the mutual aid offers in the open-air prison.[3]

Acknowledgements

Many conversations have influenced and shaped these thoughts, countless through reading, writing and thinking-with; others through encouragement, often fragmentary thoughts, movements, nudges, reorientations. In particular, I would like to thank Lisa Tilley, Anupama Ranawana, Alex Williams, Hannah Boast, Tom O'Shea, Suhaiymah Manzoor-Khan, Robbie Shilliam, Will Stronge, Jas Nijjar, Suhail Malik, Diann Bauer, Guilaine Kinouani, Shareefa Energy, Petero Kalulé, Smin Smith, Rajkumar Uthayakumar, Nick Srnicek, Francesca Peck-Williams, Ryan Huff, James Etherington, my editor Jakob Horstmann, all of my students, but particularly Casey Highfield-Smith and Saffron Naylor, my family, and especially Lynda Fitzwater, Zola Trafford and Magnus Trafford.

1
The Mouth of a Shark

no one leaves home unless
home is the mouth of a shark.
[...]
make a refugee camp a home for a year or two or ten,
stripped and searched, find prison everywhere
and if you survive and you are greeted on the other side
with go home blacks, refugees
dirty immigrants, asylum seekers

(Warsan Shire, 'Home')[1]

This is my home
this thin edge of
barbwire.

(Gloria Anzaldúa, *Borderlands/La frontera: The New Mestiza*)[2]

IN THE SHADOWS OF FLIGHT PATHS

In the visitors' room at the largest immigrant detention centre in Britain there is a mural of a shark. From the vantage point of stained board-backed chairs and tables adorned with a sharpie-scrawled numbering system, the shark – with bared teeth – stares panopticon-like over the head of the guard who checks you into the room and assigns tables. Somewhat indecorously, a large clock sits within this mural.

When you have insecure immigration status, you don't have life. Your life is not considered important. It should not be like this. Human life is more important than immigration status.

The clock haunts this space that is so fraught by time, a space of detainment without sentence or conviction. The 'tuck-shop' is closed again, staff disorganised as if caught off-guard. Today the room is opened an hour and a half late. A small crowd tensely waiting is now shuffling together into the tiny anteroom whilst one door locks before another can open. 'It's like we're going into prison', someone quietly remarks.

Just imagine, just walk in my shoes once. You have a normal life and then they detain you. Take you away from your family and your kids. It's not normal. If you're going to detain you like an animal – how can you expect them to live a normal life. It's going to be ruining their lives for ever.

This cold, dank-smelling, exhausted space of visitation is at once secured, apprehensive, anxious, but also brimming with love, desire and ache. Enfolding in the tenderness of emotion and presence, lovers, mothers, fathers, children, friends – sucking in air in the vicinity of one another, capturing fragrances of scalp, neck, spirit.

The treatment we are getting here is not right. On our anniversary my husband travelled to see me. While we were kissing they came to me saying that we are not allowed to kiss. My husband just started crying because we being treated as criminal and making life hell for us.

Just beyond a grey business hotel, sitting at the other side of a dual carriageway to a drive-through McDonald's, are the Heathrow Immigration Removal centres. Like many others, the running of Harmondsworth is outsourced to Mitie, a company now infamous for its subsumption business practices and the paucity of conditions of its immigration centres.[3] Ostensibly a holding ground for asylum hearings, Harmondsworth is a prison that witnesses sickness, mental health crises and suicide. The people detained there are often refused access to medical care, and sent away with paracetamol regardless of ailment.

We are locked up like dogs. Even animals in this country have their rights. Detention is not supposed to be like a prison. But we are treated worse than prisoners. Where is the humanity in this country, where is the human right in this country.

Harmondsworth lies in the elongated shadows of flight paths, positioned for proximity to planes that extend its carceral reach. Rebuilt and expanded in 2001 under New Labour, it was the first purpose-built detention centre in the UK. It was brought into being by the 1968

Commonwealth Immigrants Act, which had removed the right of entry for British Commonwealth citizens and made precarious the rights of many already residing in the country.

> *The people that they deport, and put on the charter flights. Those people lose their lives. Everything gets worse for them.*[4]

The centre symbolises violent attempts to refound the authority and integrity of Britain in a post-colonial world that would ultimately resurrect colonialism inside, and neo-imperialism without. Their corporate facia of hostility is intertwined with strategies of containment and punitive bordering that extends far beyond national territories – outwards across Europe and Africa, and inwards across health services, education and housing.

Britain – as nation-state – is colonialism

Put bluntly, this is the proposition and argument of this book.

Whilst this is a book that is largely about Britain, this is a Britain that is not limited to its island shores. This is because Britain has never been independent – there is no 'island nation', as Gurminder Bhambra puts it.[5] Britain was established in 1707 with the formalisation of England's annexation of Scotland forming a 'united' kingdom. By the early twentieth century, its empire dominated around one quarter of the Earth's lands, one fifth of its people, and half of all Muslims. Britain ruled over 100 colonies, protectorates and dominions, with 52 forming the later Commonwealth. Britain-as-empire involved the annexation of lands, settler colonialism, chattel slavery, extraction, genocide and expansionist commerce.

Imperial empire had been built in opposition with its 'others', making stolen land into property and commodity, and Indigenous people into a commodified reserve. This was the condition of Britain's wealth and sovereign political power. The British state was built upon inestimable wealth that was extracted across empire through forced taxation, dispossession, enslavement and forced labour. But Britain's dependence on its colonies was not limited to economy and political might. There is a paradox at the core of Britain's insistence on liberal freedoms, which empire brings to light. Defining the universality of liberal freedoms had relied on the creation of an 'other' against whom they could be measured. Not the product of an internal European character, liberal values of liberty and equality in the British metropole (the 'parent' state of its colonies) were produced through violent divisions of the world in its colonies.[6] The very image of liberal Britain rested on freedoms that were won by expropriation and enclosure, exploitation and extermination.

The 'end' of empire was a long, slow and violent process, which stuttered through counter-insurgency, uprising, installed governments, enforced trade deals and post-colonial migration. What emerged was a system of neo-colonial imperialism built through the hard-fought domination over the territories, politics and economies of newly sovereign states. The formal independence of post-colonial states was intertwined with ongoing subordination that would later become embedded in multilateral organisations and international law.

The end of Britain's formal colonies was seen by politicians like Enoch Powell as the possibility for its rebirth as a singular nation. However, at the same time that Britain fought to retain its imperial directives amidst global decolonising forces and world-making struggles, its borders were necessarily opened to inflows of capital, people and commodities. Prompted by domestic labour shortages and the desire to maintain commonwealth power, the British Nationality Act of 1948 gave some of Britain's colonial subjects the right to travel to and work in the metropole through incentivised guest-worker style schemes. These were supposed to promote the temporary movement of labour from colony to metropole, forming precarious communities whose citizenship status was in question from the start. Also under Heathrow's flight path, after the violent partitioning of Punjab by the British in 1947, Southall became *Chota Punjab* – Little Punjab. Not completely jokingly, one reason for settling there was that 'if the *gooras* [whites] ever kicked us out, it would be easy to get on a plane and return home'.[7]

This brought tensions and tactics of colonial control into the heart of the metropole. Much of this book is concerned to show that these tensions and tactics underpin both the idea and the reality of Britain as island territory and neo-imperial state since the end of formal empire. From the embers of empire, Britain was rebuilt as the continuation of colonialism. I will argue that the history of post-war Britain is also the history of colonial strategies and techniques deployed 'at home'. In tracing this deployment of *internal* colonialism, I aim to show that this was not just driven by the desire to rebuild Britain's labour force, economy and global position. Britain has been politically, economically and existentially dependent upon its colonies and their re-formation inside the metropole. To put this somewhat glibly, as existential horizon and nation-state machinery, Britain *is* colonialism.

Of aliens and universals

In the summer of 1948, Britain saw both the *Empire Windrush* bringing around 800 Jamaican people to the port of Tilbury *and* the inauguration of the National Health Service (NHS). Both were symbolic of compacts between citizen and state, with the nascent welfare state rooted in liberal citizenship as universal entitlement. The edges of this universal compact were transparent – it was never meant for the others, which British empire held within. Further still, its universalism was written *through* this exclusion and as a means of its protection. Whilst trajectories in the metropole had progressively shifted towards welfarism, leniency and equality, their colonial counterparts were subject to genocidal violence and torture against anticolonial resistance; the scrambling efforts of the colonial office to hold onto power; claims over resources preserving unequal flows of trade.[8]

The emergence of a universal compact through social reforms had been underpinned by eugenicist arguments against the likely social degradation and perishing of the British nation.[9] The National Insurance Act in 1911 sought to prevent the degeneration of Anglo-Saxon stock through social hygiene – intervening in living standards through health and unemployment provision for certain workers. Whilst advocating universalism, Beveridge's infamous 1942 report relied on a similar logic to argue that at the present rate of reproduction, the 'British race' could not continue. With eugenicist credentials and a firm belief in the pride in Britain, Beveridge understood that its continued imperial quest required intervention to install a national minimum living standard: 'good stock should be allowed to breed while bad stock would be ameliorated through state intervention'.[10] As Robbie Shilliam writes, Beveridge saw the possibility for 'the preservation of empire in the universal provision of social insurance and welfare in Britain'.[11] This welfare capitalism was financed by continuing colonial exploitation such as the reduction of plantation workers' wages in Malaya by 80 per cent, with resistance to the cuts leading to the British setting up resettlement camps.[12] In this sense, universal provision was not just a weapon of exclusion, it was a weapon for the maintenance and protection of freedoms that had been built upon exclusion.

For Britain the decolonising world was a fragile state of affairs, with the commonwealth held together largely by a trusteeship system of colonial administration that would guide nations towards their own self-determination.[13] Though the 1948 act meant that commonwealth immigrants had rights to British nationality, in reality migration was neither unrestricted nor spontaneous. With concerns over declining British stock, a waning post-war economy and labour shortages, the government formed a working party to manage the movement of labour from its prior and extant colonies. In order to incentivise limited movement, the Colonial Office organised a scheme that would select the best colonial subjects for migration under direct control of the office. For example, the Indian administration required proof of financial status and literacy through a series of checks before emigration was possible.[14] Relying on colonial governments and extra-territorial immigration and border controls at ports of departure allowed Britain to circumvent nationality laws, so they would not have to implement border controls at port of entry.

As 'children of the empire' increasingly found their way to the mother nation and as the temporary arrangement began to give way to settlement, this did not herald a universal post-colonial welfare system, but rather a series of immigration restrictions, buttressed by increasing anti-immigrant resentment. If social and economic welfare movements in Britain were grounded in racialised nationalism, then as Satnam Verdee writes, 'the golden age of welfare capitalism and the social democratic settlement was also the golden age of white supremacy'.[15] Migrant people from the old colonies found themselves in a Britain that was differentiated, living and working in zones of dis-location that operated out of sync with the universal compact surrounding them. Then, as now, they were forced to carry the colonies on their backs. Uneasily traversing the spatio-temporal connections that supposedly made Britain post-colonial, these zones were spaces of precarity and permanent temporariness – shaped for those 'never sure whether or not he has crossed the frontier'.[16]

Britain's universal compact, which had been built against and in protection from its others, now required new strategies that could maintain the 'British race' against colonial subjects *inside* territorial shores. This required a seismic shift away from a fixed relation of political belonging between state, citizen and geography and towards flexible strategies and technologies of citizenship. New battle lines were drawn, with migrant people and those with migrant heritage configured as aliens who could lead to the destruction of the nation. The close management of their economic, social and political inclusion and exclusion provided the state with legitimacy. Drawing this picture of a Britain under siege was central to Britain's new self-image as a unified nation whose ends were its maritime borders.

COLONIALISM DIRECTED INWARDS

There has been much written about the role of imperial states and corporations in the global periphery, postcolonialism and the role of development, aid and security.[17] However, these approaches have some-times omitted the role that the global periphery played in the constitution of nation-states in the imperial core. They highlight how colonialism continues to shape the current configuration of interests manifested and often violently enforced in the context of global governance. Nonetheless, whilst centring its after-effects, colonialism is often understood as something that was done *by* Europe *to* the rest of the world. It is the remnants and legacies of empire that continue to influence the treatment of those people who were once colonised. This rests on both methodological nationalism and Eurocentrism. Contemporary forms of governance are understood to have been endogenously produced in the imperial core rather than through historical and ongoing colonial processes of accumulation, exploitation and control.[18] In tracing the movements of colonialism inwards we can rectify this lacuna to foreground the transnational relationships that have given shape to the political, economic and cultural forms of power through which nation-states and global governance have manifested.

Colonial entanglements

Rebuilding Britain in the wake of a decolonising world was dependent on a combination of military support for insurgencies and wars that devastated infrastructure and peoples together with regimes of indebtedness put in place through post-Bretton Woods institutions. The latter would recognise the political authority only of those nation-states that met certain criteria allowing external access to resources. Multilateral aid packages became a necessary response to aggressive integration into the global economy via World Trade Organization (WTO) and International Monetary Fund (IMF) rules, sanctions and loans, and the ensuing petro-dollar-caused debt crisis. Structural adjustment programmes (SAPs) were put in place as conditions on aid and lending from the early 1980s. These benefitted the political and economic institutions that sponsored loans awarded by the IMF, and whose control is heavily weighted in favour of the United States, Japan, Germany, France and the United Kingdom.

The expansion of Europe and the 'development' of the colonies had bound the two together. As Walter Rodney wrote, after formal decolonisation 'many of the territories incorporated into the overseas empire were locked into providing primary products for the UK'.[19] Britain is still reliant on the extraction of labour, rents, raw materials and resources for industrial processes, and industrialised farming. Free trade agreements continue to shape export prices and wages, whilst militarised commerce and the offshoring of industry effectively subsidise our living standards and our purchasing power. This echoes across the neo-imperial relations that are now even more firmly etched than when Mississippi plantations and Manchester factories were forged into an unequal world economy.[20]

We can see this from the vantage point of Harmondsworth. Charter flights, which were introduced under New Labour in 2001, typically take place in the dead of night at the edges of airports like Heathrow, Gatwick and Stansted. The aeroplanes that are used for these violent deportations have been made using materials extracted through imperial intervention in parts of the world that Britain may never have formally colonised. Take Mozambique as example. Formally colonised by the Portuguese, British control of the wider region had been present during that period, felt acutely through the Mozambique Company, with the country joining the commonwealth in 1995. In Mozambique's capital, Maputo, lies Mozal, an aluminium smelter partially funded by UK investment and the World Bank. The smelter has been exempt from tax on profit and VAT because the investment is counted as development. Yet for every dollar the Mozambique government made from the venture, $21 is extracted from the country.[21] In total, the UK has received $88 million from the development project in addition to the original loan repayment. In 2014, Mozambique was the largest recipient of foreign direct investment in the continent. But this uneven and extractive development has created massive liabilities for Mozambique, leaving it the poorest country in the world in 1993 and second poorest in 2017 by GDP.

These material, economic and social practices operate transnationally to differentiate access to housing, food, land, resources and healthcare. As Tania Li puts it, they are practices that 'let die' in order to 'make live'.[22] It is in part for these reasons that Mozambique is so vulnerable to changes in climate that precipitate extreme weather. In early 2019, the tropical cyclone Idai led to massive-scale devastation in Zimbabwe, Malawi and Mozambique. Almost the entirety of Beira, the fourth largest city in Mozambique was destroyed, flooding demolishing entire villages, winds and floods affecting more than 2.6 million people, and taking over 1,000 lives. As Idai makes stark, climate crises are increasingly making life in the region unsustainable, whilst the destruction caused by climate change is inseparable from ongoing capitalist plunder in the name of development. However, it is likely that the Shark at Harmondsworth will never see any of those whose homes are made in the mouth of a shark. Not only do our draconian asylum regimes make no allowances for so-called climate refugees but they are increasingly securitised, enhanced and expanded globally.

These inequities and interconnections reverberate across Britain, where shifts from colonial to neo-colonial nation brought about new relations of geographical enclosure through differential citizenship and plastic strategies of exclusion. Underfunded and overpoliced, this made entire communities subject to supposedly colour-blind technologies of finance and debt, credit scores, surveillance and algorithmic and pre-emptive policing – providing the façade of anti-racist science that has led to hierarchical outcomes.

Domestic colonies

I use the phrase internal colonialism to centre the production and reproduction of colonial relations through the intensification and reproduction of societal structures and hierarchies, differential access to resources and normative limitations. Its strategies have redeployed structures that facilitated and legitimised slavery, exploitation and extermination and frameworks that suppressed dissent and resistance to them. Considering colonial entanglements in this way both draws on and differs from theories of domestic colonialism that were primarily focused on the US. Their visibility relies on a long tradition of activist and academic analysis of segregated areas (ghettos) as an internal colony in the US including activists such as W.E.B. Du Bois, Kenneth Clark, Malcolm X, Kwame Toure, Harold Cruse; and sociologists such as Robert Blauner, Robert L. Allen, Charles Pinderhughes.

In *A Negro Nation Within the Nation*, W.E.B. Du Bois argued that African Americans in the depression era required the creation of institutions whose economic and political self-determination might circumvent Jim Crow segregation. Central to his analysis was the articulation of twelve distinct features that drew together the experience of colonial subjects and African Americans as 'semi-colonial' people:

1. Physical and psychological violence
2. Economic exploitation
3. Poverty
4. Illiteracy
5. Lawlessness and crime
6. Starvation
7. Death
8. Disaster
9. Disease
10. Disenfranchisement
11. Cultural inequality
12. Exclusion from political participation.[23]

Tying together the transnational experiences of colonial subjects was core to the development of this account of semi-colonial people in the US. This was also instrumental in the making of a pan-African movement that would be directed towards the mass emancipation of Black people across the world. As Amy Ashwood Garvey stated at the 1945 Pan-African Congress in Manchester, the movement would be 'supported by the semi-colonial people in America.'[24]

What is specific about domestic, or internal, colonialism was that the biopolitical and geopolitical management of people and land occurs within the borders of an imperial nation.[25] Initially, the understanding of internal colonialism had originated from Latin American analysis of unequal terms of trade between dominant and subordinate nations as analogous with those between dominant and subordinate groups within nations. Taken up by writers in the US, the concept of a nation within a nation was mobilised to develop theories of domestic colonialism as a geographically contiguous state whose symbolic form was the ghetto.[26] In 1962, Harold Cruse used the phrase domestic colonialism to describe the problem of the underdevelopment of African American communities. The ghetto was understood as the major device for persisting anti-Black colonisation. Its underdevelopment had produced the conditions of colonialism in the US that centred on geographical segregation and the subordination of a differentiated population.

The framework offered a way of thinking about life conditions for African Americans beyond simple economics and the idea of race as discrimination or prejudice. As Blauner argued, the persistence of race in America couldn't adequately be explained by class analysis, but required tracing its conditions to those produced under colonialism:

> Western Colonialism brought into existence the present-day pattern of racial stratification; in the United States, as elsewhere, it was a colonial experience that generated the lineup of ethnic and racial divisions.[27]

This provided an explanation for the continuation of spatial segregations, economic dependence, political exclusions and excessive policing.[28] The forms of control that had been used to maintain the colonies were now being used to ensure the enduring domination of the US nation and its white elite. Systems of exploitation and control were found to form a dynamics of domination and resistance that was structured by coexistent racial antagonism. Building on this tradition, the most prominent use of the framework of internal colonialism was in Stokely Carmichael and Charles V. Hamilton's 1967 *Black Power*. Critiquing white power and locating foundational racism in the 'economic dependency of the colonised', they showed how racism constrained and shaped the lives of those contained by the internal colony. Not only descriptive, but a call to resistance on behalf of the nation within a nation, internal colonialism was developed as both theory and praxis.

Coloniality as process

Despite drawing on this lineage, the approach taken throughout this book will necessarily break with it – not least because of the substantive differences between the British metropole and the US settler colony. It should be said that the theory has not been limited to the US. Internal colonialism has been fruitfully employed to consider many contexts including Palestine, Indonesia and Sri Lanka.[29] However, the contexts in which it finds a natural home are those which allow for the relatively clear demarcation of colony and host nation. Whilst I shall return to this throughout this book, these delineations have not been so clear cut in the case of Britain. The terms of segregation produced in Britain, I shall argue, have often been far more diffuse and distributive – though just as deep.

Rather than use the framework of internal colonialism to describe the territories of a colony inside the state, I want to think of it primarily as a framework for clarifying histories, understanding processes and connections, and bringing to light the interwoven movements of colonial techniques and practices within Britain's shores. By necessity of method, this both expands our remit and forces us to consider internal colonisation as an enduring set of processes. This also builds on work that has challenged assumptions – both that we exist in a post-colonial world, and that geographical, cultural, and political distinctions separate colony and metropole.[30] By considering the transnational circulations of colonial forms of governance and practices of accumulation, we can foreground how they have been constitutive of British nationhood, and are an enduring process across the Earth.

This is to think of the violences of colonialism not as Britain's spatial and temporal other or originary past but as its 'ongoing conditions of possibility'.[31] As such, the analysis throughout weaves together strategies developed across empire with their later deployment both inside British shores *and* across external borders and neo-imperial territories. Telling this story unveils both the mass-scale and complex circuits of colonial capitalist power, and the often-silenced counter-discourses of its subjects. Far from passively subject to colonial relations, ongoing coloniality can only be understood through the lens of anti-colonial resistance and active political agency. Internal colonialism has largely been implemented as a reactive mechanism to a series of manufactured crises centring on the presence of the other now within.

The method offers significant explanatory reward. Through it, we are granted understanding of the persistently laminar contours of labour and property markets; why criminal justice reformism gave way to punitive militarism in the 1980s; the manifestation of differential racisms and their weaponisation against communities judged to be uncivil and criminal; how counter-insurgency projects have become normalised with all citizens conscripted as border guards; how the horizon of the nation continues to be staged as the only permissible ground for progressive politics; how, under pressure of dwindling resources and ecological crisis, we're headed towards a politics of green nationalism underpinned by a border regime that produces temporary and highly controlled forms of citizenship for Britain's others. This throws sharply into focus the mechanisms through which the persistence of this unequally differentiated world has been made to seem like a neutral standard, and how it is protected with increasing vehemence.

Faithful to its original intent, the framework of internal colonialism provides a way of thinking about Britain that is obscured by narratives that frame the last half a century through the lens of neoliberalism. I will return to these issues a few times, so here I shall just briefly consider approaches to this historical period through the lens of neoliberalism as market rationality writ large. David Harvey, for example, considers our history since the 1970s as a project that was taken up by the capitalist classes to 'protect themselves from political and economic annihilation'.[32] This project to repair class power supposedly became embedded in policy by Pinochet, Volker, Thatcher and Reagan by retrenching the welfare state and demolishing labour movements. This was marked by a fundamental transformation of the role of the state, withdrawing from social provision, and supposedly intervening only when neoliberal order broke down – to repair markets, prevent challenges to capital accumulation, and resolve social crises. In this light, neoliberalism has very often been made into a universal logic whose material processes transform us all into human capital.

This narrative doesn't just obfuscate and collapse trajectories and distinctions within British history, it forces an understanding of the development of socio-political formations through the narrowing conduits of class analysis. As I'll show throughout, there is an incredible wealth lying beyond this deformation which could help us to more adequately understand our contemporary predicament. But taking up the framework offered by internal coloniality does not require simply jettisoning the explanatory traction of the mechanisms that Marxist analysis foregrounds. Rather, it refuses the delegation of race to social abstraction or ideology, and actively pursues the claim made by Lisa Tilley and Robbie Shilliam that 'race has the same kind of materiality as class does in constituting the hierarchies and eviscerations of the "social"'.[33]

Internal colonialism emphasises processes of underdevelopment, differential exploitation, violence, containment and criminalisation – all of which have been central to the reproduction and reconfiguring of racialisation around 'migrants' and the spaces in which migrant communities inhabit. In this, I take heed of Patrick Wolfe's suggestion that 'race is colonialism speaking'. The specific articulations of race and racisms that have emerged in recent British histories are produced through the underlying machinery of colonialism as it is wielded within the British metropole. In many ways this coheres with the Latin American focus on the coloniality of power, in which practices of European colonialism are intertwined with the ongoing stratification of social systems and groups. Aníbal Quijano defines coloniality not as colonialism *per se* but as the systemic structuring of culture, labour, markets, intersubjective relations and normative life experience within subordinating and racially shaped relations, behaviours and practices.[34] This includes the enduring intersubjective constructions of race that were produced through supposedly objective European knowledge, and that constitute not only a subordinating relation between coloniser and the dominated, but also colonisation of knowledge and imagination. As Nelson Maldano-Torres writes, coloniality survives colonialism – 'as modern subjects we breath coloniality all the time and everyday'.[35]

This is at odds with the dominant racial formation theory of Michael Omi and Howard Winant, which rejects colonialist explanations of race. Instead, they foreground social processes through which the racial organisation of societies are produced as a complex of meanings that are under constant transformation in conditions of political struggle.[36] The result is a colour-blind approach that relies primarily on analysis of racist ideologies.[37] Their emphasis on meaning systems and ideologies fails to do justice to their material basis. In part this is motivated by a drive away from biological or essentialised accounts of race. Nevertheless, whilst denying not just that race has any biological basis but also any *material* basis, they also fail to demonstrate why racial difference constitutes a central dimension of social organisation and discourse.[38] So rather than gaining traction on the causal significance of the conditions that give rise to the reproduction of race, race becomes a floating signifier that is dislocated from its origins in colonial regimes. Against this, I hold that race is a technology that forms part of the machinery of colonialism. The reproduction and manifestations of race in the metropole have used frameworks and practices that had developed across empire, and led to '[s]kewed life chances, limited access to health and education, premature death, incarceration, and impoverishment'.[39]

This line of thought follows articulations of racial capitalism in which the machinery of capital accumulation is considered inseparable from its fundamentally racialised arrangement.[40] Drawing on Cedric Robinson, in Gargi Bhattacharyya's recent work racial capitalism is similarly not posed as a metatheory nor master narrative, but as a means to characterise the tendency of capitalism not to homogenise but to differentiate. This provides a frame through which the tendency to homogenise and universalise the machinery of capitalism can be resisted. For Bhattacharyya, this offers the guiding thought that 'in the realm of the economic, racism is an attempt to safeguard the interests of those deemed dominant or "unraced"'.[41]

This also indicates a shift in attention. Considerations of racial capitalism pose racialised hierarchy as the outcome of processes of capitalist accumulation. But in following Wolfe's suggestion that race is colonialism speaking, we are perhaps led away from questioning whether or not capitalism is inherently racist, or whether it relies on racist intentionality. For instance, against a doctrine of empire as a great civilising mission and industrialising force, it is often supposed that colonialism can be accounted for on the terms of the machinery of accumulation alone. Perhaps this is a matter of focus, but insofar as Britain is concerned, it seems necessary to understand empire as not only producing conditions of economic dependency and ongoing subsidy, but also of a sub-structural logic through which Britain's liberal self-image could be won. Capital accumulation and the ascendancy of Britishness as a model of humanity forged in violence and protected with vehemence are necessarily thought together.

BORDERLANDS TRAVERSING TIME AND SPACE

With Gloria Anzaldúa, I want to think of Britain's borders as not only physically instantiated nor just a product of fantasies of national omnipotence. Instead, I consider the dis-located zones of coloniality as borderlands that traverse transnational spaces and temporal orders. As Anzaldúa puts it:

A borderland is a vague and undetermined place created by the emotional residue of an unnatural boundary. It is in a constant state of transition. The prohibited and forbidden are its inhabitants.[42]

These borderlands stretch across occult passageways for 'those who cross over, pass over, or go through the confines of the "normal"'.[43] They are zones that intersect lives and bodies. As Sarah Keenan puts it, they involve 'taking space with you' – along the thin edge of barbwire of calculative credit scores, access to shelter and food, armed social work and threatened deportation. Borderlands are strange geographies that are imposed but also transported across air, sea and land. They are carried by certain people, and not by others, 'attaching to individual subjects wherever they go rather than bounding off a defined physical area'.[44] As Keenan suggests, this is to think of places not as enclosed spaces but as 'articulated moments in networks of social relations and understandings' as Doreen Massey writes.[45]

This prompts a mode of thinking that could engender ways of rendering visible these 'rhythms of endurance, the surges of life that carry bodies forward and back'.[46] Here, I follow Anzaldúa's considerations of these zones that are out of sync with the supposed universalisms of liberal freedoms. Slipping between and without a deadened dialectical movement between the false universality of science and logic and the reification of local experience, Anzaldúa urges us not to ontologise the other – as if an alien subject exists prior to, or under, the veil of colonial time and space. As Denise Ferreira Da Silva reminds us, whatever we suppose to lie behind this veil will ultimately be reproduced as other to be permanently excluded by, and dislocated from, freedom again. Furthermore, as Glen Coulthard points out, the parallel politics of this way of thinking – benevolently including those who were previously excluded – promises to replicate the very configurations of colonialist, racist, patriarchal state power they seek to transcend.[47]

Instead, I will attend to the 'point of entanglement' as Edouard Glissant put it, of abstract global structures and local and embedded forms of life, where these 'overspill clear boundaries in time and space [and] are marked above all by displacements – temporal, geographical, rhetorical, and technological displacements'.[48] This requires us to embed ourselves in forms of knowledge that are abrasive and undermining of a critical form that involves the manufacture of a unified subject who supposedly sits apart from worlds, and speaks without consequence. This, for Glissant, leads us to consider inhabited ways of knowing and understanding that are necessarily open-ended, mobile, consequent:

An 'intellectual' effort, with its repetitive thrusts (repetition has a rhythm), its contradictory movements, its necessary imperfections, its demands for formulation (even a schematic one), very often obscured by its very purpose. For the attempt to approach a reality so often hidden from view cannot be organised in terms of a series of clarifications.[49]

This resistance to clarifications arises from an attention to nested knowledges that traverse temporalities. Violence is done to these knowledges through attempts to wrench them into modes of knowing and criticality that typify the rational public sphere. By drawing attention to these forms of living knowledge we might also undo the supposedly transparent universality that gives structure to this sphere.[50]

This is vital when accounting for these narratives from the vantage point of an academic benefitting from the privileges of whiteness, and trained in knowledges that reify social difference and uphold social transparency – even when (and perhaps especially when) that social transparency is supposedly disabused. Noel Ignatiev argues that treason to whiteness is loyalty to humanity. But whiteness as structure of social significance and power is not easily sloughed off. Working to draw attention to the machinery through which whiteness is maintained requires us to keep a weather eye on its reproduction through material practices and social relations.[51] Whiteness is so often both too attached and too detached from its material fundament – supposedly now describing a race that requires cultural protection like any other. This is where Omi and Winant's approach leads us. For them, whiteness is not a structure produced through colonial practices that extends beyond phenotype.[52] Rather, whiteness operates as a racial group 'among many other relatively co-equal groups contending today in a horizontally arranged plurality that exists on an increasingly level playing field'.[53] Cut adrift from its colonial form and basis, whiteness becomes rewritten as part of the play of identity.

As Achille Mbembe puts it whiteness that was forged through colonialism was:

the mark of a certain mode of Western presence in the world, a certain figure of brutality and cruelty, a singular form of predation with an unequaled capacity for the subjection and exploitation of foreign peoples.[54]

In considering the mass-scale and complex circuits of colonial capitalist power, and the often-silenced counter-discourses of its subjects, I hope to show how the production and reproduction of whiteness was entrenched as core to the organisational schema of Britain. In this lie two overriding thoughts to which I shall return. The first, drawing on the work of David Roediger is that whiteness is *apophatic* – it is both empty and defined only by 'what one isn't and on whom one can hold back'.[55] The second is that 'whiteness belongs', as Guilaine Kinouani puts it – 'no amount of being born "here" will grant you access to the fortress of belonging, if you have black or brown skin'.[56] Whilst Roediger's assertion forms part of the propulsive logic underlying much of this book, Kinouani's suggestion situates its attempt to refuse clarifications, to trace entanglements, and to foreground the points of resistance through which whiteness has been made as core to Britishness at the end of empire.

So against the temptation of positing internal colonialism as theory or rational frame, I endeavour instead to situate knowledges that are emergent from the borderlands. These are more likely to arise from interstices, misattunements and dis-coherences than through the production of a unified history and meta-theory. For Anzaldúa, this is encapsulated by *La Facultad* as:

> anything that breaks into one's everyday mode of perception, that causes a break in one's defenses and resistance, anything that takes one from one's habitual grounding, causes the depth to open up, causes a shift in perception.[57]

Drawing on Rachel Carson's notion of death by indirection, Rob Nixon defines slow violence as:

> a violence that occurs gradually and out of sight, a violence of delayed destruction that is dispersed across time and space, an attritional violence that is typically not viewed as violence at all.[58]

The primary aim of this book is to render this gradual and corrosive violence visible, conceivable and accountable through the lens of ongoing coloniality. This is to follow Anzaldúa, in this subterranean understanding, attempting to cause 'the depths to open up' and to see the 'deep structure below the surface'. The hope is that this refusal of clarifications becomes part of a refusal of 'methodological whiteness'.[59]

In refusing this politics of unification, I trace attempts to generate from these depths a unified nation-as-subject: Britain – as symbol, material infrastructure and productive machine – not merely to be resisted but to be refused and abolished.

POLITICS ON A WAR FOOTING

The book is roughly split into two halves. The first traces how internal colonialism was progressively deployed on home territory. Of course, these movements did not reproduce colonial techniques exactly. They were continued and transformed in three major areas: spatial and economic segregation and differentiation (Chapter 2); policing, criminalisation and pathologisation (Chapter 3); racial differentiation and management as threat to Britain (Chapter 4). Through analysis of both the mechanisms and outcomes of these forms of internal colonialism, I show how the shape they took was determined by attempts to reforge Britain after the collapse of empire through a post-colonial cut.

In Chapter 2, 'Extractive Entanglements Across Alien Territories', I trace how the colonial categorisation of people for exploitation, dispossession and disposal has worked its way into differentiations of housing, labour and finance in the metropole. Strategies ensuring spatial segregation had been used across empire to territorialise potential threats against property regimes and colonial order. A barrage of active policies and practices, informal actions and public discourse reproduced these in England for commonwealth migrant people. I show how property regimes were not only segregated and protected, but also subsidised by this migrant labour force. Their racial cheapening forced apart a potentially homogenised working class, and made way for a growing middle class whose stability would not be dependent on social welfare but the accrual of wealth through home ownership. Where the marketisation of housing and shifts towards financialisation promoted some inclusion into systems property ownership, this was both limited and involved exorbitant charges and punitive measures. Together with existing racial stratifications of housing stock and redlining, this led to dispossessions that formed the ground for mass displacement through urban regeneration projects. Austerity measures have had the effect of accelerating these configurations, revealing a core drive of internal colonialism to be a flexibility to shift between producing relations of hyper-exploitation and those of expendability.

Whilst segregations have been core to the technologies of colonialism in Britain, this analysis centres their diffuse and non-linear form to consider the idea that a specifically *distributive* apartheid took root across this period. Chapter 3, 'Policing Empire after Empire', considers how this has been produced and enforced by forms of control, surveillance, and detainment through state and privatised violence. To begin, I show how Britain's others had always been necessary to produce the boundaries of reason and lawfulness characterising the liberal subject. A criminal justice system that tended towards reformism in the metropole relied on definitions of lawfulness that required the manufacture of an inherent lawlessness in the colonised other. This worked its way into policing migrant bodies at home through the pathologisation of entire groups of people through logics of hereditary criminalisation. Black migrant bodies were remade as essentially criminal through strategies of policing whose roots lie with colonial force. Directed toward population controls rather than addressing crime, punitive and militarised systems of criminal justice that had been developed across empire were increasingly used to govern the 'perpetual other' now inside English shores. I argue that this explains why, in the 1970s and 1980s, there was a decisive end to reformist criminal justice in England, leading to what has been termed a new punitiveness. Criminalisation and colonial forms of policing have been employed not just to exclude racialised communities but to actively produce them as pathologised and alien – protection from whom was core to stability of national belonging.

Chapter 4, 'Homeland Warfare and Differential Racism', considers strategies of multiculturalism, counter-insurgency and the expansion of bordering regimes in the context of a political logic drawn from Enoch Powell. The forcefulness of policing and containment has often been seen as antagonistic to state multiculturalism. But the privatisation of race afforded by an analytic of racial demography allowed for strategies of co-option and differential racism that consolidated the pathologisation of the racialised poor. By the turn of the century, these trajectories had worked their way into hegemonic discourses that certain migrant's values were both homogenous and threatening to the social fabric. In the context of counterterrorism, this became the basis for the implementation of counter-insurgency measures under the CONTEST scheme. I argue that this domestic strategy was both premised on Britain's internal colonialism, and that it consolidated its synthesis of criminalisation, paramilitarisation and cultural stigmatisation. I end by arguing that attempts to refound Britain through the post-colonial cut find their culmination in the expansion of bordering practices that enlist all citizens as police.

The shorter second half of the book thinks about how the account might intervene in approaches to contemporary politics. Recent political movements circulating around a socially democratic project within the Labour party have formed around the idea that we are currently witnessing the end of a specific form of globalist capitalism associated with neoliberalism, and a corresponding crisis of liberal democracy. Both are put down to a crisis in capitalist accumulation coming to a head in 2008 and its subsequent management by austerity measures. By way of response, a kind of socialism was formed that presents a politics which actively reproduces the nation as the only horizon for political change. In showing how politics under this horizon is possible only on condition of ongoing coloniality, I argue that it would be no position to imagine or practise its undoing. Staging political struggles like this misses the point of how the specific forms of capitalism at work over the last few decades have been inherently shaped by a reliance on the justification of layers of differential exploitation by a supposedly natural order. This has been enforced through quarantine, criminalisation, precarity and pre-emptive forms of power, which together produced hierarchical regimes of control. Getting this wrong affects the contours through which any hope for their resistance and transformation could be born.

Chapter 5, 'Extinction Politics', problematises the staging of political struggles on the terms of the collapse of neoliberalism. I begin by outlining a counter-narrative of shifts in Britain's geopolitical formation under what is commonly called neoliberalism by highlighting the role of the commons and its limits as inheritor of Lockean logics of development. This reproduced an order whose globalised form has relied on the system of nation-states to ensure the continuation and naturalisation of Britain's political and economic power in its neo-imperial form. Understood through the lens of the post-colonial cut, this brings to light how economic and political nationalism within the political left has been produced within this framework. I show how that project relies on a re-established natural order that is translated into a romanticised nostalgia for the welfare state bounded by national territories, and against which migration is pictured as exacerbating our current crises by driving down wages or using our dwindling resources. I finish the chapter by arguing that under pressure of ecological crisis, committing politics to this supposed restoration of the nation risks becoming a cipher for a geopolitical reconfiguration whose end is the reproduction of Britain as lifeboat state. The enemy that left politics should seek to ward off is not so much globalised neoliberalism as it is green nationalism.

The concluding Chapter 6, 'The End of Britain', considers possible strategies for the end of internal colonialism, looking first at anti-colonial nationalism, reformism and recent calls for decolonisation. I draw attention to the ways these often funnel colonialism through the framework of exclusion and inclusion, so highlighting how they fail to undermine arguments that multiculturalism coupled with overpopulation is destroying the natural order of the nation. I go on to consider the idea that a politics of global anti-subordination might be pursued through the ending of border regimes. These hold much promise, though they tend neither to account for the machinery of internal colonialism, nor to adequately estimate how they might also undermine the legitimacy of nation-states across the board. To close, I explore how instabilities at the core of the project of post-colonial Britain might be exploited to this end. Politicking tells us that nationalist horizons are merely pragmatic – that public 'common sense' is too wedded to the form of the nation. But the insistent and ongoing forces required to maintain the shape of that world are exhausting. Through rupture from within, we can identify where insurgent universality is forged from the solidarities and kinships at the end of Britain.

2

Extractive Entanglements
Across Alien Territories

take notice: the otherworld
is lustrous, like sealight
or twilight, ambiguous because
it's more than one thing at a time:

(Marie Ponsot, 'Migrant Among Us')[1]

The colonial world is a world divided into compartments.

(Frantz Fanon, *Wretched of the Earth*)

EMPIRE, WASTE AND PROPERTY

This chapter examines ongoing patterns of segregation, exploitation and dispossession in Britain since the 1960s. As children of the empire found their way to the metropole by incentive, coercion and cunning, they didn't meet inclusion but housing segregation and spatial marginalisation.

A dark room, often requiring electric light at all times of day welcomed them – if lucky. A bed, a chair, a table, possibly a cupboard. Washing in a shared bathroom that often lacked a bath.[2] For Windrush souls, British empire passports promised opportunity and advancement, against the backdrop of a home left emaciated and chaotic under supposedly post-slavery British rule. But homelessness and half-way housing separated families in the 'mother country'.

> *When we came off the boats at Southampton, we didn't walk into council houses. My room was so small I couldn't even change my mind in it, and the rent I was paying was so large I couldn't change my mind in the post office.*

If work was relatively easy to find at first, it was underpaid and exploitative. The restoration of wealth required by Britain's stagnating economy was in part created through its revenue and taxation. Whilst this propped-up welfare for white Britons, a near total colour bar segregated access to housing, aid and labour.

> *...there was the enormous creation of wealth in Britain on the back of blacks. That is the system of exploitation that I am talking about.*

I trace how operations of colonialism made their way across the metropole, with logics and practices that echo across these spatio-temporal entanglements to remake the colony at home.

> *They once colonised us in Azad Kashmir, and in some village in Africa, but they are colonising us now 15 miles from Downing Street.*[3]

These movements did not leave colonial techniques intact but reproduced their underlying frameworks. In particular, colonial logics categorised people for exploitation, dispossession and disposal. It is their reproduction in the metropole that I trace through this chapter.

Waste as matter out of place

To understand these logics, let us first consider how imperialist Britain forcibly 'remade' places as property. According to John Locke, property is defined by the transformation of land through labour.[4] In this sense, Locke's theory is antecedent to the labour theory of value associated with Adam Smith and David Ricardo. For land to be made a commodifiable asset it had to be cleared and enclosed, on which basis a system of wage labour could be formed. In England, enclosures had made way for the production of an agricultural and subsequently industrial wage labour force. At the same time, the conquest of Ireland, and to a lesser extent Scotland, had dispossessed land for English landlords. The English crown confiscated Irish lands, redistributing them to the English elite who made them into tenancies for a primarily English labour force. In part this relied on the dismissal of Irish customary law together with a legal regime that voided ownership where land was empty of 'civilised' people. As Patrick McAuslan writes, this relied on the underlying idea that:

[…] the natives have no law and no capacity to develop a modern state and society, and it is for their own good that their land is taken from them.[5]

In this sense, colonial dispossession of the Irish was the condition of capital accumulation for the English from the start. This forged a deep and long-standing division between English tenants whose labour was exploited, and the colonised Irish who were evicted and displaced to highly exploitative tenancies on the worst lands and transported to work on plantations in the Caribbean.

Locke's work provides the logical basis for this proto-capitalism, which was founded by the appropriation and reorganisation of nature and peoples into regimes of property. Expanding the colonial dispossession of Ireland, empire built the networks of trade and markets that would form the infrastructural basis for liberal capitalism, as well as instilling property regimes by restructuring material and social relations. According to these regimes, legitimate possession was formed as a relationship that could only be produced by the coloniser. Locke's definition was underpinned by a distinction between cultivated and wasted land, and vindicated by God's will:

God gave the world to men in common; but since he gave it them for their benefit, and the greatest conveniences of life they were capable to draw from it, it cannot be supposed he meant it should always remain common and uncultivated. He gave it to the use of the industrious and rational, (and labour was to be his title to it).[6]

All the lands of northern America were available for appropriation by the coloniser because there existed no commerce there, and so no cultivation or improvement of that land. Under the moral injunction of natural law, the land should be made productive and profitable. Whilst remaking places through labour instituted a regime of property that designated rights over enclosed land or other sources of surplus-value, this determination was in constitutive relation with 'waste'. The foundations of private property lie in these ideologies of labour as improvement and action, providing the means for transforming nature as waste into nature as property.

This required a subject deemed capable of shepherding the metamorphosis from nature to property – a subject who was industrious and rational. By contrast, the Indigenous other was marked by an incapacity to develop and improve nature, and so also an inability to make nature into property. According to this framework, they were rationally dispossessed by their own state of nature – a 'people arrested in their evolution, impervious to reason, incapable of directing their own affairs'.[7] Indigenous people were figured as regressive against a steady current of improvement and progress, themselves requiring improvement through the force of colonial regimes. Their relationships with land were invalidated, and their clearance and enclosure was legitimated as improving the 'waste-lands'. Land not cultivated by empire was understood as mere waste, with Indigenous people supposedly incapable of transforming land into property, so themselves becoming eradicable and exploitable. As such, by enclosure and armed removals, land *was made* property, the rights to which were ratified by law grounded in the fundamental right to exclude.[8]

Conjoined with Locke's moral justification was an economic argument that colonialism would increase land value and provide revenue for Britain. The distinction between waste and property formed the basis for dispossession and subsequent extraction of surplus-value. Not just means to acquire surplus-value through property rights, this process also marked distinctions with those who were justifiably (according to this regime) dispossessed – so articulating white Britishness as a system of power that would take the form of a property relation.[9] Those falling outside of this category were deemed waste as much as the land that was their home. The establishment of this white colonial subject in distinction with the racialised other was built through this dispossession, exploitation and erasure.

This chapter considers how these imperial logics and tactics provided the grounds for their later use in the metropole. They relied on figuring waste as matter that was 'out of place'.[10] Through this lens of waste matter as disordered and disordering, both uncolonised land and Indigenous peoples had posed a threat to the newfound social order of property and economy. I first turn to the ways that segregating and differentiating spatial geographies were produced as an attempt to territorialise these threats. I show how these logics were reproduced in England, buttressed by a tranche of policies and practices and public discourse that forged newly migrated populations as foreign threat. The racial purity of the nation was inextricable from anxieties regarding this contiguity of white Britons with their prior colonial subjects. A central drive toward this new segregation was the protection of property rights – maintaining the nation and its wealth as a white possession even in the presence of its racialised other. I go on to show these were not just protected, but also subsidised by a racial cheapening that produced forms of labour hyper-exploitation.

This leads me to consider neoliberal techniques of marketisation and financialisation as enduring forms of extraction and dispossession. The frontiers of the wastelands became despatialised and dispersed through the movement of people into the metropole. It thus became imperative to contain the wastelands in the same moment that it became necessary to rely on commonwealth labour for the restoration of the imperialist production of capital. What has resulted does not always look like the ghettoisation familiar to internal colonies of the US. Instead, the reproduction of colonialism as a property relation has resolved itself into flexible systems of distributive apartheid, which contain and disperse, exclude and include, hyper-exploit and discard.

FROM MAGIC MOUNTAINS TO THE SWAMPLANDS

Let us first consider strategies of segregation and their underlying logic as weapons against the threat of contamination. Across empire British invasion and settlement had been enforced by violence and sustained by spatial restriction.[11] The British created zoning systems for settlers, with housing for Europeans separated from colonial subjects. Since the seventeenth century, the British East India Company designated distinct areas of (then) Madras as 'white' and 'black' town. Later, more complex techniques were used to separate European and 'native' districts in hundreds of cities, perhaps the most famous examples of which are Edwin Lutyens-designed New Delhi, and the townships of South Africa.[12]

These processes of segregation are well documented across empire, forming zones that demarcate exclusion and belonging. As Fanon writes:

> The settlers' town is a strongly built town, all made of stone and steel. It is a brightly lit town; the streets are covered with asphalt, and the garbage cans swallow all the leavings, unseen, unknown and hardly thought about. The settler's feet are never visible, except perhaps in the sea; but there you're never close enough to see them. His feet are protected by strong shoes although the streets of his town are clean and even, with no holes or stones. The settler's town is a well-fed town,

an easygoing town; its belly is always full of good things. The settlers' town is a town of white people, of foreigners.

The town belonging to the colonized people, or at least the native town, the Negro village, the medina, the reservation, is a place of ill fame, peopled by men of evil repute. They are born there, it matters little where or how; they die there, it matters not where, nor how. It is a world without spaciousness; men live there on top of each other, and their huts are built one on top of the other. The native town is a hungry town, starved of bread, of meat, of shoes, of coal, of light. The native town is a crouching village, a town on its knees, a town wallowing in the mire.[13]

Their legitimation was the racialised state of nature – of waste – as enemy to be guarded against. Waste and the racialised other were bound up with one another as objects of anxiety and peril, making the enclosure of land and people imperative. This was fuelled by fears caused by the newfound spatial intimacies of colonial settlements that became woven into geographies of segregation against threats of disorder and impurity.

From colonies to the twilight zone

We often think of migrant people from Britain's colonies as forming the archetype of bodies deemed out of place. But this out-of-place-ness was not just a product of the movement of those bodies into the metropole. Migration saw the continuation of logics of waste as disordered matter out of place. These were enforced by systems of segregation, with 'slum administration replacing colonial administration'.[14]

Initially the British government attempted to draw labour from its former and contemporary colonies in a guest-worker style system to rebuild post-war economic growth. The sustained immigration that took place in the middle of the twentieth century saw increasing numbers of people living in squalid inner-city conditions in overcrowded reception areas. Determined to some extent by geographical demands for labour and post-war housing shortages, this was also caused by a near total colour bar meaning that migrant people were forced to occupy housing stock that was vastly overpriced and neglected. From the late 1950s, slum clearance orders in England and Wales led to around 170,000 people per year moved from inner-city slums to estates and flats around cities' outer rim. Predominantly white occupants of inner-city slums and council housing were moved to peripheral estates, or otherwise used the opportunity to escape from areas that had become established in the public imagination as ghettos.[15] Large numbers of white people in receipt of public housing support or in private rentals moved away from urban centres.

The state had mostly devolved responsibility for housing to local authorities who had consolidated segregation principally by barring rights to access public housing. Residence requirements and informal racism in the allocation of public housing had largely disqualified recent immigrants from council housing until the late 1960s. Migrants of colour had been forced to move into privately rented housing of below-average quality and above-average density, whilst facing huge discrimination in the marketplace.[16] Prevented from accessing housing ownership or public housing, this left them filtered into overcrowded bedsits in decaying areas, at the mercy of exploitation by landlords like the infamous Peter Rachman. Even those relatively few Black people who did live in clearance areas tended to be excluded from rehousing and were corralled into private rentals instead.

The buildings housing Black migrant people and their families would have been next to go should clearance policies have remained, but by the mid-1960s policy began to shift towards *in situ* improvement. These shifts came about as a result of increasing pressure on public authorities by legal requirements such as the Race Relations Act 1965, together with social resistance to the rehousing of Black people in new council estates. At the time, Labour politician Reginald Freeson charged local governments in areas of high immigration with behaving as though Black people didn't exist. In 1966, he argued in parliament that local authorities were failing to execute redevelopment plans because they did not want to rehouse immigrants 'living in twilight zones of major city areas'.[17] Even so *in situ* improvement policies were consolidated under General Improvement Areas (GIAs) in the 1969 Housing Act, and Housing Action Areas (HAAs) introduced in 1974 – both of which coincided with primary Black residence areas.

As a result, Black communities were largely retained in the highly segregated areas of cities to which labour settlement had drawn them. Sam Selvon captured this in his novel *The Lonely Londoners* (1956), which reframed London through creolised English and traced the contours of informal cities within the city – 'little worlds, and you stay in the world you belong to and you don't know anything about what is happening in the other ones'. These worlds are the derelict spaces that others couldn't really know, with people existing 'in a twilight subterranean enclave of cramped rooms situated somewhere between Notting Hill and the Harrow Road'.[18]

The handkerchief turns black

The colonial fear of contamination had spread to the metropole – not only of racial degradation but of threat to economy and property regimes. After the Race Relations Act, an informal colour bar limited housing options to areas that were racially tainted. This fear was written into Selvon's prose – '[w]hen Moses sit down and pay his fare he take out a handkerchief and blow his nose. The handkerchief turn black.' This was symbolic of the resurgence of the colonial logic of waste as matter-out-of-place, which supported controls on the spatial distribution of commonwealth immigrants.

This resonates with the ways that colonised populations had been pathologised, both physically and mentally, as justification for segregation:

> Uncivilized Africans, it was claimed, suffered urbanisation as a pathol-
> ogy of disorder and degeneration of their tribal life. To prevent their
> pollution contaminating European city dwellers and services, the idea
> of sanitation and public health was invoked.[19]

Bolstered by European theories of health, hygiene and disease, this desire for sanitation symbolised anxieties on behalf of the British against the degeneration of racial stock. Isolation was required to prevent the spread of diseases, whose source was supposedly the non-European. The hill station in Freetown, Sierra Leone became an experiment for the building of white towns away from the clammy air of urban areas. British settlers built widely spaced bungalows that were designed with ventilation to dispel the air and germs that were imagined to be radiating from the Black people in the valley below. In turn, urban slums were regulated or cleared and inner-city inhabitants removed to townships elsewhere.

The same underlying idea 'that African bodies, customs, and neighbourhoods were particularly likely to generate both germs and mosquitos'[20] of Sierra Leone, also underwrote the white flight of private housing as well as shaping the provision for higher standard suburban public housing for working-class white people. For example, urban planners in English development had long been influenced by the development of suburbs in colonial cities such as Madras.[21] The East India Company's monopolistic control over suburban real estate had formed the basis for defensive strategies against the supposed physical harms of the 'black plague' and cultural and economic harms caused by proximity. Familiar across cities divided by race across Africa, colonial settlers in Sierra Leone built an elevated British residence overlooking Freetown. This echoed the way that hill stations had been built in colonial India. These 'magic mountains' were chosen at higher altitudes to prevent British colonisers from becoming too intimate with 'natives' whilst also warding of the supposed mental chaos that could be produced by Britons spending too much time in tropical climates. Segregation was understood as a necessary safeguard against racial degeneration, shoring up whiteness by the architectural simulacra of the English country town.

Similar techniques had been used across empire in building cities at transport and military hubs.[22] Their physical construction and maintenance required proximity between coloniser and Indigenous population. The management of these spatial intimacies relied on buffer zones of parkland and industrial buildings. British city planners thought that these would maintain order and the demonstration of civilisation against the disorder of Indigenous ways of life. Entrenching differential spaces helped to resolve anxieties and contradictions regarding the commingling and proximity of colonisers with Indigenous people. These were fraught with fears at the intersections of racial purity, health and property.

In the metropole, parallel spatial arrangements were reproduced by so-called 'white flight'. White residents abandoned inner-city areas, leading to neighbourhoods populated by majority migrants of colour whilst the white middle class self-segregated to monocultural suburbs. Averting the disaster of contagion required their ongoing protection, with fears rising by the mid-1960s that migrant people previously consigned to crowded slum houses would try to move into white residential areas. Such fears were exacerbated by collective practices of communal housing and financing known as 'sou sou' and 'pardner hand', as well as mortgage clubs and the shared buying of properties by extended families.[23] In response, self-segregating white areas were heavily guarded from possible incursion. Tenants and residents' associations organised to keep migrant people away, and public health laws were used to dispel multiple occupancy and break up collective housing.

The threat of contamination was writ large in public discourse. Famously, Enoch Powell named this 'separate and strange population' as a threat to be guarded against by a white nation becoming undermined by alien values. He advocated for the repatriation of immigrants in his 1968 'Rivers of Blood' speech, and employed an image of race as danger – 'their colour marks them out', as he put it. In parliamentary discussion and public discourse, these immigrants were compared to pestilence and threat, with the horizon of racial extinction implicit in these debates. Thatcher had studied Powell's speeches, echoing closely his archetypal approach to the racialised other as risk to the nation in her now infamous 1978 interview:

> If we went on as we are then, by the end of the century, there would be four million people of the new Commonwealth or Pakistan here. Now, that is an awful lot and I think it means that people are really rather afraid that this country might be rather swamped by people with a different culture and, you know, the British character has done so much for democracy, for law and done so much throughout the world that if there is any fear that it might be swamped people are going to react and be rather hostile to those coming in.

Grading respectability

As was the case in the colonies, English segregation shouldn't be put down to state design alone. It was produced at the confluence of state control, coalitions between state and corporations, and informal practices supported by a burgeoning white middle class. As the threat of the other was felt to be present within the metropole, so too were the segregating practices of racial steering and a racialised offer of public housing.[24] Public sector housing remained difficult to access under Thatcher, with migrant communities receiving the worst properties – when they did so at all. Whilst a legal colour bar was officially prohibited, in effect this was translated into cultural measures hidden inside bureaucratic systems. Central to these was a respectability grading, which differentiated tenants according to culture and existing environment. This was given credence by the pathologisation of migrant populations in studies of child development and poverty in the 1970s and 1980s.[25]

In 1972, London GP Margaret Pollak carried out research on three-year-old children in her south London practice, following up with the same children at age nine. According to her investigation, allegedly poor verbal and cognitive skills in a 'West Indian' sample of children were caused by parental absences, unsatisfactory childminding, and lack of interaction and stimulation.[26] As a way of ensuring the reproduction of the nuclear family for immigrants, in 1968 restrictions had been put in place so that only children with both parents residing in Britain would be allowed entry. Even so, the familial arrangements of immigrants were subject to the scrutiny of sociological and psychological study. Analyses of behavioural disorders and emotional disturbance were undertaken, with particular concern over the ways they might contribute to the reproduction of social disadvantage in the education system.[27] In 1977 the Labour government launched an inquiry into the underachievement of Caribbean children, its partial results released under the interim *Rampton Report* in 1981. Whilst this pointed toward stereotyping and racism at work in the classroom, the controversy that resulted led the new Conservative government to force the replacement of its chairman with Michael Swann. The result, known as the Swann report (1985), had taken eight years to produce. It too noted a climate of racism in schooling, and it advocated cultural diversity in education whilst denying genetic causes for differential attainment. However, it also attributed reduced educational outcomes to environmental and cultural differences, singling out the higher proportion of single-parent households in Caribbean communities.

The poverty and life experience of Black families was supposedly accounted for by differences in family structure, parenting style and household organisation. Sociologists were not just complicit in these explanations, they actively produced them. Most significantly, Ralph Dahrendorf in 1987 helped popularise the notion of an underclass which was marked by race. This underclass was to be found in urban areas and suffered under a culmination of social pathologies.[28] The idea strengthened divisions between a deserving and undeserving poor along racial lines, distinguishing between those especially impoverished, and those just ordinarily poor. The divisions were well-established by the burdening of migrant communities with their own welfare. Whilst not actively proscribed from welfare services at this time, they were ignored and excluded by ignorance from agencies that treated Blackness primarily as a threat to the existing social fabric. The need for care of an ageing population in the 1980s relied on expectations that 'Third World values' and the extended family would deal with them. Somewhat ironically, immigration laws in the 1980s had actively worked against the existence of extended families residing in Britain.

The withdrawal from public building together with a loss of council housing stock through the Thatcherist 1980 Housing Act right-to-buy policy further entrenched this division. The subsequent commodification of housing replaced subsidies with tax relief on mortgage interest. This supported massive shifts in housing provision. In the early 1950s half of all households were in the private rented sector, but this had fallen to 10 per cent by 1980, with a majority of households owning their homes.[29] The properties most suitable for purchase were on the suburban estates almost exclusively occupied by white families who took the opportunity to enter home ownership. For instance, in Nottingham between 1976 and 1979 over 10 per cent of this 'good' council stock was transferred to owner-occupied stock.[30] The remaining public housing offer was stratified by race, with allocations limited to poor quality properties in inner-city areas so continuing the segregation of communities already installed there.

In the private sector, house prices were depressed in multicultural communities. Strategies of segregation had led to spatially differentiated patterns of racial inequality across value, mobility and risk assignment determining access to credit. Local building societies were well-known for redlining, refusing mortgages and steering migrant people to certain areas.[31] To a degree this was ameliorated by loans made by local authorities. Council loans were offered as mortgages on properties in improvement areas, so attracting Black people to buy homes there and in 1976, around one third of Black owner-occupiers were reliant on this finance. However, these were available only in these cheaper inner-city areas, and were awarded with far higher interest rates, shorter loan periods and punitive safeguards than typical mortgages. As such, Black and Asian borrowers paid more for their loans, and due to the structures of tax relief on mortgage interest received far fewer subsidies than white higher-income owners. This widened the gap between home owners and renters as well as between owners whose homes provide a source of capital accumulation and those whose homes failed to store wealth because they were tarnished by geographies of waste.

Alien territories

Communities from prior colonies were often powerless to take advantage of the commodification of housing as a direct result of the uneven development of Britain. They were unable to accumulate or even retain wealth because they were situated in segregated areas facing 'the locational inertia associated with a downward spiral of house conditions and relative house prices'.[32] Exacerbated by mortgage redlining and property inheritance, these practices, policies and discourses had led to the systematic confinement of migrant people to marginal and underdeveloped areas. These had been justified by figuring migrant people as illegitimate competitors for scarce resources – as foreign invaders who occupied 'alien territories' within the metropole. The systems that produced segregation in England were predicated on irrevocable difference of those people configured as regressive and less civilised, whilst replicating the material basis for that configuration. They continued attempts to territorialise waste against the threat to social order, which supposedly issued from claims to state provision, property ownership and the accrual of wealth.

As a result, there was no significant dispersal of Black people into predominantly white wards,[33] whilst residential location was critical in determining 'their subordinate position in society'.[34] For example, inner-city areas had huge levels of unemployment, with a 1982 study showing that Black people born in the UK to West Indian parents were four to five times as likely as their white counterparts to be unemployed.[35] This had not only been produced by migration and its resistance. Rather, these communities were already figured as threat and contagion by colonial logics that had marked them out as waste. Claims to the welfare and wealth of the metropole were prohibited and guarded against just as Indigenous claims to land had been understood as threat to the established power of empire. Migrant bodies were not rendered out-of-place through their mass movement across colonial lands, they had been so across empire.

EXTRACTIONS FROM THE TWILIGHT ZONE

In this section I suggest that strategies of segregation were intertwined with strategies to continue colonial accumulation and exploitation. As such, it becomes important to understand segregation not just as a containment strategy (of people and wealth), but also as a technique for the differentiated extraction of value.

People who had previously lived under colonial rule forged a transnational web of connections across neo-colonial territories. The twilight zones – systemically produced in post-war Britain – provide a conduit for the continuation of processes of accumulation by dispossession and specific forms of exploitation. For example, the City of London, financier of neo-colonial extraction and land-grabs in the global South, is also reliant on the exploitation of cheap migrant labour to clean its offices, nurse its workers, and to care for its children in what Parrenas terms the 'international transfer of caretaking'.[36] This is tied to practices of consumption of goods and services that produce higher incomes, such as for home owners to purchase labour to improve their homes to better store wealth. Collapsing spatio-temporal relations that had previously been carried over land and sea by white colonisers, these new forms of spatial intimacy have also led to new ways to produce surplus humanity and economic dependency.[37]

Labour and political capture

The differential access to wealth accrual enforced by segregated housing was conjoined with market logics that translated racialised hierarchies into labour hierarchies, pay discrepancies and barring of access to more secure forms of work. Thinking through these transmutations requires us to dismantle the idea that capital accumulation has been the basic motor for neoliberal societal transformation.[38] The picture we are offered by such a view is one in which the logic of capital accumulation is supposed to have formed a set of social conditions in which race and imperial relations become irrelevant, replaced by abstract relations of the market. Let us briefly articulate and dismantle this narrative.

The racialisation of immigrants has been central to the process through which national identities were formed in opposition to the imaginary threat of a surplus labour force to be drawn upon at will. This coheres in part with Marx's theory of surplus labour. The idea is that shifts toward industrialisation required the formation of surplus populations, whose size and character is governed in accordance with capital accumulation to be drawn into production or expelled into unemployment. For instance, the reduction of prices often leads to wage decreases, unemployment, and welfare retrenchment which maintain the production of surplus-value. In that case, surplus labour is used to put pressure on the workforce to accept these lower wages, shoddier working conditions and intensified production processes. This explanation foregrounds the composition of a surplus labour force through post-colonial migration that responded to temporary labour supplies in the expanding industrial economy until the mid-1970s. The thought is that deindustrialisation and the decimation of labour power in the 1980s then led to the increasing precarity and flexibility of the entire labour force.

It is certainly the case that the weakening of labour power under Thatcher relied on the myriad ways that the labour of racialised migrant communities was exploited differentially against those of the white working classes. These depended upon active and accumulated discrimination, colour bars preventing Black and Asian workers from promotions, and exclusion from union membership. Indeed, not just excluded from them, unions actively resisted the employment of Black workers, taking industrial action to defend a white labour force. In 1955, the West Bromwich Transport Corporation held a series of Saturday strikes against the employment of a single Indian trainee conductor. Supposedly more progressive unions and organisations like the TUC refused to intervene in discriminatory practices, instead blaming migrants' refusal to integrate.[39]

The resulting irregular employment and poverty fed into the pathologisation of a racialised underclass. For example, a Working Party on Coloured People Seeking Employment in the United Kingdom was set up by the Conservative cabinet in 1953. Their report suggested that work was not easy to come by for colonial migrants because of their 'irresponsibility, quarrelsomeness and lack of discipline'.[40] Sedimenting into common sense beliefs that migrants were criminal, lazy and predatory helped to justify public discourses that welfare reinforced rather than reduced poverty. This relied on an entrenched idea that the white working classes were victims of a racialised lazy underclass whose claims to state resources and instrumental use as strike-breakers had led to their own relative precarity.[41] As such, explanations of racism can be 'added to other symbolic mechanisms of class exploitation as an excessive ideological device the dominant class imposed upon the exploited', as Da Silva writes.[42]

Racial cheapening

However, neither the scapegoating of migrants nor their use as a flexible source of surplus labour can fully account for the ways that colonial relations have engendered labour stratification in the metropole. Often missing from these accounts is how the consolidation of power for working- and middle-class white Britons had been derived from revenues gained through empire, which acted like a racial subsidy to the metropole:

> The super exploitation of the Third World has brought material comforts to the white working class such as consumer goods, welfare state and a standard of living beyond the country's resources. The white workers have been incorporated in the system because they, too, get their share of the cake.[43]

The subsidy continued. The colour bar did not, strictly speaking, *bar* people from work, it segregated colonial migrants into badly paid and deskilled jobs with lowered wages through 'acceptable' forms of exploitation familiar to the colonies.[44] There, standard economic theories of the value of labour would falter due to the lack of a substantial reference point that could form the basis for measuring surplus-value. For instance, plantation economies could not rely on measurable forms of capital to regulate work and rationalise production since value was produced as a result of the capture and subjection of labour.[45] Enforcing different rates of surplus-value has been central to the unequal transfer of value in colonial and post-colonial economies.

Not confined to the colony, analogous problems manifest in the metropole regarding setting labour value in the context of migrant communities. Roughly, the rate of exploitation can be measured as the ratio of surplus-value to wages. Ordinary exploitation arises from the unequal conditions under which the exchange of labour occurs. Standard narratives emphasising surplus labour and scapegoating seemingly assume that the rate of exploitation is relatively uniform across the population, with competition in the labour force motivated by labour valued at the same rate. But labour time and economic value have not operated in a linear relationship with each other. Rather, the value of labour for racialised communities was set in conditions of unequal exchange that gave rise to forms of hyper-exploitation. For the hyper-exploited, wages are set below the value of labour power.[46] With a differential ability to enforce the rule of exchange produced under conditions of barred access to labour and unions, racialised communities were systematically paid less than their white counterparts for the same labour.

As the Race Today collective wrote in 1974, the employment of Black and Asian people reproduced colonial relations through:

> ...low pay, the fiddling of bonuses, the constant harassment of the workforce for more productivity, the imbalance in the production targets given to blacks and whites, the non-existence of Asian shop stewards, the restrictions that made up their daily working lives as compared to those of the white workers – washing time, tea breaks, lunch breaks, toilet breaks, dignity.[47]

The market value of labour was set by a moral economy of racial cheapening, allowing for differential rates of exploitation from the active work force.[48] This racial cheapening of labour was both produced by and productive of logics of people as waste products. They formed an underclass whose ultra-cheap labour power produced value that was captured, rather than created, by British workers, companies and the state.

Importantly, the hyper-exploitation of this racially cheapened labour allowed a white majority labour force to operate at class levels, and accumulate wealth, higher than they would have otherwise been able.[49] White British workers were able to leave lower-paid jobs, or to take supervisory roles for higher wages. Labour stratification thus made possible unequal exchange transferring surplus to subsidise labour and capital for largely white middle classes. It is through the dynamics of this combination of subsidy and the production of a racialised underclass that the reserve price for white labour was set. This process was central to producing the conditions under which welfare retrenchment would later be able to get off the ground. The erosion of the welfare state was made feasible not just by undermining labour power, but by forming a safety net that had made it possible for white Britons to receive higher wages and status, better-skilled positions and property.

Ongoing deindustrialisation and deregularisation of employment law led to large-scale shifts that began to replace long-term and stable work with flexible forms of employment. Companies employed fewer core staff with a broader flexible staff, and subcontracted labour to prior colonies. These differential production costs and local workers' rights have been core to the accumulation of capital in the imperial core, with borders not just excluding workers, but producing uneven geographies that are manipulated to facilitate labour arbitrage. That is, to move industry to create jobs in areas where wages and business costs are less expensive. Conjoined with increasingly restrictive visa and immigration policies and the stigmatising and racialisation of cheapened labour, this has allowed for migrants in Britain and wage-workers in the periphery to be hyper-exploited, propelling an already segregated populous toward informal and marginal economies. In other words, the mechanisms through which surplus-value was produced require us to recognise how the reproduction of colonial logics have forced a potentially unitary labour force apart.

The accumulation of capital has relied on a structured labour force that is not indifferent to race, but works through the 'social production of "difference"', as Lisa Lowe writes.[50] Neither operating only at the level of ideological superstructure, nor only an effect of economic structure, the formations of race work sub-structurally to organise the material and structural basis for capital accumulation. In other words, the remaking of racialised populations in the metropole was inextricable from the production of a de-homogenised working class. This was a social articulation that relied on distinctions between the working class and a racialised underclass, whilst reproducing divisions that had been instrumental to the formation of proto-capitalist systems of property and labour. Borrowing from Patrick Wolfe, these can be articulated in terms of a difference between an exploited labour force whose reproduction is required, and a hyper-exploited racialised underclass who is ultimately consigned to expulsion and exclusion.[51] The logics of waste had become attached to migrant bodies, pitting a subsidised working and middle class who could sell their labour and compete within markets, against an underclass whose fate lies in the balance between hyper-exploitation and disposability.

MODULATIONS OF EXCLUSION AND INCLUSION

In this section, I show how these distinctions between people exploited and expelled continued to be manifest by the complex dynamics of racial exclusion and inclusion in property acquisition and financial systems since the 1980s. These involved continuing the carving up of lands into heterogeneous geographies and discrete spaces, with the attachment of 'different versions of the human to different places'.[52]

Extortionary inclusion

Previously excluded by mortgage redlining and neighbourhood devaluation, the refusal to lend to migrant populations was gradually replaced by extortionary inclusion. This had the effect of bringing money and savings that had been circulated within communities through collective purchasing of properties and lending into banking and financial systems. Shifts in the financialisation of lending markets and the privatisation of development made this possible, with people drawn into the financial system as it became easier to obtain credit.

By financialisation I do not mean to create a distinction between the operations of abstract economics and 'real' capital accumulation. Rather, I am interested in how wider financial industries and banks operated on broader economic systems and social practices to form a set of specific and systemic tendencies through relations of interaction and exchange. First, this allowed corporations not primarily concerned with finance to reduce their reliance on bank loans and acquire financial capacities. Second, banks expanded activities into financial markets and household lending, and, in particular, to act as an intermediary between the two. Third, ordinary people and households were increasingly involved in finance, both as debtors and asset holders.[53] So financialisation was intertwined with individuals and households, not only via mortgages, but by student debts, payday loans, hire purchase, credit cards.

This followed techniques that had enabled the transfer of lands into capital investment through privatisation and the strictures forcing the liberalisation of resource markets in peripheral economies. Since the 1960s, a frequent tactic was to use debt to restructure states through punitive intervention and conditions on lending. Lending between US and Latin American countries during the oil crisis was a means to make relations of indebtedness into a disciplinary device to restrict taxation and nationalisation and to ensure US dominance. In the metropole, debt was also used to restructure communities and economies. Where the debtor has seemingly entered into an agreement of their own volition, power asymmetries exist between debtor and lender – the relationship itself forming a new set of affordances and capacities for intervention. One aspect of these is what Costas Lapavitas describes as financial expropriation. This is the ability for the direct extraction of profits from workers' revenues and accumulated wealth – through mortgages, credit cards, hire purchases and loans. This has since become systemic practice. Regimes of permanent indebtedness are grounded in asymmetrical social relationships that exacerbate precarity and expropriate future incomes.[54]

Deregulating markets

As mentioned above, Thatcher introduced the transferal of housing association properties to Registered Social Landlords in the late 1980s. Together with the 1988 Housing Act, which defined housing associations as non-public bodies, this gave private companies overarching control over properties, depleted housing stock and opened up housing to finance.[55] This allowed for the expansion of finance to areas of the housing market that had previously been off-limits. For example, mortgages were offered in rundown inner-city areas, and for houses in decaying public sector housing estates under right-to-buy legislation.[56] These shifts also made way for a move from mortgage lending at the level of local savings and decision-making to national, market-wide criteria. Relational lending that had entrenched segregation through informal redlining gave way to supposedly colour-blind criteria, thresholds and risk assessments. One way this was established was through a reduction of bank branches in low-income communities. Around 17 per cent of bank branches closed in Britain between 1982 and 1992, mostly concentrated in major urban areas.

The translation of lending decisions into objective and centralised criteria failed to abstract from the differentiations that had led to racial redlining. Instead this process obscured and expanded differential economic inclusion. Modelling the value at risk for lending decisions relied on the statistical manipulation of risk that was mediated between banks and customers. The ground level of these financial technologies was predatory lending practices and risk assessment that reproduced racialised difference within socio-spatial risk pricing. In effect, the assessment of loan applications quantified prior racial discriminations and historical structures that had segregated and devalued racialised communities.

Contextualised within 1980s Britain, financialisation linked workers' revenue to slow wage growth and welfare cutbacks, but also to forms of wealth accumulation that were primarily realised through home ownership and rising house prices. This served to consolidate markets that had been unevenly distributed by rising house prices by largely white property owners in more affluent areas, against stagnant lower-priced areas marked by race, This translated differentially configured spaces into seemingly commensurate systems of value, reproducing them on the terms of a market hierarchy that forced higher interest rates and more punitive measures on mortgages granted in those areas. As a result, capital from segregated communities was exported at accelerated rates. For decades this had been made possible by charging far higher rents for poorer properties, but now it was administered by greater interest charges and large numbers of mortgage defaults.

As this liberalised lending market began to swing back in the 1990s, finance was increasingly restructured toward the more stable middle-class heartlands. Levels of debt in the UK in the early 1990s surpassed net income, so demand for debt-related products like loans and credit lines fell, and insurance firms began to raise premiums or refuse policies. At the same time, New Labour set in motion mass-scale development projects in urban areas. Under civil pressure, the essentially untouched twilight zones finally received recognition from politicians to deploy plans for urban renewal. But in this context, these were written as strategies designed for expropriation and dispersal. Tony Blair's urban renaissance strategy (1999) translated discourses of ghettos into 'sink estates', and pushed through redevelopment projects that would open up inner-city housing to wealthier renters. These so-called regeneration projects were underpinned by public–private partnerships such as private finance initiatives (PFIs).[57]

Operating on prior stratifications, divisions were created between preferential banking and investment services that privileged those with wealth, and the end of free banking, increasing levies and charges, for those without. This served to further police the boundaries of the financial system, with those who had been allowed inside financial markets in the 1980s now forced outside by punitive charges. Many people were forced into highly unequal dependency relations with financial institutions. Left reliant on banks yet abandoned by them, people often needed to look beyond market regulated financial systems and so poorer communities became rife with exploitative and predatory services – offering annual interest rates of over 1,000 per cent. These sub-prime credit markets employed risk pricing strategies that specifically employ call centres to target non-standard borrowers.[58] The barring of access to standard financial systems supported existing economic power – larger financial institutions were again incentivised to lend only in higher income areas, and to people deemed financially proficient. Predatory lending continued to operate at the other end of the market to larger financial institutions and banks, whilst both nonetheless safeguarded financialisation as a disciplinary mechanism and highly asymmetric social relation.

Privatised segregation

The segregation and underdevelopment of inner-city communities was compounded by their privatisation, with ever dwindling public funding backed up by an inability of communities to access funds to maintain the built environment. Where there still exists public housing, residential qualifications have returned through the Localism Act (2011), and are exacerbated by choice-based letting schemes run by private companies. The cumulative nature of selective credit provision in which decisions to lend money involve determining their long-term value have led to downward spirals of decline.[59]

Today, as a result, whilst 32.5 per cent of white households own their property outright only 8.3 per cent of Black households do.[60] Not just ownership, the situation and condition of housing are racially differentiated, with a quarter of Black and Minority ethnic households living in pre-1919 homes, often in poor repair, harder to heat and situated in deprived neighbourhoods.[61] Nearly 27 per cent of Black and Minority ethnic population live in the 25 per cent worst neighbourhoods in England, while the corresponding proportion for white population is 8.6 per cent, and children who live above the fourth floor of high-rise blocks in England are most likely to be Black or Asian.[62]

Housing stock is an equally important indicator of racial discrepancies, with Black and Minority ethnic groups more likely to live in flats, maisonettes and apartments (29.8%) and terraced housing (29.1%), whilst white households more frequently live in detached and semi-detached housing (26.1 and 34.7%, respectively).[63] In 2001, the charity Shelter reported that nearly half existing bedsits were inhabited by asylum seekers, many of which were cockroach-infested, damp and overcrowded.[64] Racialised housing deprivation remains unaccounted for by geography, socio-economic status, age, household structure or date of arrival in the UK.

BLACK HOLES OF EXPULSION AND ERASURE

This section ends this chapter by showing how the configuration of differentiated populations as controllable, hyper-exploitable and expendable has been rapidly accelerated since the late 2000s. The segregated conditions of housing and wealth accrual since Windrush have formed the basis for the rapid reorganisation of society not just to hyper-exploit, but increasingly to expel racialised communities.

Unhoming

At the confluence of segregation, home ownership projects and racial subsidy, a white middle class was consolidated. It was in their material interests to uphold policies and reinforce systems leading to higher home prices in a context of diminished state support and financial discipline. As detailed above, this was inextricable from the mass-scale redistribution of wealth away from racialised communities. This has since been embedded by the package of redistribution and restructuring forming the austerity programme since the late 2000s. Wealth that migrant communities had fought to accumulate has been systematically extracted and eradicated by austerity measures leading to massive-scale cuts to public service funding, and reshaped discourses and practices of exclusionary social citizenship.[65] Jobs have become more precarious, with real wages reduced, people who had worked more than one low-waged job losing one or more of them, high levels of anxiety, and lack of access to the same benefits as British citizens.

Changes to the system of universal credit that we have witnessed in the UK sit atop a series of cuts to benefits and alterations to tax systems, all of which have disproportionately affected Black and Minority Ethnic women. As a result, Black women (employed or not) stand to lose £5,030 a year – around 28 per cent of net individual income of those not in employment and 20 per cent of those in employment.[66] A study carried out by the Women's Budget Group shows that Black families in the poorest fifth of households will see their living standards fall by over £8,400 a year on average between 2010 and 2020 due to cuts to benefits and services. The results of these cuts are already stark – in 2017, 59 per cent of Bangladeshi children, 54 per cent of Pakistani children, and 47 per cent of Black children in Britain live in poverty.[67]

Across the board, housing, planning and immigration legislations brought in since the 2008 crisis have involved an accelerated program of social reorganization that codifies social entitlement and exclusion. Secure tenancies in social housing are being phased out, with higher earning tenants having to 'pay to stay'; local authorities forced to sell low-rent higher-value properties to subsidise voluntary right-to-buy programmes; eviction powers are to be extended; residential qualifications are to be expanded, which are directly discriminatory to asylum seekers and indirectly to recent migrants.[68]

These work in tandem with major development projects in urban spaces. Partnership schemes between rapacious developers such as Landlease and councils like Southwark have seen the mass-scale process of housing demolition and rebuilding. The estates regeneration project that was put in place under the 2010s Conservative government sold local authority properties, and particularly housing estates, to private companies. Redevelopment and commodification have resulted in people forced from communities, made to leave places like the Aylesbury estate, which had been carefully managed through a steady process of decline.[69] Huge numbers of people have been displaced, as far as from Elephant and Castle to Hastings. Still others are expropriated from their housing and businesses by massive rises in rents. Echoing practices of mass eviction occurring across the global South, this displacement is a violent material and emotional rupture.[70] Between 2012 and 2015, this great unhoming saw more than 50,000 families (over 150,000 people) evicted from London boroughs.[71] In the process, multicultural communities have been broken up and dispersed whilst their remnants see exacerbated levels of poverty and are increasingly vulnerable to destitution.

Of matter out of place

Inner-city areas that were produced as waste through downward decline have been renewed through the return of the wealthy. Privatisation, enforced decline and redevelopment are well-worn colonial efforts, appropriating land and subsistence to force people into dependency, precarity and hyper-exploitation. So-called urban improvement renews civilising discourses and colonial exploits. The urban wastelands are transformed from corralled spaces for hyper-exploitation and predatory exclusion to sites of improvement and development through expropriative displacement.

Emerging in the work of 1950s Latin American economists like André Gunder Frank, theories of domestic colonialism have long centred economic underdevelopment.[72] Social stratifications were understood as the consequence of designed underdevelopment, leading to the isolation of Indigenous communities and their unequal incorporation into the machinery of racial capitalism. Similar mechanisms were found to be at work in 1960s US. Most famously, Stokely Carmichael and Charles V. Hamilton foregrounded an underdeveloped people whose colonised status was maintained by relations of economic dependency. For example, John Lindsay, then mayor of New York City, wrote that:

> The basic similarity between Harlem and an underdeveloped nation is that the local population does not control the area's economy, and therefore most of the internally generated income is rapidly drained out. That money is not returned or applied to any local community improvement.[73]

Spaces of uneven development continue to be a matter of white (re)-settlement, enclosure and exclusions. As charted above, the ongoing inflections of development and underdevelopment form the racialised geographies of contemporary British landscape. I have drawn attention to the regeneration of colonial ordering through alliances between state and finance, anti-migrant policies, white resentment and the pathologisation of the alien within.

The evolution and ultimate demolition of so-called sink estates was made possible through the slow violence of disinvestment and state attrition – of destruction at a pace that evades that of the spectacle. The underlying logic supporting this violence has been the economic and social differentiation of spaces into places for neglect, exploitation and disposal. Drawing on Mary Douglas's idea of 'dirt as matter out of place', Ben Campkin argues that dirt and the classification of order continue to inform these architectural practices and spatialised demarcations. They are manifested by the purification of the sink estate and the reclassification of housing and land as waste. For example, the 2015 Institute of Public Policy Research report *City Villages: More Homes, Better Communities* argued for the rezoning of council estates as brownfield land, allowing their value to be better maximised. Brownfield land refers to land that may have become contaminated, so requiring clearance before redevelopment – it is by definition land that requires cleansing from contamination.

These processes have been given popular justification by claims that increasingly isolated racial communities are 'literal black holes', as broadcaster and former chairman of the Commission for Racial Equality Trevor Phillips put it, 'into which no one goes without fear and trepidation and nobody escapes undamaged'.[74] The psychosis of whiteness, as Kehinde Andrews writes, consistently avoids the realities of the production of white monocultural suburbs as well as the revanchist expansion of the wealthy into spaces occupied by the racially condemned.[75]

Distributive apartheid

According to writers and activists based in the US, the geographical segregation and subordination of a differentiated population was necessary for internal colonialism.[76] The ghetto was understood as the major device for persisting anti-Black colonisation. However, in the account of post-war Britain given above, whilst such separation was present, it has not been so clear cut. Given the pervasive redeployment of colonial strategies of segregation, hyper-exploitation, expropriation and expulsion, this suggests that linear segregations aren't necessarily features of internal colonisation. In Britain, at least, their underlying logic is one of exclusion, extraction and erasure that operates across molecular and molar worlds.

I have shown how relations of contiguity and dispersal were forged through colonial exclusions and intimacies. Coloniality continued through the reconstruction of whiteness as a property relation that operated through exclusion, exploitative inclusion, geographic containment and diffusion – Selvon's little worlds are nested and labyrinthine. As we have seen, exclusions exist in cases of regional co-existence: through the management and modulation of segregations across wealth, housing and access to resources. What starts to emerge in this account is a picture of *distributive* apartheid.[77]

On 14 June 2017 Grenfell tower in affluent North Kensington became a site of death and despair. Fire spread rapidly upwards because of the flammable cladding that had been installed to make the building more attractive to nearby developments. This was cheap and substandard. It was installed without requisite safety measures, leaving an air-gap between the cladding insulation and building that prevented firefighters access to the fire. Protestations about the cladding and fire safety of the tower had been ignored by local council and government, deaf to the voices of the racialised poor. Colloquially called the Moroccan tower, those living in Grenfell were caught in conditions of coloniality – confined to 'lives of poverty in a dilapidated and dangerous building in one of the wealthiest places in the world'.[78] Grenfell had already been rendered waste at the fulcrum of the reverberations of colonialism, forming an open wound 'where the Third World grates against the first and bleeds'.[79]

As argued above, at the heart of colonialism's annihilative drive has always been a flexibility to shift between relations of hyper-exploitation and those of expendability.[80] The dispersal of colonial spaces and bodies across the metropole carries with them this logic of potential erasure – as Fanon recognised:

> The zone where the natives live is not complementary to the zone inhabited by the settlers. The two zones are opposed, but not in the service of a higher unity. Obedient to the rules of pure Aristotelian logic, they both follow the principle of reciprocal exclusivity. No conciliation is possible, for of the two terms, one is superfluous.[81]

The corollary of this is the enforcement of control, surveillance and detainment through state and privatised violence – it is this to which we now turn.

3
Policing Empire after Empire

We are the disobedient
we overspill and overspeak
we are unboxed, unharnessed, unfathomable
        (Suhaiymah Manzoor-Khan, 'A Virtue of Disobedience')[1]

The struggle of our new millennium will be between the ongoing imperative of securing the well-being of our present ethnoclass (i.e., Western bourgeois) conception of the human, Man, which overrepresents itself as if it were the human itself, and that of securing the well-being, and therefore the full cognitive and behavioral autonomy of the human species itself/ourselves.

        (Sylvia Wynter, 'Unsettling the coloniality
        of being/power/truth/freedom')

CONTIGUITIES OF VIOLENCE AND REFORMISM

This chapter traces how strategies and logics underpinning violence and policing across empire were fundamental to the reproduction of colonialism in the metropole. In the previous chapter, I sketched how the logic of colonialism led to the segregation, hyper-exploitation and disposal of racialised communities in Britain. This chapter shows how the pathologisation of entire groups of people was reproduced and consolidated through logics of hereditary criminalisation, together with practices of social control, surveillance, militarisation and containment.

The great insohreckshan

In January 1981 in New Cross, south London, a house fire at a teenager's birthday party was likely caused by a racially motivated arson attack by one of the right-wing groups active in the area. Following a number of fire-bomb attacks on the homes of Black people, the fire killed 13 Black children and injured 26 others. Subsequent police investigations were wholly inadequate, denying that a crime of racial violence had even taken place.² The Metropolitan Police suggested that the party had been gate-crashed by drug users in a cover up that preserved a long-held complicity between police and the far right. This led Black activists and community groups to organise as the New Cross Massacre Action Group.

*Come what may, we are here to stay.*³

Recalling the Southall march that had culminated in the police murder of Blair Peach two years earlier, a 'Black People's Day of Action' was organised for 2 March that year. Around 20,000 mostly Black people marched from New Cross to Hyde Park – a spectacle that clearly unsettled the police. Headlines the next day led with the *Daily Mail*'s 'When the Black Tide met the thin Blue Line', and the *Daily Express* describing the march as 'the rampage of a mob'.

it woz in April nineteen eighty-wan
doun inna di ghetto af Brixtan
dat di babylan dem cause such a frickshan...

Just a few weeks later, the Metropolitan Police launched Operation Swamp 81. Deliberately evoking Thatcher's infamous phrase, this involved mass police presence in Brixton, which was a centre for Black social and political life in England and an archetypal example of the distributive segregation discussed in the previous chapter. Plain-clothes police officers patrolled the area making indiscriminate stop and searches of nearly 1,000 people – mostly Black young men. On Friday 10 April, the onslaught on the community led Black young people to fight back against the police. The next day, later known as bloody Saturday, saw even greater police presence. A routine search on the Saturday afternoon led to a large-scale uprising, leading to 65 civilian and 299 police injuries, and over 1,000 police officers eventually flooding the area.

...an it bring about a great insohreckshan
an it spread all ovah di naeshan
*it woz a truly an histarical okayjan.*⁴

Below, I show that this act of anti-colonial resistance – this great 'insohreckshan' – was not just the culmination of colonial policing brought into the metropole. Rather, it resolutely set in place trajectories of policing whose regimes had reverberated across the Imperial state-at-large. Directed toward population controls rather than addressing crime, more punitive systems of criminal justice that had been developed across empire were used to govern the perpetual other now inside English shores.[5]

Metropolitan liberalism, colonial punishment

There has been an overriding myth about the civilising force of British empire that persists in some quarters today. This relies on the idea of a liberal metropolitan culture existing *prior* to empire that was subsequently being exported across the world. At first glance, narratives of British policing seem to support this imaginary. As J.M. Moore discusses, nineteenth-century shifts toward liberal reforms, education and welfare in the metropole led to the emergence of alternatives to imprisonment, declining prison receptions and declarations of its possible abolition altogether.[6] As result, the early twentieth century saw substantive moves toward penal reform, decarceration and welfarism in the metropole. In the 1910s, then home secretary Winston Churchill argued for decreasing the number of convictions leading to imprisonment by one third; to reduce the existing prison population; to abolish imprisonment for shorter sentence terms.[7] Churchill was part of a much broader movement towards penal reform, which between 1908 and 1939 saw the prison population of England and Wales halved from 22,029 to just over 11,000.

Borstals, understood as progressive methods for the reformation of young offenders, were looked to as preparing the ground for prison reformation. The Probation of Offenders Act 1907 allowed the imposition of probation, rather than imprisonment, for many offences and London probation service became a social service for finding homes, family reuniting and finding employment. The conceptual ground for these shifts was a combination of moral scepticism regarding imprisonment together with an impetus to return workers to society against the proclivity of imprisonment to produce recidivism. The humanitarian movement emphasised decarceration for prisoners' welfare, self-respect and social progress, against the prison method and deprivation of liberty as extremely cruel. With support from wealthy benefactors such as Alexander Paterson and the Howard League for Penal Reform, alternatives were promoted in place of imprisonment, and by the 1920s an emphasis on rehabilitating prisoners was entrenched across the prison system.

However, the 'civilised' and socially liberal tendencies of nineteenth- and early twentieth-century England occurred at the same historical moment as the Jallianwala Bagh massacre of peaceful protestors on 13 April 1919. That act of vindictive ruthlessness recalled events of the 1857–58 Indian rebellion, where participants were 'tied to the muzzle of a cannon before its discharge spectacularly terminated their lives'.[8] Brutal violence, punitiveness and imprisonment were endemic to colonial rule across empire.

Othering lawlessness

Moore argues that this colonial excess was justified by the supposedly universal principles of liberalism and their exclusionary exceptions. J.S. Mill famously argued that 'despotism is a legitimate mode of government in dealing with Barbarians, providing the end be their improvement, and the means justified by actually effecting that end'. This is borne out by practice. For example, in the nineteenth century self-claimed guardian of political and religious liberty Lord Acton proffered the justification that the British were working with 'nations in which the elements of organisation and the capacity for government have been lost'. Instilling this capacity required that they were 'educated anew under the discipline of a stronger and less corrupted race'.[9]

However, this sort of critique coheres with the idea of colonialism as 'civilising mission' – whether understood as misguided and racist, or as beholden to (Eurocentric) justificatory structures 'of its time'. The exceptionalities of liberal political philosophy and their outworking in colonial practice could be understood as lacunae in an otherwise universal humanism. Explaining the viciousness of empire by means of exceptionality hence offers a get-out clause that liberalism could retroactively suture. The wounds of colonialism could be figured as an unwelcome breach in an otherwise universal doctrine whose aims were reformism for all.

In distinction, I want to foreground how liberalism was functionally dependent upon the maintenance of coloniality. The creation of Britain as a liberal society required the existence of its others. As discussed in the previous chapter, the consolidation of property regimes relied on colonial exclusion and enforcement, so the conditions of liberal freedom were also born through this elimination and exploitation of Indigenous lands and peoples. This required the absolutisation of a specific form of the human subject who would be defined in opposition to its others. The distinction does not itself *result* from the logics and dispossessions driving colonial property regimes. As Sylvia Wynter argues, it results from the 'answer to the question of what is human and the present techno-industrial, capitalist mode of production is an indispensable and irreplaceable, but only proximate function of it'.[10]

Answering the question of what is human relied on ideals that emerged during the Enlightenment period.[11] In *Perpetual Peace* (1795) and *Idea for a Universal History with a Cosmopolitan Purpose* (1784), Kant had laid out a theory of universal social development with Europeans at the highest and most developed stage thus far, together with a judicial theory of a single system of laws whose protection against less-developed states should be financially and violently enforced. At its core lies an image of the European in the image of liberal humanism, common to which was a 'commitment to *man*, whose essence is *freedom*':

> Liberal humanism proposes that the subject is the free, unconstrained author of meaning and action, the origin of history. Unified, knowing, and autonomous, the human being seeks a political system which guarantees freedom of choice.[12]

Knowledge, rationality and autonomy are bound together according to this picture of freedom as both determined and constrained by objective laws. According to Kant, rational morality is universal, so our actions are subject to critique under objective laws that demand our conformity with them. Whilst lawfulness and freedom are inextricable from one another, they are resolutely cast as distinct from causal events or processes.

This is because reason, according to Kant, must be autonomous and subject only to its own standards in order that it can give laws to us. The 'only uncompromised use of reason is the one in which the principles of its use are not forced upon it from the outside'.[13] Lawfulness demarcates the separation of the realm of reason from the realm of causation by means of freedom, which is to say, through reason's self-determination. However, this articulation is famously circular – the legislative approach to reason yields to a vicious regress which requires the causal exercise of power to stop.[14] The pre-emptive solution to this problem relies on the coupling of objective laws to a developmental theory of natural order through which objective laws might emerge.

Kant argues that development from 'the lawless state of savagery',[15] and towards this European ideal, would be guaranteed by the natural order of war and conquests that would spread Europeans across the world and impose European law. As such, he argues that even in case the foundations of a European state are unjust, there is an absolute duty to obey the law. This duty is a practical principle of reason according to Kant, 'requiring men to obey the legislative authority now in power, irrespective of its origin'.[16] As James Tully writes, justifying this principle is the idea that unsociable beings must 'have the law coercively imposed upon them by a master in order to establish the basis for the development of a lawful and rightful order in the first place'.[17]

So to define an objective realm of lawfulness also required the institution of lawlessness by force. This relied on the creation of two mythic worlds – civilised societies which had the capacity for rational and lawful government, and societies that existed outside of history which were lawless and despotic. It was only by writing the social systems of non-European countries out of the lawfulness required by reason that the exercise of colonial freedom could be produced – the structure of the laws of reason requiring the vigilant demarcation from that which is unreasonable: the domain of nature, affect and uncivilised forms of thought. Configured as inherently exterior to civil society, non-European people signified this outsideness to the 'territory of the universal principles'.[18] The colonised other occupied this sphere of mere causality – that which is intrinsically affectable and outside of the realm of lawfulness. Not only were the capacities of the 'lawless savage' considered to be less developed and thus subject to imperial rule, their resistance to the imposition of that rule was taken as evidence of their supposed lawless freedom. In other words, the Indigenous other was constructed as an object of the law who could not be protected under it. Resistance to the law was understood as a regressive resistance to reason that confirmed a state of nature and lack of socialisation that could see them progress towards rule-governed beings, which is to say, human.

Let me sum up. The self-image of the liberal subject was reliant on the symbolic and material configuration of groups of people as essentially lawless. In this sense, liberalism wasn't so much developed endogenously by the metropole and exported outwards, as it was fashioned through distinction, and protection from, the lawless, illiberal and despotic other.

The broader systems of political liberalism thus provided the foundation for a civil polity whose authority lies with democratic reasoning. But as David Theo Goldberg argues, the supposedly progressive liberal principles of liberty, equality and fraternity, correspond to a 'multiplication of racial identities and the sets of exclusions they prompt and rationalize, enable and sustain'.[19] This explains why liberal freedoms and reforms in the metropole were coupled with the violent erection of boundaries against an uncivilised world in the colonies – they were actively sustained by them. The liberal metropole was dependent on the colonies not just for imperial theft and subsidy, but for its logical integrity.

The liberal order required preservation against the constant threat of an irrational and lawless exterior – where both orders were produced through the construction of those boundaries. In what follows, I'll trace how this was used to police migrant bodies in the metropole, first considering strategies that remade Black migrant bodies as essentially criminal. The violent production of the racialised body as criminal other has been produced by strategies of policing whose roots lie with colonial force. Rationalities of lawfulness and lawlessness have been fundamental to the construction of liberal Britain. Through these practices, they have manifested a specifically post-colonial form of British belonging that has relied on the reproduction of the colony at home.

This pathologisation of Black criminality and the need to quell internal colonial uprisings underpinned shifts towards an increasingly militarised police force. I'll argue that this also explains why, in the 1970s and 1980s, there was a decisive end to reformist criminal justice in England, leading to what has been termed a 'new punitiveness'.[20] In a supposedly post-colonial and post-war metropole, the apparatuses and technologies of colonial violence were translated and modified, attempting to reproduce the uncivilised and lawless other *within* the metropole.

Shifting from reformism to the remaking of populations as surplus has been central to this 'new punitiveness' – indicated by shifts from decreasing prison populations even whilst crime rates remained high under a lenient criminal justice system oriented toward reform, towards penal expansion and the reappearance of the central social role of prisons. This has sometimes been explained by domestic shifts from welfarism to disciplinary neoliberalism. However, explaining these shifts requires us to expand away from considering only the internal machinations of the metropole, and to also take into account the non-linear spatio-temporalities of empire. To this end, I show how the formation of surplus populations continues colonial practices and logics. These are manifest by the manufacture of urban 'gangs' and the flexibility with which networks of suspicion and data are used to create lawlessness. Criminalisation and colonial forms of policing have been employed not just to exclude racialised communities, but to actively produce them as pathologised and alien – protection from whom was core to stability of national belonging.

(RE)PRODUCING HEREDITARY CRIMINALITY

Whilst historians have often regarded colonial India as a 'laboratory of mankind', this is particularly pertinent when considering what Jasbinder Nijjar describes as 'Britain's punitive and exploitative history of constructing, controlling, and punishing colonial subjects as criminal collectives'.[21] Through this, we can trace strategies that have produced populations as criminal and consider their redeployment by metropolitan systems of policing.

Criminalising tribes

Under the state–capital coalition forming the East India Company, large areas of India were controlled by its massive private armies. In 1835 the Thuggee and Dacoity Department was set up under civil servant William Sleeman as an intelligence collecting department targeting suspect criminal groups. This responded to the figure of the thugee – the idea of a native criminal intent on robbing and murdering their victims.[22] Later, under the British Crown, the Criminal Tribes Acts (CTA) of 1871 awarded powers allowing for entire tribes to be subject to exclusion and control by their classification as criminal when there was some reason to think there were 'thugs' amongst them. The act allowed for the registration, surveillance and control of tribes, with 13 million people classified under it by the early twentieth century, and no recourse to remove the designation.

Building on earlier campaigns against Thugs, the CTA provided a way of dealing with threats to the colonial state, not just by individual criminals, but entire tribes.[23] This relied on a deeply held belief that the tribes had a hereditary and biological propensity to crime. Further credence was provided to this belief by the development of the pseudo-science of eugenics in England. Conjoined with the CTA, this allowed for entire sections of society seen as a threat to colonial order to be indissolubly branded as criminal – using systems for the supposed pre-emptive identification of criminals using measurements of the skull and arm-span.

As a result of these logics, policies and execution, tribes like the Mappilas of Malabar in south-western India were considered irredeemably lawless and criminal. J.H. Stephens, a member of the viceroy's Executive Council in 1871, described the CTA as follows:

> It means a tribe whose ancestors were criminals from time immemorial, who are themselves destined by the usage of caste to commit crimes and whose descendants will be offenders against law, until the whole tribe is exterminated or accounted for in the manner of Thugs. When a man tells you that he is an offender against law he has been so from the beginning and will be so to the end. Reform is impossible, for it is his trade, his caste, I may almost say his religion is to commit crime.[24]

The causes of criminal activity were thought to inhere in the very nature of colonial subjects. This was an embodied and essentialised criminality, which could overcome all evidence to the contrary – 'reform is impossible'. Whilst supposedly scientific, the criminalisation of tribes was thereby constructed to lie in the realm of nature so they could not possibly be reformed.

Liberal failures and sus laws

I want to think about how similar techniques have marked people as inherently criminal and beyond reform as part of the reconstruction of colonial strategies in the metropole. This can be brought to light in considering the context of the 1981 Brixton uprising. Discussed less than the later miners' strikes, the uprisings in Brixton and subsequently across England became a central symbol in Margaret Thatcher's law and order strategy, which used state violence to repress and control their 'alien violence'.[25] As Tara Brabazon describes it:

> For many historians researching Thatcher's first term, Brixton appears an aberrant implosion in the economic rationalist narrative. It was a moment of unravelled consensus, when violent clashes between

police and protestors were the only means possible to protect the Thatcherite state.[26]

Tapping into Powellian language, the uprising was presented in public discourses as riots ending law and order and British ways of life. Lord Scarman's report on the 1981 Brixton uprising was more liberal, speaking to the 'understandable' failures of Black communities to deal with oppression and poverty, having 'no doubt that unemployment was a major factor [...] which lies at the root of the disorders in Brixton and elsewhere'. Scarman saw that Black communities faced similar disparities regarding education and unemployment as broader working classes, but far more severely, so 'young black people may feel a particular sense of frustration and deprivation'.

Scarman also found evidence of individual malpractice and the disproportionate use of stop-and-search powers against Black people. As might be expected, Scarman failed to criticise police practices at anything more than a superficial level, arguing only that 'racial prejudice does manifest itself occasionally in the behaviour of a few officers in the streets'. He drew attention, for example, to the use of a colonial tactic with a police battle cry of chanting, shouting and rhythmic beating.[27] This was most blatant in his pronouncement that '[i]nstitutional racism does not exist in Britain', leading to critique of the document as 'a liberal report, but one within entirely racist parameters'.[28]

The implementation of specific strategies of saturation and deterrence policing were foregrounded as the incendiary leading to the uprising. Nonetheless, whilst these are important, to adequately explain the increasingly punitive nature of policing in this era requires us to consider the barrage of practices used to maintain the segregation and control of Black and Asian people. Policing techniques familiar to the colony were reproduced through the criminalisation of Black young people as central to increasingly confrontational policing. The use of sus laws has rightly been highlighted in this regard. Directed toward individuals with an intent to commit any felonious act, whilst drawn from the Vagrancy Act 1824, the deployment of sus laws was descended from strategies employed under the CTA. Its use was reinforced by the revival of other laws like affray, conspiracy and blasphemy. Together these were used to flexibly accommodate much Black behaviour as criminal.[29] As a result, in 1979 in London, of 1,894 sus arrests, 767 were of Black people – at that point making up just 4.2 per cent of London's population. As a practice, their use operated as a form of social control and exclusion – to instil fear, control and deter. Their disproportionate use against Black people reinforced societal marginalisation and helped to recast them as an 'internal colony within the nation'.[30]

Born criminal

Whilst inflected with liberal condescension, Scarman's report effectively reproduced the predestined criminality of Black British communities – citing the 'rising tide of black crime'. This was compounded by Kenneth Newman, who was commissioner of the Metropolitan Police in the early 1980s, talking of Jamaicans in the UK as 'a people who are constitutionally disorderly'.[31] As Cecil Gutzmore argued at the time, the jollity of Black cultural forms were themselves seen as enough to warrant police targeting and intervention.[32]

In colonial India, the framework of hereditary criminality had given rise to an irresolvable tension that formed the basis of colonial policing. Groups of people were subject to the increasingly stringent and violent force of law whilst at the same time understood as not possibly subject to it. In this context the function of policing was not reform. Nor was it the prevention of criminal activity, since these were groups of people understood to be 'destined by the usage of caste to commit crime'.[33] Rather the function of colonial policing was the controlled separation and hierarchisation of colonial subjects and the identification of groups of people as born criminals.

Echoing the CTA, the same logics were reproduced in England. Black people were configured as axiomatically lawless, uncontrollable and outside the law, yet subject to its harshest implementation. Recalling the manufactured figure of the thugee, mugging had been staged as a widespread crime across urban Britain in the 1970s. As described in the landmark book *Policing the Crisis*, street robbery was remade in popular discourse as a crime perpetrated by Black young people.[34] As Cecil Gutzmore argued, the press and courts orchestrated the link between mugging and Black youth by dramatising deterrent sentences that were passed on specific cases. Subsequently, the Metropolitan Police reconstructed their statistics backwards several years, conflated crimes that didn't belong together, and recorded data on victims' perceptions of race of their assailant. In the mid-1970s, these statistics were released to evidence an exponential rise in mugging, principally carried out by

Black young people. In 1976, the Metropolitan Police claimed that early reports stating that the 'West Indian crime rate is much the same as that of the indigenous population' were incorrect.[35] Black crime was reported to be rife, particularly in multicultural areas. These were used to confirm the criminalisation of Black young people, with media narratives using the barely coded colonial language of their 'hunting' of victims. This drew on logics of hereditary criminality to foreclose racialised subjects under what Paul Gilroy describes as an 'inbred inability to cope with that highest achievement of civilisation – the rule of law'.[36] They were exacerbated by the consolidation of an increasingly static surplus population, whose irregular employment and poverty were read as inherently predatory and criminal.

Criminalisation ensures that people are maintained and controlled as a separate population whose claims on the state are carefully corralled.[37] Where hereditary criminality was linked to religion and caste in colonial India, in Britain it was engulfed by discussions of nation and belonging. The racialised migrant (or descendant of) from previously colonised countries was marked as the permanent outsider. The 'outsider' was rewritten as a folk devil subject to an increasingly punitive form of state regulation via the criminal justice system in what Gilroy called the myth of Black criminality. In this era, ideas of Black criminality emerged as central to racist 'common sense', so providing justification for pervasive, illegitimate, discriminatory and illegal police practices.

As such, policing was part of a set of practices that defined and protected the nation's boundaries from the enemy within, as Powell's 1970 election speech named them. The distinction was central to the criminalisation of migrant communities as *fundamentally* lawless. As Gilroy puts it:

[t]he subject of law is also the subject of the nation. Law is primarily a national institution, and adherence to its rule symbolises the imagined community of the nation and expresses the fundamental unity and equality of its citizens.[38]

The convergence of policing with logics of criminality and lawlessness produced populations that could not possibly be integrated into British society because they were configured as 'no-bodies'.[39] These communities were forged as a transcendental signifier for social problems and disorder, so requiring excessive quarantine and control.

Policing the nation

That the protection of the British nation looms in the background of these events is perhaps clearer against the backdrop of successive Race Relations Acts 1965, 1968 and 1976. These were core to a tranche of practices intended to deal with migrant populations. The Race Relations Acts conjoined increasingly stringent immigration controls targeted at quelling the amount of people migrating from former colonies with integration measures designed to appease the existing population. As Labour MP Roy Hattersley put it in 1965, 'integration without control is impossible, but control without integration is indefensible'. In other words, integration was a means of managing race relations that required, and was supported by, the increasingly violent policing of England's migrant communities.

Echoing these unstable relationships between law and lawlessness characterised by the imposition and flexibility of imperial law-making, the closing down of citizenship made migrant people increasingly susceptible to state violence. Under powers awarded by the Immigration Act 1971, a category of migrants with the right to work but not settle had been carved out. This made way for grounds of suspicion to be applied to practically anybody who looked like they might be a migrant. Stricter controls on immigration were enforced by passport raids in workplaces and homes in the 1970s and 1980s. People suspected of breaking immigration laws could be detained and questioned, and so the powers were used to disproportionately detain, stop, search and question non-British-appearing people, with entire communities rendered inherently suspect. Later immigration reforms in 1981 included imposing charges for the use of any NHS service on anybody who had resided within the UK for less than three years. As a result, racialised people were often required to provide proof of their eligibility prior to being given access to the health service.

Notably, police powers were exempt from the Race Relations Acts until 2000. This is unsurprising given that punitive policing was required to maintain the social order created by harsher immigration controls. Yet, their absence makes explicit policing's functional aim as guarantors of the state against the dangers of the immigrant other. Scarman's report was generally thought to indicate the ways that Thatcher's neoliberal cuts to welfare and increased unemployment had simply hit Black young people the hardest, so forcing them toward criminality. Not only does this misunderstand the functions of policing and the material construction of criminality, it also fails to account for the violent and paranoiac ways that policing had become the policing of nationhood itself. As Salman Rushdie noted in the early 1980s, '[f]or the citizens of the new, imported empire, for the colonised Asians and blacks of Britain, the police force represents that colonising army, those regiments of occupation and control.'[40]

In this context, Brixton highlights attempts to resist and to maintain imperial supremacy. Not only had this not abated under the Race Relations Acts, but it had been made difficult to redress since racial discrimination was deemed officially non-existent. Moreover, non-white citizens had been progressively stripped of the formal equality that had been awarded by the British Nationality Act 1948 conferring the status as Citizens of the United Kingdom and Colonies. In the wake of Powell calling for the UK to 'curb the influx of immigrants', the Callaghan Labour government went on to restrict non-white immigration through the Commonwealth Immigrants Act of 1968. Officially, Callaghan repudiated 'emphatically the suggestion that it is racialist in origin or in conception or in the manner in which it is being carried out', but cabinet papers recently released show that the legislation was specifically targeted at 'coloured immigrants'. The Commonwealth Immigrants Acts 1962 and 1968 meant entry into Britain could be denied for anybody who did not hold an employment voucher, or who could not prove they had the means to support themselves whilst in the country.

With the mass migration of Asians from Kenya and Uganda during the late 1960s and early 1970s, Conservative prime minister Edward Heath declared Britain to be in a state of emergency because of the immigration of people of colour. In response, Heath passed the 1971 Immigration Act, which entrenched the racialised differentiation of migrants across the Commonwealth and former British colonies. Where the 1968 Act had brought Black migration under control, it had not yet created the conditions for temporary workers. The 1971 Act achieved this by granting foreign workers a permit for a specific job for an initial period of twelve months. This shift from settlement migration to temporary citizen produced an explicitly hierarchised labour force along with far greater controls on migrants.[41]

Moving through parliament at the time of the uprising, the 1981 British Nationality Act removed automatic *jus soli* (birthright citizenship) and consolidated the category of the right of abode, building on the

1971 Immigration Act restriction to 'patrials'.[42] This had restricted right of abode through male descent to the United Kingdom. In effect this meant that white commonwealth subjects would be granted freedom of movement (from Australia, Canada and New Zealand, for example) whilst excluding those made British subjects under colonialism from Asia, Africa and the Caribbean. Legally defining British citizenship for the first time, this was written through hereditary bloodlines and the severing of imperial and neo-imperial interconnection. This was compounded at the time by calls in parliament to repatriate commonwealth citizens, supposedly to deal with the 'immigration problem' and forge Britain as a white nation disconnected from its form as part of a larger empire. The 1981 Act rewrote British identity as whiteness, whilst the criminal justice system materially produced Black people as alien and lawless outsiders: 'Black Britons were cast as the perpetual other within the nation – a colony within the metropole.'[43]

TRAJECTORIES OF POLICING AND MILITARISATION

According to Moore, it was around the time of the uprising that the rehabilitative ideal collapsed. In the 1980s, a focus on inclusion and welfare gave way to exclusion and containment enforced by increasingly militaristic policing.[44] Whilst things weren't really so clear cut, these shifts require us to understand their novelty in the metropole but also their continuity across a broader perspective on British policing. In this section, I show how these movements are best understood as the outworking of coloniality – not as a continuity that simply returns to the metropole, nor as rupture and developmental progress from it, but as condition and aim of policing.

Militarised temporalities

The concrete networks of migration across the new textures of the colonial world consolidated the use of techniques from elsewhere, now applied at home. Both personnel and strategies developed in the colonies were imported back from empire, with home policing ultimately converging with colonial practices.[45] The Police Overseas Service Act (1945) intended to maintain British policing in territories outside of the UK. This involved the secondment of British police officers to Britain's remaining colonies where forces were often facing crises of control. The movement of personnel also saw repatriated colonial officers slotted into senior positions in the homeland police force, with successive appointments to commissioner of the Metropolitan Police of ex-military men who had been central to counter-resistance operations across empire. In the mid-1980s, ex-Ugandan police commissioner Michael Macoun reflected that:

> So many UK officers over the last decade and a half have served overseas that some of them must have learned something about public order tactics which presumably they brought back with them.[46]

In Michel Foucault's somewhat fleeting analysis of colonialism, he borrows from Aimé Césaire the idea of the 'boomerang effect' to describe how colonialism returns techniques and strategies to their European home. For both, this is understood as a kind of inexorable return of colonial depravity, which could not be quarantined to the colonies 'over there'. As such, the tools of colonialism would be applied in European contexts, particularly in the context of authoritarian rule. As Foucault puts it:

> […] while colonization, with its techniques and its political and juridical weapons, obviously transported European models to other continents, it also had a considerable boomerang effect on the mechanisms of power in the West, and on the apparatuses, institutions, and techniques of power. A whole series of colonial models was brought back to the West.[47]

Whilst seemingly consistent with the narrative presented above, the metaphorical 'boomerang' is antagonistic with it for two interrelated reasons. First, it suggests an inevitability to the return of colonial techniques, rather than explaining them. Second, it attaches colonial techniques to a rise in political authoritarianism across the board, rather than analysing their interaction with other forms of policing and control. It is clearly the case that the colonies formed spaces in which experiments of surveillance, extermination and concentration camps were honed, as Césaire incisively clarifies. However, on its own, the 'boomerang' fails to explain how belonging in Britain was reforged through techniques of power, dispossession and control, as well as how specific and concrete strategies have been utilised in the reconstruction of coloniality at home.

It is well established that Britain's colonial policing of the Irish was used as a kind of test-bed for the later establishment of British police forces.[48] In the 1830s, Whitehall had established two police forces, one as law-keepers in mainland Britain, and the other, the Royal Irish Constabulary, to repress and control the Irish republican rebellions. The force was armed and had a military form that involved drills and marching. The Irish force offered the British government a ready-made model for policing in the colonies, which it drew on more formally from the middle of the nineteenth century. Ireland became a base for colonial police training, with officers of the constabulary travelling globally to provide training, and some senior officers from Indigenous populations journeying to Dublin for instruction.

A coalition between police and military was commonplace across the colonies, with military tactics used to control and repress, and policing integral to the maintenance of colonial power once in place. The use of excessive methods against Indigenous populations, and particularly those deemed a threat to the socio-political order of dependent territories, meant that 'colonial policing culture [was] distinctly political in nature'.[49] The force of policing lay not in the protective shape of liberal welfare, reform and the emergent socio-democratic consensus familiar to the metropole, but in active strategies of state control and violence that had been developed across empire in a range of locations and contexts.

In recent history, this was perhaps most blatant in 1950s Kenya. There, the British state carried out thousands of judicial executions – often in absence of concrete proof, and through the dubious categorisation of activities as terrorism.[50] The battle against the 1950s Land and Freedom Army (known by the British as the Mau Mau) rebellion in Kenya involved mass containment, torture and genocide. Presided over by Conservative prime minister Harold Macmillan, this employed techniques familiar to responses to colonial resistance in India, the Caribbean and South Africa. As Elkins describes, this was part of a 'murderous campaign to eliminate Kikuyu people, a campaign that left tens of thousands, perhaps hundreds of thousands, dead'.[51] This was backed up by a politics of forced containment of around 1.5 million Kenyans to a network of detention camps and enclosed villages. British settlers forced Kenyan people into specific areas such as tribal reserves, from which the Kikuyu tribe, who were thought to provide a network of support for the rebellion, were removed by burning down villages, and resettled into camps that were surrounded by barbed wire fences and spiked trenches.

The British did not only deploy tactics like these in the context of so-called 'emergencies'. Rather, policing cultures in the colonies were primarily of a paramilitary character. The colonial police acted as a kind of state military – in contrast with the image of the British policeman as essentially civilian bobby on the beat – which required policing by consent in order to retain legitimacy for the political regime. The militarised policing of Kenya expanded on structures that had been developed across empire where excessive policing was common – involving spectacular executions, illegal raids, extortion, corruption and 'mindless brutality', as Cole puts it.[52]

Tracing colonial inflows

In the 1980s, the two traditions of policing became increasingly conjoined. In the period that followed the 1981 uprising, policing models were developed that targeted populations supposedly at risk of participating in future violence drawing on public order tactics tested in the remaining colony of Hong Kong. In September 1981, the Association of Chief Police Officers (ACPO) met for their private annual conference in Preston.[53] The director of operations of the Royal Hong Kong Police, Richard Quine had been asked to present strategies used in their paramilitary approach to public disorder. Their approach distilled decades of British colonial policing into command and control networks, riot suppression units who were armed and flexibly deployed, and street patrols for curfew enforcement. As Northam writes,

> Its public order tactics are a compendium of methods which have been tried and tested for forty years in all the former colonies. They have repressed dissent and put down uprisings in the Caribbean, up and down Africa, in the Middle Est, the Indian sub-continent and in the Far East.[54]

Quine recommended forming an elite squad to be trained in tactical exercises and transformed into a paramilitary unit. At the conference, the ACPO formed the *Community Disorder Tactical Options Inter-Force Working Group* who were tasked with the compilation of the *ACPO Public Order Manual*, which was approved by then home secretary William Whitelaw, as well as a range of training materials including the system resulting in the *ACPO Public Order Training Manual*.

Whilst thousands of officers were trained using the manual, this had been conducted in secrecy, with the decision to shift policing towards a paramilitary approach known only to the Home Office and higher-ranking police officers. The manual advises tactical options in the face of serious rioting that include use of smoke, baton rounds, tear gas, and in the case of lethal rioting, firearms. The ACPO found justification in Scarman's report, where he had written that '[t]he police must be equipped and trained to deal with this [disorder] effectively and firmly whenever it may break out'. This added to the legitimation of more explicitly deploying colonial approaches to policing, and training the police to fight as soldiers on the streets of England against possible future colonial uprisings.

Newman, who had been appointed Commissioner of the Metropolitan Police in the wake of Scarman's report had previously worked for the British Palestine Police, and most recently as Chief Constable of the Royal Ulster Constabulary. Under his direction, the Metropolitan Police was restructured, with criminalisation and militarisation essential to transforming Black and Asian communities from enemy of the state into enemy of 'the people of Britain'. The enemy within would therefore become the enemy of all, since, as criminals, they embodied a struggle against social order. As Newman stated, 'it would be better if we stopped talking about crime prevention and lifted the whole thing to a higher level of generality represented by the words social control'. New regulations ensured similar changes across Britain, bringing social services under the banner of community policing, expanding surveillance powers across public bodies, and legitimating extensive stop and search.

Importantly, these shifts focused as much on community policing as paramilitarisation. Crucial to generating legitimacy in an era of race and class-based struggles was the development of seemingly innocuous projects like Neighbourhood Watch. Emerging from strategies used in Northern Ireland and the response of white communities to civil rights movements in the US, Newman made Neighbourhood Watch integral to his multi-agency reorganisation of policing. The seemingly antagonistic drives toward individual acquisition and community action were made interdependent in service of marshalling differential power over space, property, and the means of accumulation. Suburbs shaped in part by white-flight needed their middle-class self-defence league to embed surveillance into everyday life and continue to draw distinctions and limits within and between communities.

As such, the pervasiveness of policing across people's lives strengthened the legitimacy of coercive force whilst delegitimising political action against the state. For example, Douglas Hurd would go on to use the scheme to exemplify 'Active Citizens', and in 1984 Thatcher proclaimed that 'Every citizen has to help. No-one can opt out. If you want our country to be safe, you cannot afford not to get involved'. However, this sort of community political-policing crossed political divides in the period, becoming embedded in a shared common-sense. The uptake of neighbourhood watch schemes was not divided by partisanship but by wealth, property-ownership, and proximity to the urban wastelands. Alongside Crimestoppers and Crimewatch, the movement implicated many into routine and formalised low-level intelligence gathering. Intelligence gathering through the scheme was used to justify passport raids, raids on black clubs and meeting places, and arbitrary arrests.

Information collection was central to the paramilitary approach imported from Hong Kong, with intelligence units operated in 'peace-time' situations before public disorder broke out. Drawing on this, the British would construct an intelligence gathering machine that was put together from police information and public data. Whilst using telex and data management techniques, the ACPO looked forward to an auto-mated future. These special branches used classification systems that calculated the risk of outbreaks of public disorder alongside the use of focused policing and surveillance. Targeted policing was determined by these criteria, which included 'a high density of population of ethnic minorities; frequent trouble between gangs; hostility towards police as manifested by the incidence of complaints and difficulties in making arrests'.[55]

The initial meeting between the ACPO and the Hong Kong Police led to a formal relationship, with regular meetings leading to an exchange programme of operational officers. The control structure developed by the ACPO drew directly on theirs, with the chief constable able to transform a police force into a paramilitary unit in the context of an emergency. Models of paramilitarised policing that developed through the ACPO training were used to deal with subsequent rebellions in 1985: in Handsworth in Birmingham, Brixton, and the Broadwater estate in Tottenham. Police response was armed with guns loaded with plastic bullets and CS gas. Though they were not given the order to fire, this would be the first time that plastic bullets would be deployed on mainland Britain, and a precursor to the arming of police forces across the country. In the Broadwater uprising, more than a thousand police officers had been transformed into riot gear and suppression units within a few hours. In 1987, the Metropolitan police developed its own riot suppression units in the form of *Territorial Support Groups*. These were (and still are) trained tactical groups that could be transformed from ordinary police officers to a paramilitary group equipped for fast and flexible deployment. As Northam puts it, this requires the police to think of themselves 'as members of an army rather than a constabulary'.[56]

On riots and reason

The use of force had again been legitimated by discourses of the enemy inside – with Oliver Letwin famously arguing that the 1985 uprising was caused by the 'bad moral attitudes' of Afro-Caribbean rioters. Since Scarman, and into the 1990s and 2000s, sociologists and politicians had considered feelings of powerlessness and frustration on behalf of Black cultures in the face of being shut out of mainstream society and at the bottom of the economic ladder.[57] This might appear to do justice to the social and economic conditions under which racialised communities were living. But implicitly in this sort of evaluation is the idea that criminal justice was not capable of functioning as it should do; that policing and the courts couldn't operate as a reformatory and rehabilitating service for criminals because of the epidemic of violence and criminality that was largely confined to Black young people in urban environments. This understood criminalised behaviour as a kind of pathology, a lawlessness that was reproduced by economic hardship and social marginalisation. Steadily built on through the 2000s, this would increasingly inform social control and regulatory responses towards the perpetual outsider. In turn these legitimised and rendered sensible policies that were designed to discipline and further marginalise supposedly 'maladjusted' Black people and families. Politicians and popular media have foregrounded 'zero-tolerance' law enforcement driven by stories of youth violence that, whilst making no reference to race, are implicitly racialised by the accompanying use of images of Black and Brown faces.[58] But most blatant was Tony Blair's 2007 declaration that London's violence is caused by a 'distinctive black culture'.[59]

The English uprisings that occurred between 6 and 11 August 2011 are symbolic of the convergence of paramilitarisation and this pathologised criminality. During the uprising, thousands were involved in looting, arson and anti-police violence across England, answered with strengthening shifts toward military-style policing. The uprising was rooted in a protest focused on the request that Metropolitan Police meet the family of Mark Duggan. The police had shot Mark on 4 August 2011, and protests were exacerbated by police refusing to meet with his family and other protestors. By 11 August, more than 3,000 people had been arrested, with 1,000 people subsequently issued with criminal charges; there were five deaths and 16 others were injured as a result.

In the popular press the riots were derided for their feckless irrationality, sheer criminality and racial degeneracy.[60] But many rioters actively claimed their role in a struggle against more punitive policing. For instance, a 19-year-old Black student from Bromley stated:

> Everything the police have done to us, did to us, was in our heads. That's what gave everyone their adrenaline to wanna fight the police […] because of the way they treated us, we was fearless […] Same way they forget to think about us is the same way we forgot to think about them during the riots.[61]

The militarisation of the police response served to enforce the criminality of the uprisings framed as riots, with their supposedly apolitical nature confirmed as inhering in the psycho-pathological character of those involved. In colonial Kenya, the severity with which the Land and Freedom Army had been surveilled, expelled and exterminated had been legitimated by framing support for them as pathological and potently epidemic.[62] In experiments on captured Kenyan rebels conducted by the psychiatrist J.C. Carothers in the early 1950s, evidence was supposedly found which demonstrated that the uprising was not of a political nature, but due wholly to these pathologies of the mind. The pathologisation of English rioters similarly undermined their potential power as uprisings against police violence. Political pronouncements on them ranged from criminal, 'pure and simple' by then prime minister David Cameron, to members of a 'feral underclass' by then justice secretary Ken Clarke. This pathologisation of rioters was ingrained into the inner workings of the policing of public order units since the early 1980s. For example, the training of the London Territorial Support Group relied on the idea that rioters are fundamentally lawless and irrational. This unit had already been accused and found guilty of assault on children and young people on several occasions.[63] As a 29-year-old Black male rioter put it:

I've been beaten up in the back of one of them territorial support group war buses as we call them. These big black buses where they come and they kidnap us [...] And they beat us in there [...] They're monsters. Absolute monsters. And they don't have no law and justice in their heart. They look at us. They look at us as scum.[64]

Across the board, the uprising was understood as inimical to politics because, reframed as riots, it would be seen to lack reason, lawfulness and political force.

The framing and policing of the uprisings as riots exemplifies their sanctioning and control in order to enforce and demarcate lawfulness and lawlessness. Typified by disruptive, partisan and often violent action, riots are relegated to the result of irrational belief, the affect of crowds and social pathology. However, there is scant evidence for thinking that uprisings are not shaped by social norms, and mobilised through intransigence against 'consensus' politics. As mentioned above, the supposed rational sphere of liberal politics requires a line to be drawn between actions taking place in accord with meaningful rules, and actions that do not. This allows actions to be judged according to how lawful and reasonable they are. But if actions are driven by emotion and compulsions then they can't even be judged by these standards. This is apiece with the ways in which political liberalism monitors the boundaries of politics proper. Liberal reasonableness has been built upon spaces of democratic reasoning that are immunised against the import and content of certain statements, actions and people. In other words, the political content of those actions judged as lawless is pre-emptively neutralised as apolitical.

As one of the authors of a major report on the riots pointed out, judgments pronounced on the uprising served to annex it from the domain of the political, and very quickly return to the status quo:

You don't need to look below the surface here because there's nothing to find. This is just people behaving criminally and immorally. As soon as the cops have learnt to do their job, it will all be fine.[65]

Yet, the virulent force of the statements and subsequent sanctions on the rioters belie a recognition of their potential power. For example, Novello Noades, chairman of the bench at Camberwell magistrate's court, argued for a directive to make custodial sentencing on rioters harsh because 'the very fabric of society was at risk'. On the one hand, this recognises the agency of rioters as disruptive to current social power, and on the other, sanctions their activity as simply criminal and external to the domain of the socio-political domain. Such 'anti-normative' behaviour is castigated as both irrational excess and 'too' political.[66]

The sanctioning, police violence and legal censure of that action in the aftermath of the uprising does not result from the external misapprehension of its antinormative behaviour, but rather it awards it recognition as counter-normative, so requiring explicit and impositional power to recuperate the domain of lawfulness and lawlessness. This has been central to the redeployment of colonial strategies of policing in the metropole that work as an attempt to reproduce the nation against the spectre of the enemy within. For example, in the wake of the uprising came David Starkey's now infamous *Newsnight* diatribe that:

the whites have become black, a particular sort of violent, destructive, nihilistic gangster culture has become the fashion [...] which is this Jamaica patois that has intruded in England. This is why so many of us have this sense of literally a foreign country.[67]

Here, the pathologisation of Black criminality becomes contagious – recalling the justification for moving settlers to the magic mountains of colonial India. Maintaining the integrity of the nation against this epidemic legitimated a logic of social quarantine whose corollary was the militarisation of policing.

SHIFTING NETWORKS OF RECYCLING TO DISPOSAL

In this section, I show how this sort of epidemiological approach to Black criminality continues to underwrite the formation of surplus populations through the manufacture of 'gangs' and the flexibility through which data is produced to create conditions of lawlessness.

Remaking populations as surplus was familiar territory for British colonialism.[68] This relied on intelligence-gathering techniques that had been long central to dealing with political insurgency and particularly in the context of later decolonising resistance. The powers brought about under the CTA, for example, were made possible via techniques of surveillance and information collection. That had included census data and the development of fingerprinting technologies – first used in the context of criminal justice by the fingerprint bureau established in Kolkata in

1897 as part of the identification of criminal records. More broadly, ever-vigilant surveillance was central to the operation of colonial control – working to identify those seen as potential risk to colonial 'harmony'. Police intelligence units were created, with information collected on all subjects who were thought possible to threaten the political order coupled with stricter enforcement of what Mark Brown characterises as colonial 'penal excess'.[69] For instance, the British in Kenya imposed mass surveillance and stop and search practices against Black people, together with intelligence-gathering practices employing both inducement and torture. Analogous strategies work towards the containment of racialised communities and their consolidation in the symbolic and material fabrication of gangs as cause for violent crime.

The race–gang nexus

The 'race–gang nexus', as Patrick Williams puts it, was entrenched through the 2000s with specialist police (gun and) gang units employed throughout England and Wales. These include Trident in London, Ventura in Birmingham, Stealth in Nottingham, the Matrix in Liverpool and the Xcalibre Task Force in Manchester.[70] The set-up of these units was combined with the development of gang databases used to build up intelligence to inform policing as well as to increase conviction rates for members of gangs. Gang data is shared across agencies, having a generalised impact on young Black people – particularly since, as Amnesty put it, the addition to gang databases involved 'ad hoc and inconsistent standards and procedures'.[71] For example, grounds for inclusion in the gang matrix include intelligence gathering of social media activity, often involving the development of fake personas and befriending without a warrant. According to research on Greater Manchester Police gang 'intelligence', the majority of those named in connection with supposed gang members were associated through social rather than criminal links, such as family and friendship, whilst still receiving police attention due simply to risk analysis defined by proximity.[72]

These forms of policing produce gangs through an information-gathering machine that constitutes an archive for flexible and convenient deployment. Disparate and largely innocuous information is combined to make risk-profiles, which supposedly determine the potential to commit crime. Membership in a gang is made synonymous with Black and Asian young men, whilst violence and criminal activities carried out by white young people are defined out.[73] So the collective lawlessness of entire Black communities is translated into networks of criminality through risk analysis that is grounded in spurious connections that are remade as empirical data. This police-craft translates racialised criminalisation into objective criteria for pathologised violence.

In part as response to the 2011 uprising, David Cameron announced an 'all-out war on gangs and gang culture'. However, whilst violence in general is considered a gang issue, data suggests that less than 5 per cent of youth violence can be attributed to have any connection with a gang.[74] Even so, significant funding was again awarded to anti-gang policing. This led to the development of problem profiles, whilst increasing the use of the gang as a platform for legitimising the criminalisation of young Black men. The gang database also includes topographic mapping, which masks racial profiling by determining hotspot locations, with gangs determined by mere proximity to high ethnic heterogenous communities.[75] As Stafford Scott of The Monitoring Group in Tottenham put it, if 'you're black and born on an estate, nowadays the system automatically sees you as being in a gang'.[76]

As Nijjar describes, this has led to a situation in which '[b]lack people are disproportionately subject to a frightening mix of militarised antigang policing measures, including armed policing, stop-and-search practices, gang injunctions, and multi-agency forms of surveillance'.[77] An Amnesty investigation in 2018 found that 87 per cent of people listed in the gang matrix in London 2014 were Black or Asian, and 78 per cent Black only.[78] The long-held idea that economic marginalisation underpins punitive policing also loses its explanatory traction when we consider that the racial make-up of those on the gang database fails to reflect the ethnic composition of deprived communities.[79] Moreover, this is not just a matter of bias in its compilation, as Lee Bridges argues:

> As the police themselves turn increasingly to so-called 'intelligence-led' operations at a time of reduced manpower and resources, these databases feed directly into the ways that policing policies and priorities are being targeted on particular groups. In other words, the racial bias in the databases becomes institutionalised in police practice.[80]

This becomes particularly pernicious in conjunction with the joint enterprise law. This allows many people to be prosecuted for the same offence – so making way for the ability of the state to prosecute groups of people according to 'common purpose'. In other words, groups of people could be prosecuted together whenever there exists an association of all suspects (in a gang, for example) who had 'foresight' of the offence, together with intent (though the latter was added only in 2016). Given the over-representation of Black and Asian people in the gang database, it is unsurprising that, together with joint enterprise, there has resulted a hugely disproportionate use of the latter on racialised groups, with 76 per cent of people convicted via joint enterprise being Black men.

Spatial control

One way that this has been institutionalised is through targeted policing. For example, the 2017 Knife Crime Strategy worked with chicken shops and other fast food restaurants to 'control Wi-Fi and phone charging facilities' and 'play classical music' in an attempt to calm down risky adolescent subjects.[81] This was part of a wider plan to work with businesses, particularly in areas of London going through the kinds of urban renewal and regeneration projects discussed in the previous chapter. A scheme was introduced in these areas called Met Patrol Plus, which would increase the police force within a local area by allowing businesses and local authorities to match-fund policing in a two-for-one deal. Quite clearly, the state enforcement of racial profiling operates in direct collusion with capital and expropriative displacement. This was codified most explicitly by the proposal made by Home Office minister Victoria Atkins in June 2018 to remove council housing from families of listed gang members.[82]

A parallel logic is in operation with nascent concerns over 'county lines'. These have become increasingly used to describe the selling of illegalised drugs by primarily city-based operations expanding into suburbs and small towns. The techniques to do so typically involve younger workers transporting along 'deal lines' from city out of county. In public discourse, this has been presented as a new modality of gangs whose origin was at least partially constructed under the auspices of a war on drugs.[83] Importantly, however, this lies at the confluence between discourses of gangs and their dis-location from criminalised urban environments. Discourses around county lines embody the idea of Black invasion into spaces formed through white flight and associated shifts described in the previous chapter. Here, criminalisation meets the racialisation of white suburbs and Black urban spaces, with the policing of bodies out of place

– as alien invaders of white purity – imperative against their becoming infected by racialised disorderliness.

With these logics forming a basis of legitimacy, Trident have used pre-emptive incapacitation and disruption tactics to pursue supposed gang members prior to any criminalised act or the existence of possible evidence. They work through engagement with public sector partners to seek 'Anti Social Behaviour Orders – Hard Stops – Super Gang Injunctions – Stop and Searches – Evictions and even having children removed from the home'.[84] In the London borough of Haringey, this supposed pre-emption has led to gang members not being allowed to travel out of borough, and the Driver and Vehicle Licensing Authority (DVLA) being used to remove driving licences under the pretext of suspected drug use.

With the detective chief superintendent of Newham in London stating that '[g]angs are more dangerous than paedophiles' in 2018, we have also seen even greater militarisation of the policing of Black communities. London Metropolitan Police now carry out routine armed foot patrols in areas that are judged to be high in likelihood of gang activity. According to a 2018 investigation, the Metropolitan Police employed violent force such as handcuffing, stun guns, CS spray, batons and guns 41,329 times in April to August, a rise of 79 per cent compared with the same period in the previous year.[85] Of these, 39 per cent were incidents involving Black people, many of which were part of stop and search practices.

From recycling to disposal

From the 1980s onwards, policies and strategies put in place under both Conservative and Labour governments have seen a swelling prison population. Gang databases, joint enterprise and the flexibility with which criminal profiles are put together from disparate datasets have been conjoined with the creation of massive numbers of new offences. As a result, UK prison populations have doubled over the last couple of decades. There are currently 92,400 people incarcerated in UK prisons, with thousands of others in detention centres, young offenders' institutions and psychiatric units.[86] Weighted by proportion of population, Black people in the UK in 2015/16 were proportionally more likely to be in prison than Black people in the US. British Black people were four times more likely to be in prison than would be expected given their proportion of the total population.[87] Of under 18s in custody in the UK in 2017, 45 per cent are from designated Black and Minority ethnic groups, up from 24 per cent in 2007,[88] with rates of prosecution and sentencing for Black people three times higher than for white people in the UK in 2016. Perhaps most blatant is that Black men are 228 per cent more likely to be arrested, plead not guilty, and be sent to prison by the Crown Court than their white counterparts.[89]

Despite still using discourses of employability skills, education and rehabilitation, these are places of punishment and repression – '[p]rison is about punishing people who have committed heinous crimes', as justice secretary Liz Truss put it in her 2017 'biggest overhaul of prisons in a generation'.[90] The same discourses have been used to generate a mass prisoner workforce, more familiar to discussions of the prison-industrial complex in the US, where corporations extract free or ultra-cheap labour from convicts.[91] Familiar to colonial rule, containment has long been used to integrate people into the racial capitalism of empire through enforced penal labour. Here, under the Conservative–Liberal Democrat coalition government, what was euphemistically called the 'rehabilitation revolution' was designed to increase the employment of prisoners.

Over 300 businesses make use of prison labour, brokered by the New Futures Network (NFN). These businesses often draw attention to their use of prison labour as a way of suggesting they are using more ethically appearing practices. However, using a discourse of reintegration, this mass workforce is hyper-exploited, with no unions or strikes possible, and increasingly placed in the hands of private security firms like G4S, which now runs 14 UK prisons. If a prisoner works a full working week, consisting of ten morning, afternoon or evening shifts, or five night-shifts, and is considered to demonstrate adequate performance and effort in all activities then they are paid by the prison a minimum rate of £4. In other words, they earn 80 pence a day for a full working week.[92] Supposedly central to the functioning of (neo)liberal forms of democracy, this production of a contained workforce is directed at exploitation extraction rather than rehabilitation, and it is disproportionately Black.

Running counter to discourses of reintegration, prison-leavers are released into systems that systematically produce poverty and homelessness. Between 2015 and 2018, nearly half of the 220,411 people leaving detention were either classified as unsettled or left for accommodation that wasn't tracked.[93] There was a 25-fold increase of rough sleeping amongst those who had served short sentences between October 2016 and June 2018, with a quarter of short-sentenced prisoners released homeless – almost double the rate in October 2016. Abandoned by the state, one person under post-custody supervision takes their own life every two days. This is a sixfold increase since 2010, with 153 self-inflicted deaths in 2018–19 compared with 24 in 2010–11.[94] The purpose of incarceration is primarily to remove people from society, with incapacitation rendering the convict 'suitable for disposal rather than recycling'.[95]

THE FLEXIBILITY OF VIOLENCE

In the above, I've suggested that a common line can be traced across movements of policing and lawfulness from colonies to metropole through their use of hereditary and pathologised criminalisation of entire groups of people. These continue to underpin mass roll-out of surveillance cameras, DNA databases, communications monitoring and electronic tagging, techniques such as stop and search as form of social control, increased militarisation and excessive containment. Across the criminal justice system, state policing achieves specific modes of quarantine, control and disposal.

A central role of policing has been to remake colonial subjects and develop strategies for their removal and distinction from citizens proper. As such, the strategies and techniques discussed above were not simply returned to the metropole, rather they were utilised and developed in order to maintain the integrity of a constitutively imperialist nation-state through a period of manifest change. The structures of policing form points of convergence between colonial and liberal democratic experience, not as linear effects, but as encoded in forms of the political that we should call colonial.[96] That is to say, the configuration of policing concerns both order maintenance and the production and reproduction of colonial power in a context where the colonies are no longer at a distance but dispersed and intimate.

In this sense, policing is interwoven with broader structures of power and security, many of which are obscured as peaceful violence that is justified and normatively acceptable. That is, a violence that became rewritten as part of the natural order by logics of hereditary criminality and the pathologisation of Black communities. To a degree, this coheres with Jacques Rancière's analysis of the police *as* established social order.[97] What is normatively acceptable as lawful is both produced by broader structures of policing and is retained and continually forged through policing – with the borders of belonging modulated and flexibly managed – not simply as restrictions, but as productive of *modes of life*.

As such, strategies of coloniality have been transmuted and reconfigured in the context of new forms of sociality in England. The legitimacy and justification of liberalism required a significant change in order to deal with the increasing intimacy of a violence that had before been held at arm's length. Where liberalism required the vigilance and violent policing of liberal lawfulness and reason against the threat of the multitude outside, a neoliberal era has required much more labyrinthine ways into subjectivity that continue to render these distinctions possible at home. Here, the Enlightenment struggle between reason and unreason finds its figure in the shape of a law-abiding society set against the threat of an ignorant and uncivil population judged incapable of such behaviour. Cohering with the characterisation of distributive apartheid found in the previous chapter, tracking this populace has involved the metamorphosing production of lawlessness through its pathologisation within epidemic networks of gangs. This police-craft produces subjects not just as included and excluded, but as distributed threats, risks, deviants and differentially pathologised.

Belonging and non-belonging in post-colonial Britain has relied on the ongoing construction of distinctions between lawlessness and lawfulness. In a historical moment characterised by spatial closeness, the enemy within seemingly threatened the integrity of the nation. British policing has required the movement of exterior colonial violence in confrontation with this immanent other, whilst their basis for citizenship rights has been made increasingly precarious. Whilst fragile, this movement was a necessary part of the forging of supposedly 'post'-colonial Britishness. It is to this that I turn in the following chapter.

4

Homeland Warfare and Differential Racism

> call it crystalline, call it
> empire call it
> salt honed call it
> calais onward
> london
>
> (Asiya Wadud, 'Calais, onward')[1]

> But under what practical conditions is the right to kill, to allow to live,
> or to expose to death exercised? Who is the subject of this right?
>
> (Achille Mbembe, *Necropolitics*)

POST-COLONIALISM AS COUNTER-INSURGENCY

In this chapter I consider strategies of multiculturalism, counter-insurgency and the expansion of bordering regimes in the context of a political logic drawn from Enoch Powell's attempt to refound Britain through the post-colonial cut. Whilst supposedly inimical to Powellian nativism, I'll argue that state multiculturalism manifested differential forms of racism through an analytic of racial demography. In the context of counterterrorism, this became the basis for the adoption of counter-insurgency as a domestic strategy that was premised on, and consolidated, Britain's internal colonies. Building on this, I argue that attempts to refound Britain through the post-colonial cut find their culmination in the expansion of bordering practices that enlist all citizens as police.

A Trojan Horse

In 2014, a hoax letter was leaked to the *Sunday Times* that purported to be from a Muslim parent in Birmingham boasting of a plan for a hard-line Muslim takeover of several high schools in the area. Whilst an obvious false flag, a media frenzy whipped up panic around an Islamist plot to take over schools, radicalise young children and undermine fundamental British values.[2]

> 'Taught to Hate' – the Spectator cover story ran with a picture of a child holding a sword in one hand and a copy of the Qur'an in the other.

The allegations triggered a series of investigations into the schools under then Conservative education secretary Michael Gove. Gove's earlier policies had expanded the formation of academies first introduced under Blair. These were schools directly funded by the Department of Education and independent of local authority control.

> ...the nuances that separate us are irrelevant. We are all brown P***s basically, who wanted to take over schools that served majority Pakistani Muslim children, and push Islam upon them when they were already Muslim.[3]

The school at the centre of the allegations – Park View Academy – was located in east Birmingham in an area of extreme poverty where almost 80 per cent of residents are Muslim. Teachers and governors had worked against all odds to see massively rising achievements, in part by integrating aspects of pupils' home life and language into the school environment.

> We observed posters written in Arabic in most of the classrooms visited by the team and in corridors, advertising the virtues of prayer and promoting the Friday prayers (Jummah). Staff we spoke to said that the loudspeakers in the school were used to broadcast the call to prayer (Adhan) across the school, but were turned off on our visit because of a malfunction.[4]

The roll-out of academies had enabled this integration by allowing for a much greater role of communities in the shape that education could take. This gave rise to a dialectic of inclusion and exclusion, meted out along the political spectrum of liberal progressivism to social conservatism – the epitome of liberal multiculturalism being gradated forms of inclusion. At Park View, this stratified and precarious inclusion was wielded as bludgeon against them.

Students are not taught citizenship well enough or prepared properly
for life in a multi-cultural and diverse society.[5]

Reports fabricated narratives through the mishandling of evidence and gross cultural and linguistic misunderstanding. Antagonism towards supposed British values and a fantastical insurgent Islamic force were weaponised against the flourishing of young Muslim people in Birmingham. But in the process, what became known as the Trojan Horse affair points us towards fundamental instabilities at the core of Britishness as defined by and against its others.

Michael Gove argued that then home secretary Theresa May should
'drain the swamp' and not wait for 'the crocodiles to reach the boat'.[6]

The argument in this chapter develops those made in the previous two, suggesting that the shape of internal colonisation has been determined by attempts to forge Britain as post-colonial nation.

The post-colonial cut

I have already shown that a fundamentally colonial order was projected, submerged and transfigured across a post-war settlement within British shores. In this context of reverberating imperialism – of guest-workers and the narrowing confines of commonwealth – post-colonial nationalism became the pervasive horizon through which Britain would be remade and its antagonisms managed. This is particularly stark given that this moment perhaps held the potential both for acknowledgement of the colonial shape of Britain *and* its dissolution as imperial state-at-large. Yet the post-colonial cut was entrenched in practice and hegemonic common sense, with mass non-white immigration and the loss of empire filtered through a common drive to reformulate the purity of Englishness. In this way, the articulation of this post-colonial cut set in place political trajectories that attempted to remake Britain on the basis of the end of empire, but which nonetheless fundamentally relied on the continuation of colonialism inside British shores and imperialism beyond them. For this reason, Powell is symbolic of an enduring political philosophy that cannot be sloughed off as an ethnonationalist anomaly, but rather underlines the fragile tension at the heart of this moment of

Britain's refounding. As Bill Schwartz eloquently puts it, 'Enoch Powell became, in Gramscian terms, a political party in his own right.'[7]

For Powell, Englishness could be granted rebirth only by being cleansed of its colonial extravagances. As such, the post-colonial cut relied on the myth of a pristine island whose inner nature was contained by seas untouched by empire – dismembering empire was prerequisite for the reaffirmation of English nationhood.[8] So the post-colonial cut required the repudiation of any sort of colonial legacy that could be construed as more than the emaciated narratives of capitalist accumulation or the attempted proselytisation of the higher-orders of liberal civilisation and its railways. In response to challenges that Britain's economic advantage had been won at the expense of impoverishment of colonised nations, Powell decried '[i]t is nonsense – manifest, arrant nonsense'.[9]

This was possible because Englishness had supposedly remained intact and unaltered by empire – its intimacies not affecting its immutable core.[10] In Powell's hands, the English nation was defined by sovereign power, which was demonstrated by cultural characteristics that were exclusively inherited and maintained as white. Whiteness was the transcendental core of the nation – 'the English are a white nation' as Powell stated, both as eugenic principle and declaration of cultural accord. However, as the organising principle and foundation of Englishness, whiteness was defined apophatically – against that which it is not. Whiteness could only be animated by its other, intimacies with whom had threatened to corrupt the integrity of Anglo-Saxon stock.

If the manufacture of sovereignty after empire was to be won through the purity of the island nation, it was under threat from non-white commonwealth immigration. As such, it has become typical to trace abrasions and vehemence characterising citizenship and belonging to this singular moment – of post-war settlement that was fractured by the inwards travel of the colonies. Bill Schwarz encapsulates the thought as follows:

> ...just at the moment when the English were able once more to imagine their nation, not as diaspora, but as home, they were confronted with a presence at home which could not have been more unhomely.[11]

This doesn't quite square with the story given in previous chapters. The sovereignty of the British state at large had from the start been born from the assertion of power and authority over its others. As described in the previous chapter, the manufacture and virulent policing of this other was not accidental, but was rather a necessary exterior used to prop up the order of the social world.[12] Britain was economically, politically and logically dependent on its colonies. It was this which compelled Britain's refounding at home.

The exercise of sovereignty, as Amy Niang suggests, 'is not a fixed and unchanging fact but a flexible, mutable, negotiable, and layered normative principle.'[13] In the context of extreme instability post-colonial Britain renegotiated the terms of sovereignty through the ongoing legitimation of extreme and violent subordination of non-Europeans. The conditions that were productive of British sovereignty had long relied on logics and hierarchies of matter out of place, together with practices producing their naturalisation through violent enforcement. Knowing little of itself beyond empire, it is unsurprising that Britain's navigation of nationhood would continue to be funnelled through these same frameworks. As I've argued in previous chapters, what followed was a phase change within colonialism rather than a break from it. In a sense, the cut was already available within the foundations of colonialism. English exceptionalism had always relied on a paradoxical universalism. The distancing of empire from Britain was possible through logics already available to it: of the racialised other who was produced as waste, segregated and violently policed.

In an attempt to reproduce the cut as post-colonial, this fundament was translated into an underlying tension: between the myth of a pristine island nation and the 'necessary evil' of bringing colonial subjects back into the motherland alongside continuing socio-economic intervention abroad. This tension was the condition of post-colonial Britain. The presence of those made 'unhomely' was not antithetical to Powell's nation-building project – it was its prerequisite. The movement of a colonial outside inwards was itself a production of attempts to calcify a new image of Britain around its island edges, and Powell was instrumental to this formation. The coherence of Powellian Englishness – as immutable whiteness – relied on the reproduction of basic 'structures of colonial thought'.[14]

In this chapter I follow this line of thought to first show that, whilst moves towards state multiculturalism have often been positioned as antagonistic to Powellian nativism, they reproduced a threat to English nationhood that was framed by racial demography.[15] The privatisation of race made way for the pathologisation of specific cultural formations which, by the early twenty-first century, were increasingly singled out as problem for social disintegration, segregation and lack of 'community cohesion'. Together with concerns inflamed by the discursive weapon of Islamic 'terrorism', this fixed in place a long war at home. The war did not issue from a ready-made nation that was under attack, but as the manifestation of antagonisms essential to the coherence of a nature under reconstruction. For example, in 1970, Powell had argued as follows:

> Britain at this moment is under attack. It is not surprising if many people find that difficult to realise. [...] When we think of an enemy, we still visualise him in the shape of armoured divisions, or squadrons of aircraft, or packs of submarines. But a nation's existence is not always threatened in the same way. The future of Britain is as much at risk now as in the years when imperial Germany was building dreadnoughts, or Nazism rearming. Indeed the danger is greater today, just because the enemy is invisible or disguised, so that his preparations and advances go on hardly observed.[16]

Held on a precipice, the integrity of this new Britain would require paranoiac vigilance to ensure its stability. With this historical background, counterterrorism reinforced the progressive synthesis of criminalisation, paramilitarisation and cultural stigmatisation – finding their home in strategies of counter-insurgency. Though demonised by the Conservative government at the time and more liberal political formations since, I finish by arguing that the core logic of Powellism continues to drive the formation of Britishness. The British nation is not only guarded by borders of exclusion, it is a fabrication reliant on the proliferation of borders beyond national territories and across all of society – borders carried by people who are at once metropolitan citizens and colonial other. The nation continues to be built as a normative principle and material assemblage through an alloy of protectionism, securitisation and counter-insurgency against the other within. The remaking of Britain as a fantasy ethno-state and neo-imperialist infrastructure has produced internal colonies whose tensions have led to the collapsing together of total policing and total warfare.

CULTURAL VALUES AND DIFFERENTIAL RACISMS

Powell's nationalism has long since been dismissed as a nativism consigned to cultural and political conservatism, and supposedly cast off by multiculturalism. In this section, I'll suggest that the latter hasn't undermined attempts to produce Englishness through the post-colonial cut. Rather, this has been reinforced by the way state multiculturalism operated as a mode of control producing differential racisms. In this context, Gove's invocation of the 'swamp' is not an anachronistic aberration, rather it reveals the basis on which multiculturalism and its alibi in British values have always operated as tools for harm.

A line of defence to a mode of control

In 1966 then Labour party home secretary Roy Jenkins gave a speech on race relations that set out the coordinates for what has since become known as multiculturalism. As Charles W. Mills puts it, this has always been less a set of policies and more a conceptual grab bag that has come to symbolise practically anything relating to race in Britain since.[17] Jenkins advocated for integration over assimilation of migrants from the New Commonwealth, arguing that it should be defined by 'equal opportunity accompanied by cultural diversity, in an atmosphere of mutual tolerance'.[18] Putting race-talk aside, Jenkins emphasised the value of cultural differences, and considered equal opportunities legislations to be a means of ensuring their integration. These were enshrined in the Race Relations Act two years later, finding opposition in Powell's *Rivers of Blood* speech in the same year. The act made the state arbiter of what could count as racial prejudice. Perhaps unsurprisingly, the founder of the Racial Adjustment Action Society Michael X was charged and imprisoned for anti-white racism under the act just a year after it came into effect.

Multiculturalism provided a way to launder race-talk whilst propping up the integrity of Englishness. Invoking the presence of diverse cultures within a sovereign nation, multiculturalism offered a language where culture became a cipher for race and difference from a white core. Central to state discourse was the suppression of biological bases for racism together with the safeguarding of their supposedly epiphenomenal outworking as cultural difference. For example, the *Colour and Citizenship* report published in 1969 by the Community Relations Commission set up by the act explicitly foregrounded cultural difference, whilst assuring people that it should not be equated with inferiority. As Jodi Melamud writes,

[t]he replacement of white supremacy's biological paradigm with a liberal paradigm defining racial formations as cultural formations has long been heralded as a victory against scientific racism.[19]

Initially, however, activists and writers had foregrounded Britain's multiculturalism as a way to challenge Britain's supposed ethnic purity and form a bulwark against racist movements and Powellian nativism. Multiculturalism evoked the continued and unabated existence of Black and Asian people. From the late 1960s, this had been consolidated around the political stance and cultural category of British Blackness, and grounded in a shared experience of oppression and a discourse positioning them as 'coloured'. In this context, as Gilroy argues, the appearance of multicultural policies in the wake of anti-racist movements was far from accidental.[20] As a response to the 1981 uprisings, multiculturalism was used by the state to move 'from a line of defence to a mode of control'.[21]

Multiculturalism took hold as an aspirational ethos that foregrounded the recognition of cultural difference. State sponsored multiculturalism sought to integrate anti-racist movements with alliances with community leaders and forums for cultural expression. One way this happened was through representatives from racialised communities entering the criminal justice system and other positions of power. In the wake of Brixton's anti-imperialist rebellion, the Home Office suggested that liaison officers should be appointed to overcome 'cultural barriers' between racialised communities and the police. By the end of the 1980s, people from these communities were increasingly positioned within state administration, politics and criminal justice systems. This was coterminous with a growing (if small) Black and Asian middle class. According to Arun Kundnani's analysis, this was a designed attempt to create a 'parallel society' mirroring the British class system, which could be 'relied on to maintain control'.[22]

Long discussed in the context of internal colonies in the US, one strategy used by the state and corporate elite to deradicalise Black political revolutionaries was through a recognisably colonial operation that combined militarised attack with co-option and indirect control. Drawing on Kwame Nkrumah's work, Robert Allen reflects on the diffusion of dissent in the US by co-opting people into positions within colonial frameworks, who would 'run the black communities and keep them quiet for you'.[23] England was similarly primed after the Brixton riots. Existing forms of anti-racism could be co-opted to form support for community-based practices as a way to mediate unproductive engagement with the state.[24] There was good reason for community-based policing in the face of decades of violence and stigmatisation, thinking that political and social responsibility in the public arena could help to shift the tide of racism, and that capitalist gains are the single most sure way to stability and inclusion. As a result, as Alana Lentin writes,

> policies aiming to take 'ethnic minorities' under the state's wing, a step forward from seeing 'immigrants' as temporary guest workers soon to return home, extinguished the fires of dissent lit by a generation coming to political consciousness in the 1980s.[25]

The complex structures of co-option operated to actively undermine community and racial solidarities through the necessity of engagement, and ultimately complicity with, systems that maintained colonial forms of control.

Differential racism

Under the cloak of multicultural doctrine and Race Relations Acts, anti-racism ascended to a social value, becoming absorbed into a broader 'common sense' for many. However, in the process, communities were both homogenised and fractured, leading to the disintegration of alliances and the solidification of hierarchies that were increasingly defined by ethnicity and religion. Interpreting the strategies of ongoing colonialism discussed up to this point through a lens of racialised culture translated coloniality into regimes of integration and formal equality. As Nisha Kapoor writes,

> [the] increasing stratification among non-white groups and the positioning of racialized minorities within the upper echelons of state administration, in particular, have come to symbolize all the burden of proof required for those advocating we have now entered a 'post-race' era.[26]

The formation of a parallel society seemingly consolidated multiculturalism as both aspirational ethos and disciplinary structure. The 'celebration' of ethnicity became a cipher for the dissolution of race as a stratifying signifier, with cultural groups narrativised as the beneficiaries of supposedly multicultural Britain. At base, this was a 'municipal anti-racism', as Gilroy puts it, whose core strategy was to produce *differential* racism that became consolidated around distinctions between 'multicultural world citizens' and 'monocultural others'.[27] The former category seemingly demarcated a strata of people deemed capable of cohering with the values of contemporary British society, and so given access to a politics of inclusion. The latter relied on the stigmatisation of people considered incapable of sharing these values, of freedom of speech and religious or sexual tolerance.

The coexistence of these distinct categories served to reinforce each other:

> [the] existence of racial minorities in professional occupations is taken to be a sign that racism is no longer an issue, and if racial minorities are poor it is because they are not working as hard as these 'model minorities'.[28]

The 'honorary humans' who occupied relative positions of power functioned as meritocratic alibis for municipal antiracism. Their signification actively secured multiculturalism as a mode of control against the majority. In the process, as Stuart Hall remarked, class institutions that had been divided by race were fractured further still, in an attempt to neutralise the possibility of resistance by 'confining them to strategies and struggles which are race-specific, which do not surmount its limits, its barrier'.[29] This both framed discriminatory practice through a lens of inclusion and exclusion, and rationalised the latter as a product of dysfunctional cultural traditions and individual behaviour. Lending further justification to the pathologisation of poorer Black and Asian communities and woven through a supposedly post-race landscape, this sought to delegitimate the public role of race and race-based complaints altogether.

The Labour commissioned Macpherson report (1999) after the murder of teenager Stephen Lawrence in 1993 briefly returned a discourse of structural racism to the political spotlight. The report both named racism and linked it with the structuration of institutions. But echoing Scarman's report, racism was again delimited by individual attitudes and prejudices. Whilst the terms of race were considered once more, response to the report drove them further into the private realm, enabling their continued evaporation from the public sphere.

Community cohesion

As state multiculturalism swiftly unravelled towards the end of the twentieth century, its systems of differential racialisation came to the surface.[30] Successive governments since the 1990s have relied on distinctions between deserving and undeserving migrants, calling for community cohesion as protection against disorder, and decrying a lack of integration. In 2001 the Cantle report, entitled *Community Cohesion*, laid out a strategy for the Labour government to secure order across northern towns like Bradford.[31] There, an uprising had taken place earlier in the year in response to police failures to protect young British Asians from racist violence. The report stated that segregation and community divisions were deeply entrenched across England. The onus for integration was placed with migrant communities, with self-segregating whiteness, political policy and economic exclusion nowhere to blame.

Echoing Locke, these communities were again positioned as regressive and hostile to modern civilisation – as Cantle wrote, '[i]f you want to change a community, the community must want to change'. First-generation migrant families were supposedly answerable for failures to learn English and adequately integrate into British society. As such, they were judged responsible for maintaining poverty and deprivation that could supposedly have been avoided – their hereditary cultural pathologies had been reproduced through their children.[32] At the time of the report's publication, David Blunkett, then home secretary, introduced compulsory citizenship exams with mandatory English language testing and a possible oath of allegiance to the nation for all people applying for British citizenship. These sought to establish collective belonging by a slightly less brutish version of Norman Tebbit's infamous 'cricket test', which conceived of patriotism as support for the England team.

The New York attacks in the same year led to an intensifying 'war on terror' that would increasingly centre British Muslims' cultural and religious 'values' together with their supposed lack of integration. The cultural fixity of those who had been pathologised under multiculturalist regimes was forged into more explicit forms of threat to British values and social harmony. As Claire Alexander writes,

> While questions of race and racism largely fell off of the agenda, issues
> of religion, ethnicity and identity moved centre-stage, with evocations
> of 'parallel lives' and 'community cohesion' conjuring familiar and

well-worn tropes of cultural difference and incompatibility [...] but now with a global securitized sheen.[33]

The precarity of good character

Where the 1981 act had written British citizenship as whiteness, this had subsequently been translated into regimes of control that enforced connections between citizenship and political belonging. Citizenship would operate as a means to constitute the exclusion and hierarchical formation of subjects and aliens. The Nationality, Immigration and Asylum Act 2002 made naturalised British citizenship conditional on 'cultural' knowledge and language, whilst implementing a tighter system of governance of asylum. This included increased powers of deportation, removing the right to appeal in cases seen to be 'clearly unfounded' (where the country of origin was deemed to be 'safe'), introducing biometric information requirements and establishing immigration control powers at other ports in the European Economic Area (EEA).

The act rendered explicit the idea that citizenship should be earned and demonstrated, whilst also putting in place a barrage of policies and legal measures that increased state powers over citizenship deprivation, passport removal, refusal of naturalisation and extradition.[34] These were written into the 2005 Home Office report *Controlling Our Borders: Making Migration Work for Britain*, which was a five-year strategy for asylum and immigration. The report unequivocally justified the measures by reference to a British nation who was 'under threat from those who come and live here by breaking our rules and abusing our hospitality'.

Gordon Brown's 2009 Borders, Citizenship and Immigration Bill, and the *Path to Citizenship* then further enhanced state powers and introduced a staged citizenship process requiring a demonstrable commitment to British socio-economic life. A greater emphasis on 'good character' was put in place across immigration and nationality legislation. This was enforced by policies such as automatic deportations for non-EEA nationals who were sentenced to twelve months or more in imprisonment under the UK Borders Act 2007. The good character requirement didn't only align with strategies of criminalisation – with even misdemeanour convictions constituting grounds for citizenship refusal – but also cultural strategies reflecting those involved in the construction of gangs such as affinities and associations, social networks, geographical modelling, and financial status. Amidst crises of multiculturalism as mode of control, mandatory Britishness and an emphasis on good character formed part of a broad set of policies that had withdrawn rights and introduced a permanent status of precariousness for asylum seekers and migrants of colour.

Whilst the logics of Powellism had largely remained submerged under New Labour, the war on terror returned focus to the conjoined threat of an enemy within and the enemy at the border. A submerged Powellism became visible once more, with the figure of the terrorist now joining the ranks of enemy within. It is here that we find a decisive shift in the mechanics of internal colonialism as they become bound up with strategies of counter-insurgency against an increasingly precarious population.

ECOLOGIES OF CIVILIAN COMBATANTS

The confluence of immigration policies, criminal justice and weaponised multiculturalism came to the fore in shifts in strategy from counterterrorism to counter-insurgency (COIN) techniques that were manifested by the CONTEST strategy.[35] Developed since 2003, the strategy's two primary domestic components are *Pursue* and *Prevent*. The former is mainly composed of military intelligence and investigation and the latter with a hearts-and-minds approach to terrorism. The turn is important for several interrelated reasons. First, it draws explicitly on strategies developed through colonial military and police control (many of which I've discussed in the previous chapter); second, it considers a generic atmosphere and ecology of insurgency to have taken root in Britain, but also globally (through the idea of global jihad, for example); third, it develops both targeted and distributed approaches that produce multicultural communities as latent enemy insurgents.

In this and the following section, I argue that the use of counter-insurgency strategies implicitly relies on the premise of non-white Britain as forming an internal colony of the kind described by previous chapters. In the process of employing these strategies, this is consolidated, normalised and made explicit. In other words, the regime of multiculturalism and its 'failures' have formed the conditions for a continuing war at home.

CONTEST as COIN

Techniques of counter-insurgency were consolidated in the context of resistance to colonial violence and control, particularly in attempts to quell uprisings that had not been dealt with by colonial policing.[36] These were honed in the mid-twentieth century in struggles to maintain colonies in Malaya (1948–60); Indonesia (1948–62); Cyprus (1955–59), Kenya (1952–56); Northern Ireland (1969 to present); Palestine (2001 to present). Robert Thompson's *Defeating Communist Insurgency* describes tactics developed from his experience in the Malayan Emergency, and subsequently used to underpin those employed in response to the Mau Mau uprising in Kenya. Core to both approaches was a clear and hold strategy – clearing an area of possible insurgents, policing it against subsequent incursion, and using information warfare to gain popular support from civilians who remained in the area. In the context of Malaya, and more visibly in Kenya, the strategy also included a network of intelligence collection posts, cordons, frequent stop and search, detainment and the use of undercover pseudo-gangs to gather intelligence.

As described in the previous chapter, the slippage between military combat and policing was familiar across empire, with 'normal' and 'exceptional' circumstances often collapsing into one another. After his retirement from a military career, Charles W. Gwynn wrote of the need to continually maintain the fragile foundations of British rule, arguing that colonial order necessitated restoration at all times.[37] This fluidity of order and disorder was prevalent in the framing of insurgency, with 'natives' becoming 'insurgents' becoming 'peasants', as suited context and objective. The simultaneous coexistence of resistance, neutrality and support across colonised populations were the grounds upon which irregular warfare was developed. Counter-insurgency strategies arose from this inferno of racialised anxiety – as C.E. Callwell's classic text on colonial rebellions *Small Wars* (1896) puts it, in 'expeditions against savages and semi-civilized races'. As Radhika Natarajan writes, 'Britishness and insurgency are two sides of the coin of empire, one reaching out with the possibility of inclusion, and the other the sign of persistent exclusion.'[38]

In these contexts, several features of counter-insurgency were developed and used to train a domestic *haute police* that would draw on the expertise of military personnel who had served in the colonies. Most significant of these were: the integration of civil and military power; the use of intelligence; the role of communications; the use of exceptional legislation; the exercise of pre-emptive controls. All of these are found in contemporary iterations of counter-insurgency, but they are perhaps most clear in the work of military consultant David Kilcullen. A considerable influence on Gordon Brown and Ed Miliband, Kilcullen had worked in counter-insurgency contexts for the Australian army in East Timor and the Middle East. Since developing a career as a strategist and consultant, he has consistently advocated policies of counter-insurgency over counterterrorism. To do so, he promotes a renewed understanding of counter-insurgency that removes it from the limitation under colonialism to a single well-defined territory. Instead, counter-insurgency is required, according to Kilcullen, to forge an emergent warfare across entire ecosystems of potential insurgents.

In *Countering Global Insurgency*, Kilcullen argues that Islamic terrorist networks comprise a mass-scale insurgency in which 'the global *jihad* represents a federated virtual state'.[39] The domestic parallel society mapped out in the previous section is here reformulated as a kind of shadow state, whose distributed networks cut across territorial boundaries:

> In classical counter-insurgency, the ecosystem was the nation-state. In globalised insurgency, the ecosystem is all of world society. Therefore liberal democracies are inside, not outside the *jihad* ecosystem. We are part of the system of global *jihad* – we provide inputs that sustain the insurgency, are affected by its boundary interactions and outputs, and are actors in the broader environment.

By this measure, we are all implicated within these wider ecosystems of potential civilian combatants.

Deradicalisation as weapon of war

Through research driven by conservative think tanks such as The Centre for Social Cohesion and Policy Exchange, theories of radicalisation have been developed in service of state security to consider the process through which the 'terrorist' is made. These new terrorists are not thought to derive their malice from political motivation but from an incorrigible antipathy toward the 'West'.[40] A decade after Cantle's report, in 2011 then Conservative prime minister David Cameron argued that state multiculturalism had failed because it had given rise to the toleration of segregated communities. In this narrative, multiculturalism became identified with the degradation of the social fabric of England, as threat to Britishness as whiteness. The post-racial discourse of segregation gave support for an emergent consensus that Muslims are generically at risk of radicalisation and so pose an inherent threat to security. As such, frameworks that had been productive of criminalisation and lawlessness were rapidly translated into the context of terrorists and insurgents – both subject to the law's highest orders, whilst their actions are not possibly shaped by them. Radicalisation's root cause had been identified as a 'cultural psychological disposition'.[41] In this way, discourses of radicalisation continue the metamorphosised pathologisation of migrant populations as a kind of depoliticised terror that is rooted in religion and culture. Radicalisation is not considered a process rooted in socio-political contexts so much as the awakening of an innate predisposition.

Since the Conservative government relaunch of Prevent in 2011, shadow units such as the Extremism Analysis Unit (EAU) were set up to implement state counterterrorism policies.[42] Primarily a research organisation, the EAU operated under the direct authority of the home secretary to provide advice and analysis to several departments within government: Prevent Delivery Unit (PDU); Joint Terrorism Analysis Centre; Foreign Office; Department for Education; Department for Communities and Local Government; Department for Health; Police. Operating across criminal justice, military and social domains, its data is regularly disclosed to other agencies within the criminal justice system as well as foreign governments.

The primary aim of the EAU is to characterise Islamist extremism by considering several factors that together may lead to radicalisation. These include systems for measuring adherence to British 'values', the critique of core values and anti-Western sentiment, which are used to create typologies for scrutinising communities and demographics within Britain. Using the tools of surveillance, profiling, tracking and data collection, these typologies are mobilised through Prevent to supposedly stop people from becoming terrorists in the first place, and are backed by Channel, which works as a program of 'deradicalisation'. Through the Counter-Terrorism and Security Act 2015, Prevent and Channel were placed on a statutory footing.

With information operations integrated into the wider security apparatus by the Ministry of Defence in 2009, information has become used in domestic contexts not just as a mode of analysis, but as a mode of influence or 'weapon of war'.[43] Continuing the erosion of distinctions between violence and coercion (Pursue) and information collection (Prevent), information operations are used as part of an aggressive approach to defeat insurgents through tactics such as electronic warfare, profiling, deception, physical destruction, information security and Key Leader Engagement (KLE). In 2007, the Research, Information and Communications Unit (RICU) was set up to work across police internet referral units and media organisations to produce strategically focused counter-narratives that involve propaganda and community-based relationships.

The UK counter-narrative campaign began with a series of research projects carried out under the RICU regarding Muslim identity, belonging, Muslim people's use of the internet and media consumption, and community credibility.[44] Subsequently, organisations invested in deploying counter-narratives were recipients of Home Office support, with the content produced then promoted to targeted users of online platforms. RICU ensured consistency in promoting messages like 'Terrorists attack the values that we all share' and countering messages like 'Terrorism is not a real and serious threat to us all. The terrorist threat is exaggerated by the UK government.'[45] Breakthrough media is the primary company used by the Home Office to deploy these counter-narratives, by working through a network of grassroots community organisations.[46] They also engage specialist PR companies to aid in the production of campaigns, including members of the M&C Saatchi group.

Central to the efficacy of this programme has been ensuring the appearance of authenticity of the content as authentic voices within targeted communities. For instance, the account @thisiswoke functions across social media platforms to pose as a popular Muslim project involving Muslim activists with posts about Hijab and racism. This is a Home Office-funded project run in conjunction with Breakthrough Media. Similarly funded by the Home Office, *Super Sisters Mag* is an east London magazine discussing Muslim feminism, which operates with white staff members regular posting as Muslimahs. In 2014, the #MakingAStand campaign was launched by an organisation called Inspire. Its objective was to encourage Muslim women to make a stand against terrorism, to feel empowered in their communities against radicalisation. At the time, Inspire were adamant that they were independent from the government, but internal documents revealed that it was a RICU counter-narrative product. A particularly clear example of state-funded discourse-manipulation transpired in the context of an attempt to resist Somalian asylum seekers in 2013. Somalian refugees had already been long maligned by the media as the most dangerous refugee community in the UK. RICU used a UK NGO called the Anti-Tribalism Movement to promote the message that Somalia was now safe and stable, and with Breakthrough Media helped produce a documentary for the NGO to be aired worldwide. The Home Office later declared Somalia safe for the deportation of refugees.

Broader strategies work to create links between state, police and community leaders (religious leaders; local councillors; youth workers). Building a Stronger Britain Together (BSBT) is a fund that is part of the Counter Extremism Strategy. BSBT funds groups involved in counter-extremism projects working to 'create more resilient communities, stand up to extremism in all its forms and offer vulnerable individuals a positive alternative'.[47] In her withdrawal letter from the BSBT-funded Bradford Literature Festival, Suhaiymah Manzoor-Khan understands that community projects and Muslim groups are often drawn to this as a source of funding in the context of austerity. Nevertheless, as she writes:

> this is a part of the apparatus of tools used by the government to legit-imise counter extremism […] the ways we are able to work with our own communities become dependent on the very project which sees us as criminal by default.[48]

The funding requirements involve information collection and the provision of evidence of counter-extremism related outcomes. This implicates and conditions community groups to reproduce the discourses and practices of their own criminalisation, making them complicit in discourses that Muslim communities are at once the inevitable source of violent extremism and should be working to undo its causes and conditions.

Concretising threats

Continuing the pathologisation of 'problem families', Prevent social workers engage in supposedly civilising and domesticating work. This purports to improve racialised communities and pre-empt the possibility of radicalisation by identifying cultural practices that might create vulnerable children. Of the 7,318 people referred to the Prevent programme in 2017–18, 2,426 came through education and 57 per cent were aged 20 years or under.[49] Induction into Prevent training was rolled out into the private sector in 2019, targeting employees in retail, travel and entertainment. Now compulsory to report against indicators of radicalisation across the public domain (and increasingly incentivised in the private domain), since 2012 a Muslim is nearly 80 times more likely to be referred by Prevent for Channel deradicalisation.[50]

This disproportionate targeting of Muslim people has often been used to show that Prevent is a racist set of policies and practices that have little basis as counterterrorism strategy. But racism and Prevent are much more entangled than is suggested by the idea that Prevent is racist, or even that it leads to racist outcomes in an ambient media environment that routinely vilifies Muslim people. Rather, Prevent is part of a broader series of mechanisms that craft racialised pathology, stigma and inferiority. This has the result of differentiating entire demographics as potential threat. We can think of this discourse of threat in terms of the equation of migration with the erosion of liberal British values framed as a struggle between increasingly concrete demographic blocks.

For example, notably reactionary academic Slavoj Žižek contends that '[w]e have to be clear they are in our culture [...] We should be more assertive toward our values [...] Europe means something noble'. This is also ventriloquised in the recent work of Matthew Goodwin and Roger Eatwell's argument that '[i]mmigration and hyper-ethnic change are cultivating strong fears about the possible destruction of the national group's historic identity and established ways of life'. And, perhaps most clearly, Sam Harris articulates the position of sedimented demographic threat intertwined with defence of liberal values:

> Throughout western Europe, Muslim immigrants show little inclination to acquire the secular and civil values of their host countries, and yet exploit these values to the utmost – demanding tolerance for their backwardness, their misogyny, their antisemitism, and the genocidal hatred that is regularly preached in their mosques.

This had been stoked in recent years by the profusion of media stories about inner-city no-go zones in British cities supposedly free from the rule of police and under Sharia law. Fox News pundit Steve Emerson claimed that parts of London and the entire city of Birmingham were entirely under Muslim control, into which non-Muslims simply don't go. Reproducing Powell's analytic demographics, the atemporal core of Britishness as whiteness is increasingly animated by the mythic idyll of a pre-immigrant English community.

In 2016 Ted Cantle and Eric Kaufmann produced a report that lent supposed empirical weight to these claims, arguing that segregation was increasing in Britain. According to the report, white populations were decreasing in several areas such as Slough, where the white population fell from 58.3 to 34.5 per cent, Birmingham, where it went from 65.6 to 53.1 per cent, and Leicester, where it decreased from 60.5 to 45.1 per cent. In the London borough of Newham, just 16.7 per cent of residents were white. Segregation was defined not in terms of diversity of ethnicity, but in terms of a white British majority who supposedly felt increasingly isolated. The strategies of internal colonialism that had produced segregation and criminalisation were aggressively routed into evidence of a regressive migrant nature that was antithetical to the supposedly liberal and tolerant Britain which had been discursively secured by regimes of multiculturalism.

Here, as Nandita Sharma observes, race is increasingly fixed to place.[51] Bodies are territorialized as subjects of specific nations and sovereign power, and migration is again seen as a form of miscegenation and cultural degeneration. Again, this relies on frameworks of waste that position the immigrant body as out of place and out of time – as backwards, illiberal, anti-modern and superfluous. Islam is considered to reject the values of life itself, representing the threat of death and social dissolution fundamentally. A weaponised multiculturalism comes to the fore, with newly concretised demographic blocks quantified and judged for their lack of integration and degree of separation from British values.

Pre-emptive power

The translation of racial analytics into quantified data has been written in to core operations of Prevent, with communities and bodies encoded in the supposed neutrality of algorithms and risk assessment. They underpinned the development of pre-emptive strategies that have formed a fundamental tenet of counter-insurgency – to identify threats and intervene *prior to crimes taking place*.[52] Emphasising prevention has facilitated shifts towards the explicitation of pre-emptive power that could ground anticipatory strategies 'beyond the threat of violence or detention'.[53] Moreover, the authorisation of coercive action prior to the manifestation of crime has legitimated the routine elision of legal protections and processes under the force of national and economic security. For instance, Tony Blair vividly stated that:

[w]hat we are desperate to avoid is the situation where at a later point, people turn around and say: 'If you'd only been vigilant as you should have been, we could have averted a terrorist attack.'[54]

As a result, terrorism legislation since 2000 and especially under the Terrorism Act 2006, has allowed for suspects to be held without charge for up to 28 days, people prosecuted for expressing unacceptable opinions or supporting foreign charities or individuals to be extradited; closed courts to be used with suspects having access neither to legal representation nor even to the evidence against them. In this context, as Zedner writes, 'the post-crime orientation of criminal justice is increasingly overshadowed by the pre-crime logic of security.'[55]

The anticipatory logics of preventative frameworks rely on the expanded intelligence-gathering capacities of multiple agencies, together with the development of 'crime science' that analyses datasets to provide criteria for the determination of threat. Working with theories of radicalisation, and with culture already translated into a stand-in for ethnic background and religion by multiculturalist narratives, systems of risk assessment are produced. From the CTA to gang databases to CONTEST, the informational marking and remaking of bodies has been a persistent feature of the demonisation of racialised communities. The collation and combination of bits of knowledge under network analysis, risk prediction models and kinships are given meaning as indicators of risk, whose contingency has worked through colonial logics of the pathological other. Continuing practices that had been embedded in strategies of criminalisation and racialised policing, race, ethnicity and religion became proxies for risk.

The creation of this data relies on the employment of service-providers as makeshift risk-assessors. For instance, Blair's 2007 Britain's Preventing Violent Extremism programme supported the formation of the database through partnerships enlisting Muslim community organisations, youth workers, health workers and teachers to refer through to Channel. The Prevent Training and Competencies Framework for the NHS opens as follows:

Prevent is part of the Government's counter-terrorism strategy CONTEST and aims to stop people becoming terrorists or supporting terrorism; as such it is described as the only long term solution to the threat we face from terrorism. Prevent focuses on all forms of terrorism and operates in a pre-criminal space, providing support and redirection to vulnerable individuals at risk of being groomed in to terrorist activity before any crimes are committed. [...] Staff must be able to recognise signs of radicalisation and be confident in referring individuals who can then receive support in the pre-criminal space.[56]

Supporting documentation for these partnerships lists signs of potential radicalisation as: abandoning current associates in favour of a new social network; experiencing a crisis of identity or family separation; expressing real or imagined grievances.[57] These pre-criminal space operations then provide the material for a formerly secret government database, accessible by police and other agencies, of thousands of people referred through Prevent primarily due to what they were perceived to believe.

Through surveillance, data analysis and categorisation, policing would reach back from the future to protect against the possibility of threat. The pre-emptive futurity of Prevent is dependent on seemingly neutral techniques that attempt to evade any possible characterisation as racism. However, their technological containment has allowed for the resurfacing of racialisation inscribed in biological bodies – the potentiality of Muslim extremism hypothetically captured by brain scans, for example.[58] The bedrock of multiculturalism provided the conditions for these fluid racial torsions. Reinforcing one another, the simultaneous concretisation and making fluid of racialisations – of demographic blocks and algorithmic affinities – converge to produce new forms of differential racism.

There is substantive evidence that these systems don't just fail to identify potential threats, but actively hinder the detection of terrorists.[59] The sheer magnitude of mass surveillance has seemingly sabotaged the ability for the state to identify 'real' terrorists. For instance, police facial recognition systems consistently falsely identify non-white faces. Even more damning is that the tiny number of terrorism-related datapoints in comparison with the entire dataset leads to a false-positive paradox – false positives are far more likely to be returned by predictive systems than true positives. However, predictive analysis is not just a process that could identify an existing threat, it is inherently productive – working to piece together and correlate data to define the potentiality of threat. Since 2015, when Prevent was placed on statutory footing, around twelve people a day have been referred to Channel. These flows of information don't just form systems by which people can be enclosed and immobilised, they provide the machinery necessary to produce new forms of social composition and interaction through statistical affinity and suggestive correlation.

Patterns of movement, content and forms of communication, religion, downloaded apps, search activity, friendships, facial hair – these reach beyond phenotypical generalisations to form a constellation of data through which the Muslim terrorist has been made into a measurable category. The complex convergence of algorithmic markers and the distributed responsibility for policing communities has produced abstract and variable categories for the fluid transcription of race. Submerged and neutralised, differential racisms haunt our socio-political formations inherently – they have become 'both spectral and fractal'.[60]

In this way, the power of pre-emptive policing is not just constrictive, it is also productive and flexible. I am thinking of power as an intersubjective relation, operating as a background modulation and orientation of our practices in which a 'field of responses, reactions, results, and possible inventions may open up', as Foucault wrote.[61] In this sense, power operates as 'a way of orienting bodies in particular ways'.[62] As McCulloch and Pickering write,

> The 'preventive' counter-terrorism framework is concerned less with gathering evidence, prosecution, conviction and subsequent punishment than in targeting and managing through disruption, restriction and incapacitation those individuals and groups considered to be a risk.[63]

Pre-emption operates as an explicit form of control, working not to single out potential threats so much as gain hegemonic control over the manipulation of the social and political environment for all citizens. Drawing on Kilcullen's work, NATO defines COIN as 'a complex form of security operations to enable stability using all available instruments of power to create a secure environment, and to enable promotion of legitimate governance and rule of law'.[64] This is a far broader aim that that suggested by typical counterterrorism strategies of unmasking and unveiling. If state hegemony is the aim of COIN, then its primary achievement would lie with an ability to conscript the consent and complicity of British citizens in its broader work.

As Stuart Hall noted, producing hegemony over social order requires shifting social dispositions within 'contending forces in a field of struggle and the articulation of that field into a tendency'.[65] Central to this struggle has been the manipulation of economies of fear, as Miller and Sabir write:

> the laws and programmes that underpin these strategies have been created intentionally and purposefully to coerce and instil fear within the Muslim community and those who stand with it.[66]

If coercion and fear are the intentionally racialised results of Prevent – rather than its symptoms or side effects – these are predicated on much broader systems of fear. As discussed previously, the interplay of fear and threat have reverberated across the post-colonial cut as both the effect and condition for creating new 'surfaces or boundaries of bodies and worlds' in the metropole.[67] In the wake of a 'failing' multiculturalism, the post-colonial dread of intimacy with the unknowable other is increasingly animated by Powellian fears of white genocide, miscegenation and ruptured borders. Security is the outworking of this aporetic logic, now finding its figure in the spectre of the terrorist who has 'taken on a god-like power, equivalent to the plague of earlier times'.[68]

Whilst radicalisation is embedded in segregated communities positioned as threat, it is also understood as a contagious pathogen. As Jasbir Puar writes,

> Terrorist bodies as a 'statistical population' coagulate through an imagined worldwide collectivity – the Muslim world – that perversely transcends national boundaries and is metaphorised through viral networks of contagion, infection and the frustration generated by inaccessibility of sleeper cells that need to contact to reproduce themselves: rampant, uncontainable, spontaneous.[69]

Muslim populations are concretised as the home of civilian combatants, whilst these domestic zones also form the contexts in which racialised presence is forged through algorithmic processes that are not attached to singular bodies but to probabilistic affinities. Dread is dispersed over unknowable and invisible threats. Whilst proliferating paranoia in their failure to capture this invisible enemy, this has also legitimised the infiltration of massive yet ineffectual surveillance systems. As such, fear is dis-located from a specific locus and a specific time, fear is anticipatory and haunted by the 'danger of not-knowing'.[70]

Kilcullen's ecosystemic approach makes fear become ambient, its affective economies enveloping us. Fear is unconfined and intensified by the impossibility of containment. As such, fear is both expansive and constricting – it upholds the ambitions and incursions of state security operations whilst constricting and stratifying the movements of their subjects. These processes may be felt subjectively, but they are objectively structured – as embodied sensations that reverberate across abstractions and motile bodies, communities and socio-political structures. The supposed failures of CONTEST as counterterrorism therefore underwrite its expansion through circuits of racialised paranoia that are fuelled by the conjoined threats of internal proximity and external intrusion.

SPECTRAL BODIES BECOME BORDERS

I want to end this chapter by considering how bordering practices more generally fit into the machinery of counter-insurgency. The above shifts in racialised power help to explain how the COIN has operated within the context of a Powellian strategy for maintaining Britishness against an enemy who is reproduced by strategies and economies of fear. In this section, I consider whether the systems through which national security is maintained have animated a protectionist framework that might also be characterised as a form of COIN.

Total policing/total warfare

Counterterrorism provided a route through which counter-insurgency would continue the erosion of the boundaries between police and military that had steadily begun in the metropole since the 1980s. The integration of national security and criminal justice has required cooperation across military, policing and public bodies. Operation Nexus, introduced in London in 2012, embeds immigration officers within police stations to gather information and identify people who could be deported even without criminal offence. The operation involves immigration status checks and police-questioning for non-criminal purposes and without any procedural protection. Through analysis of spent convictions, withdrawn charges and police encounters, people who are classified as 'high harm' threats are then referred to deportation procedures.[71] Whilst this preventative framework fortifies boundaries and consolidates segregations on the inside of the state, the integration of immigration, police and military also underpins the pursuit of national security beyond territorial borders.

Since the 'migrant crises' of the mid-2010s, the UK has vastly expanded its involvement in the militarisation of borders of 'fortress Europe': in surrounding non-EU states (Morocco, Turkey and Libya) as gatekeepers through humanitarian aid; at key migratory routes in northern Africa; attempted prison-building projects in Jamaica and Nigeria for deportations of their UK-incarcerated nationals. More broadly, the EU's Frontex border management agency has attempted to externalise and outsource bordering by establishing a system of security enforcement beyond its territorial edges. Primarily situated in northern Africa, the EU has exported surveillance technology, engaged in information exchange and installed border guard units.[72] As a result, whilst thousands of people from sub-Saharan Africa attempt to make their way toward Europe each year, many are trapped within a northern Africa buffer zone across which the EU supports detention centres and camps. The EU strategy was perhaps clearest in the proposed plan to create disembarkation zones that would immediately return migrant people to their supposed country of origin in exchange for finance and technological support. Though the project was ultimately opposed by leaders of African states, similar projects in Niger and Libya already support migration partnerships with countries such as Nigeria and Ethiopia to assist the return of migrant people, with aid often conditional on their cooperation.

Whilst outside of the Schengen zone, Britain is part of the Schengen Information System. Though Britain only has observer status on the Frontex management board, it has been active in several operations through information gathering, assistance and practices of non-assistance. Peripheral member states of the EU such as Hungary and non-European states such as Libya now pre-empt migration reaching heartland Europe, acting as 'wardens of the European border regime'.[73] Meanwhile, as Jennifer Hyndman details, the UN has adopted a containment approach to human displacement since the 1990s, attempting to keep refugees in their regions of origin through strategies of 'preventative protection'.[74] As of 2017, 30 per cent of global refugees were detained in sub-Saharan Africa as part of the European Union–African Union–United Nations joint programme.

At the intersections of foreign action and domestic criminal justice, bordering becomes productive of the shape of the contemporary nation-state. Foregrounding this 'world-configuring function' of borders brings to light the bodies that are reconfigured through these regimes, both domestically and far outside of British island territories.[75] In consequence, as Mbembe writes,

> Contemporary movement restrictions are not limited to national boundaries. They are at work on a global scale. They are deepening the space and time asymmetries between different categories of humanity while leading to the progressive ghettoization of entire regions of the world.[76]

Empire and internal colony are intertwined at these sites of bordering and movement – the detention centre imprisons those subjects who are situated on the outside of the nation whilst being subjected to the most vehement force of its sovereignty.

Illegalisation

Policies and practices of securitising borders have progressively remade refugees as 'irregular migrants'. As Harsha Walia writes, they are:

> displaced as a result of the violences of capitalism and empire, and subsequently forced into precarious labor as a result of state illegalization and systemic social hierarchies.[77]

The Immigration Act 1971 made legalised migration from poorer countries nearly impossible, with migration often permissible only through seeking asylum. Nonetheless, Britain does not accept asylum applications lodged abroad, but neither does it provide aid for travelling to make the petition in Britain. Moreover, the British visa regime is particularly stringent for countries producing large numbers of asylum seekers such as Afghanistan, Egypt, Ethiopia, Eritrea, Iran, Iraq, Pakistan, Syria, Sudan. Within this regime, migrant people without visas are never able to legitimately enter the UK and so they are produced as illegal migrants who are not possibly genuine refugees.

The regime relies on the fluidity even of Britain's physical borders. For example, according to the 2001 Channel Tunnel Order and 2003 Le Touquet Treaty, control zones operate between French and UK borders. Within these zones, either state receiving asylum claims is not required to process them, and can refuse entry in accord with that state's immigration policies. This allows for the wielding of differential power through the ability to choose amongst competing state regulations. This means that migrant people potentially never enter UK territory and so have no access to the machinery of appeals or other legal aid. The punitive nature of this border was ramped up in 2014 with the 20 September joint UK–France declaration to: '[s]tem the flow of illegal migration into Europe […] deter illegal migrants from congregating in and around Calais'.[78] Subsequently, the infamous Calais Jungle was violently disbanded in late 2016. This involved substantial police and social abuse against migrant people, which limited access to shelter, food, healthcare and clean water – removing drinking fountains from public parks, for example. As a result, migrant people were forced into public spaces and informal economies, where they have been subject to regular physical violence by the police-become-border-guard.

More recently, on 24 January 2019, the UK signed a declaration with France building on the Sandhurst treaty of 2018. The declaration foregrounds additional support for the *Centre Conjoint d'Information et de Coordination* who work against irregular migration in northern France and the Pas-de-Calais, and the *National Maritime Information Centre* and *Prefet Maritime* who will share threat assessment and engage in joint operations in the Channel. In addition, Britain promised additional funding of £44.5 million for fencing, CCTV and detection technology in Calais and other Channel ports. Whilst this border work makes migration into Britain more difficult, it does not make it impossible. The securitisation and expansion of border regimes shape journeys towards increasing peril, precarity and death. For example, the introduction of thermal imaging monitoring at British ports has led to people making the journey over the Channel in refrigerated containers. As direct result of this, in November 2019, 39 people were found to have suffocated to death at Purfleet port.

Once physically inside British territory, migrants are subjected to 'an active process of inclusion through "illegalisation"'.[79] Since 2002, asylum seekers have no longer had the right to work in the UK (or volunteer), whilst also having differential access to the means of survival such as healthcare, finance, legal aid and freedom of movement.[80] In May 2012 coalition home secretary Theresa May told the *Daily Telegraph*:

> The aim is to create here in Britain a really hostile environment for illegal migration. Work is under way to deny illegal immigrants access

to work, housing and services, even bank accounts. What we don't want is a situation where people think that they can come here and overstay because they're able to access everything they need.

The Immigration Acts 2014 and 2016 expanded executive powers against irregular migrants so that minor crimes are increasingly used as grounds for deportation or detention. Since 2014, between 12,000 and 15,000 people are forcibly removed from the country each year. Britain has also seen a dramatic increase in citizen deprivation and nullification over the past ten years, with nearly 200 cases of nullification occurring in 2013 alone and many of which were later judged unlawful. Since the early 2000s, both Labour and Conservative governments have overseen the mass expansion of immigrant removal centres, with the Home Office now cataloguing and surveilling all asylum seekers through strategies of mandatory reporting, asylum housing and electronic tagging.[81] Tagging asylum seekers administers a mandatory curfew, with both tagging and detention having no limit on their duration.

These strategies of illegalisation are enforced by the 27 Immigration Compliance and Enforcement (ICE) teams across the UK. The teams perform raids on residential addresses, often under cover of night, as well as at restaurants, shops and factories. The latter illegal working raids see thousands of people arrested each year, the majority of which are quickly overturned when people are found to be not removable. In these raids ICE teams often collaborate with employers, with reductions of fines for employers of illegalised immigrants in return for cooperation. In 2016 Byron Burgers complied with a plan to lure workers to raids under the guise of a staff meeting launching a new burger. However, as leaked Home Office intelligence documents from 2014's Operation Centurion suggest, the majority of operations begin with uncorroborated tip offs from members of the public.

As discussed in Chapter 2, Britain has relied upon migration for cheap labour, and has both enabled transnational capital accumulation and tacitly accepted irregular migration as part and parcel of this:

Illegal workers are at the heart of the UK economy: building workers, office cleaners, food pickers and packers, warehouse lifters, drivers and couriers, the menials in every service industry. The 'discount' on illegal workers makes a fundamental contribution to every business model.[82]

With up to 720,000 irregular migrants currently in London, Britain's role in shaping migration regimes has facilitated the creation of a permanent and large-scale illegalised workforce. Whilst Britain's labour needs have to some extent been satisfied by the eastern expansion of the EU, they have also been met by irregular migrants who are included in Britain as economic participants but 'denied the status of insiders'.[83]

Citizens become police

The intersections of immigration and differential access to the basic means of survival are firmly built in to the everyday bordering practices legally required by the Immigration Act 2014. This aimed to ensure Britain is a hostile environment to immigrants, requiring landlords to conduct immigration checks and establish that new tenants have the right to rent in the UK. These checks enact borders across point of access to shelter, legally backed up with the expansion of deport first, appeal later policies. As part of this hostile environment strategy, in 2013 vans were dispersed by the Home Office across London bearing the message: 'In the UK illegally? Go Home or Face Arrest.' Outsourcing specialist Capita was then charged by the government with sending text messages telling people 'You are required to leave the UK as you no longer have right to remain.'

Bordering, and the socio-political spaces produced through it, cannot be grasped through the concept of territory – as if space is a container for organisation and categorisation of exclusions and inclusions.[84] Borders are carried by people as they attempt, or are deterred from attempting, to access welfare, education, health, justice, paid labour, housing. In this way, bordering practices are productive of pre-crime spaces writ large. They are produced across vast assemblages of actions, agencies, objects and affective economies. These pre-crime spaces are differentiated by relative ease of movement – not the *end* of movement so much as its channelling, control, stability and flexible adaptation. As Mbembe writes, this has the effect of making social and physical spaces progressively more viscous and perilous for Black and Brown bodies:

> Such bodies are kept shifting between invisibility, waiting and effacement. They are trapped in fragmented spaces, stretched time and indefinite waiting.[85]

Economies of fear sustain and give shape to this pre-criminal space through which certain bodies are bound together, unified and made intelligible as objects of threat. Not just Muslim bodies, but all migrants of colour have been produced as an 'endless series of threats'.[86]

Complicity in bordering practices is supposedly state enforced, but it is rendered legitimate under fear of pervasive threat. Even just our passive consent embeds and institutionalises fear, creating affinities between certain bodies and the ways in which they navigate social space. Since we are all implicated within these ecosystems, our engagement – both with CONTEST and everyday bordering from their distribution to points of access to state services and workplaces, to announcements of 'See It. Say It. Sorted' on our daily commute – maintains a social order that is required to give stability to their hegemonic power. Implicated in this landscape of power, we are all involved in some aspects of its reinforcement, however partial this may be. These complex networks of insinuation, co-option and pre-emption legitimate pervasive strategies that declare war on our 'will to dissent or resist'.[87]

Pressed towards conscription into total policing, Britain increasingly witnesses the brittleness of these differential regimes of time and space as the tendency that turns 'discounted bodies into borders'.[88] The social death and disappearance of precarious citizens transpires alongside the genocidal tendencies of border regimes. The Mediterranean and Aegean Seas are mass graves – between 1993 and 2019, at least 36,570 refugee deaths are attributable to European border policies.[89] Empire is acutely spectral – haunting Britain – not as quantifiable, factual, statistical mass, but through an experience of loss and disappearance – of extraditions and deportations – of 'state-sponsored procedure for producing ghosts to harrowingly haunt a population into submission'.[90]

With national security rewritten as counter-insurgency, this implicates all citizens into complicity with these massive ecosystems of racialised power. If Powellian logics reach their apotheosis in bordering as COIN, then as Zoé Samudzi and William C. Anderson put it,

> White people are not simply those the state protects and serves: white people are themselves a part of the policing structure, and the notion of public safety cannot be separated from this deep complicity and investment in this form of state violence.[91]

It is here that citizens become police.

The inexorable logic of spectral empire

Whilst the colonial roots of COIN are readily acknowledged by both advocates and detractors, it is not uncommon to see explanations of its failures put down to its unfeasibility *outside* of the context and support of colonial institutions and practices.[92] In the above discussion, I've argued for a kind of reversal of this position: that the adoption of COIN as domestic strategy both relied on and reproduced Britain's internal colony. But also, in turn, that the refounding of Britain through the post-colonial cut has found its culmination in COIN.

To consider this history briefly, it should be noted that the 'successes' of mid-century counter-insurgencies like those in Malaya are widely understood to have depended on the promise of Britain's withdrawal from that colony. In this light, consider again Fanon's proposition that 'the colonial world is a world divided into compartments' discussed in Chapter 2. If my characterisation of Britain's internal colonies is correct, then these compartments are fluid, viscous spaces, not frozen but perhaps tending towards zones of petrification. These spaces are mediated by exclusions that are not defined only by spatial borders but by more flexible regimes of space. Broader systems of bordering constituted under COIN work not only to confine and territorialise people, but 'to inscribe them into temporalities and spatialities that are disjointed to the point of giving these populations the illusion of being territorially separated', as Cédric Parizot writes.[93] These differentiating and disjointed spatio-temporal regimes are manifest where '[d]ivision *already exists* and *is undeniable*; it is embedded in the architectural markers of everyday life in the colony'.[94] Echoing Fanon, the successes of COIN seem, at first glance, to lie in the absolutisation of this division – the ends of this perpetual war could only be found in forms of figurative and literal ethnic cleansing.

However, as Fanon goes on, drawing upon Sartre, 'this general clean-up destroys the thing one wants to save'.[95] Translating into our context, the absolute purification and cleansing of Britain of its internal colonies would be 'the perpetual absurd temptation of the colonialists'. Even if it were possible, this would 'amount to the immediate destruction of colonization'.[96] As proffered in discussion of the post-colonial cut above, whilst this might seem *prima facie* desirable to the Powellian, it is a structural impossibility. The nation narrativised through the post-colonial cut has been a fabrication reliant on the proliferation of borders, viscous spaces and differential regimes. Britishness-as-whiteness is possible only in its identification with its other. How could the Powellian nation possibly give up its logic of existence and condition of being? The incessant tendency towards purification, containment and repression is therefore necessarily incomplete. Inescapably haunting the Powellian project, this incompleteness forms the tension through which 'we're notified that what's been suppressed or concealed is very much alive and present, messing or interfering'.[97]

5

Extinction Politics

Existence is resistance
humans should not be at risk of extinction
(Shareefa Energy, 'Displaced Development')[1]

I hear the storm. They talk to me about progress, about 'achievements'; diseases cured, improved standards of living. I am talking about societies drained of their essence, cultures trampled underfoot, institutions undermined, lands confiscated, religions smashed, magnificent artistic creations destroyed, extraordinary possibilities wiped out.
(Aimé Césaire, *Between Colonizer and Colonized*)

INTRODUCTION

Colonial strategies of regulation, containment and exclusion have attempted to reproduce Britain as a space primarily for white Britons against those whose labour, lands and resistance built Britain from the outset. This has been tangled up with eugenicist approaches to non-white immigration as a threat to the purity of the nation. These threats were understood in terms of an alien insurgency and translated into financialised circuits of extraction and hyper-exploitation, the policing of Britishness as mode of life, and supposedly race-neutral algorithms of risk and insecurity.

In this chapter I am interested in recent political formations that have pitted themselves against a regime of neoliberalism that is supposed to have been at work since around the mid-1970s. The support for former Labour leader Jeremy Corbyn formed part of a broader socialist project arising in a context that is frequently associated with hopes for the end of specific forms of globalist capitalism and a crisis of liberal democracy. This found its narrative arc in the rise of the right and the idea that we are witnessing an increased authoritarianism. It has become commonplace to see the root cause of this alleged crisis in post-industrialisation,

economic downturn, the financial crisis in 2008 and subsequent austerity policies. This section of the left has responded by considering welfare
to be bounded by national territories, and migration to exacerbate our
current crises by driving down wages or using dwindling resources.

In the last 10 years, there has been a gigantic experiment at the expense
of ordinary workers. Countries with vast historical differences in wage
rates and living standards have been brought together in a common
labour market. The result has been sustained pressure on living standards,
a systematic attempt to hold down wages and to cut the costs of social
provision for working people. (Len McCluskey, 20 June 2016)

This presents a very different story about Britain than the one I have
given in previous chapters. The result has been a movement that relies
on the nation-state as its basic political unit, and which, I shall argue,
produces the nation as the horizon for political change. In light of this,
I want to ask how thinking about our central struggle as between neoliberal global markets and national welfare has come about; what are its
ramifications; what trajectories does it push us toward?

What there wouldn't be is the wholesale importation of underpaid
workers from Central Europe to order to destroy conditions, particularly
in the construction industry. (Jeremy Corbyn, 23 July 2017)

Ultimately, I shall argue that whilst an increasingly *explicit* authoritarianism does seem to characterise the trajectories of British politics as
discussed in the previous chapter, this is best explained as a phase change
within the management and control of Britain's internal colonies and its
coloniality further afield. I first outline how neoliberalism allowed for the
re-forming of the geopolitics of the British state. Reliant on logics of natural
limits and waste, as well as practices of bordering and hyper-exploitation,
the neoliberal era worked to reproduce a natural order whose globalised
form relies on the sedimentation of the nation-state.

The next Labour government will rebuild communities ripped apart by
globalization. (Labour party, 2017 Manifesto)

The inner-workings of neoliberal capitalism that supposedly led to the
crises driving contemporary politics have been inherently shaped by

their reliance on the justification for layers of differential exploitation by a supposedly natural order. This has been enforced through quarantine, criminalisation, precarity and pre-emptive forms of power working to produce hierarchical regimes of control.

To win we must revive this progressive patriotism and solidarity in a form fit for modern Britain. (Rebecca Long-Bailey, Labour leadership pitch, 2019)

In the wake of the 2019 election defeat of the Corbyn-led movement, hard-fought attempts within the party to shift Labour away from the horizon of the nation look likely to be set aside. Political pragmatism is set to pitch an even stronger nation-state that will protect the interests of working- and middle-class Britons. An embedded imperialism can be found at the heart of progressive politics: the hegemonic reliance of political movements on the everyday imperial practices inside and outside of the British state that serve to differentiate and control, which form the necessary condition for Britain's ongoing sovereignty and citizenship.

…adequate protection and security for its people's well-being and the nation's future – to secure the solutions needed to avert catastrophe and protect the future. (Extinction Rebellion, 2018)

I finish by arguing that, under discourses of climate crisis, these political trajectories risk becoming a cipher for geopolitical reconfigurations whose end is the lifeboat state. Politics under the horizon of the nation is thus produced through distributed architectures of sovereignty and differential governance, and therefore, is in no position to imagine or practise their undoing.

NEOLIBERAL LIMITS AND LIMITATIONS

There is a narrative becoming commonplace on the left which tells us that since around the 1970s we have both seen the ascendancy of the totalising power of the neoliberal 'disenchantment of politics by economics' and that its hegemony is now in tatters.[2] This relies on a commonplace view that the neoliberal era was largely consistent with neoclassical approaches to economy and globalist approaches to trade. For example, David Harvey argues that:

The neoliberal label signaled their adherence to those free market principles of neo-classical economics [...] Neoliberal doctrine was therefore deeply opposed to state interventionist theories.[3]

Neoliberalism is very often understood as an embedded set of power relations that remade society and subjects in the image of the market, and as entrepreneurial actors in every sphere of life. This leads to the view that economic rationality is entrenched across all society, in which humans are remade as *homo economicus*.

It has been supposed, therefore, that neoliberalism 'was not inherently ethnonationalist, authoritarian, or plutocratic', as Wendy Brown puts it.[4] The rise of contemporary forms of nationalism must be 'profoundly antagonistic to the neoliberal agenda' according to Harvey. Implicitly, the suggestion is that, for the most part, neoliberalism has held nationalist and racially charged movements at bay, whether working as a civilising and progressive force for its advocates, or eviscerating the social domain through the logic of capital accumulation and restoration of class power for its critics.

Its demise is seemingly evidenced by the nostalgia for a nation-state pitted against global finance; anti-migrant politics in the name of labour protection; mainstreaming far right arguments; data-driven immigrant valuations; anti-Muslim alliances; the resurgence of race science as intellectual discourse. As Will Davies puts it, over the last few years, we have:

> witnessed popular movements diametrically opposed to the economic common sense that has held sway in the UK and US since the 1970s. These movements are fervently anti-neoliberal [...] inasmuch as neoliberalism embeds particular forms of economic rationality.[5]

What holds these movements together is a political emphasis on nations and the securitisation of borders over the economic programme of neoliberal globalisation.

In this section, I seek to problematise the dramatisation of our contemporary struggle that is situated in the so-called collapse of neoliberalism. To do so, I first provide a counter-narrative of shifts in Britain's geopolitical formation under what is commonly called neoliberalism by highlighting the role of the commons and its limits as inheritor of Lockean logics of development. I briefly outline how the globalist order emerging in the 1960s and 1970s emerged as an alibi for the continual restoration of natural order tied to neo-imperial power and population control. Far from dismantling it, these required the restoration of the state under the post-colonial cut. This has ramifications for understanding the economic and political power of Britain in its neo-imperial global form.

Managing a global commons

In the wake of a decolonised and destabilised world order, the emergence of the idea of a global commons was consolidated in the 1970s in the context of attempts made by dominant states to create the possibility for global governance. The concept of the global commons had emerged from concerns to put in place shared standards for global trade and international relations that would work through post-Bretton Woods institutions and the Washington Consensus. Whilst advocates of globalisation theory have emphasised how this made way for globalised free markets beyond the limitations of nation-states, this new form of governance is better understood as locking-in regulatory sovereignty and anti-democratic movements and promoting global capital mobility.[6] New forms of knowledge had emerged that cohered with the idea of a global commons, emphasising local interaction and ecological interconnectedness whilst abjuring top-down interventionism.[7] Drawing on cybernetics and ideas of self-organisation, the image of the world produced was one of information flows simultaneously breaking down boundaries across a global ecosystem, whilst also naturalising their reproduction as the emergent manifestation of underlying processes.

Since the middle of the twentieth century, architects of neoliberalism like Friedrich Hayek had developed a similar analysis of spontaneous organisation – of crystals, markets, nature and society. Global order would emerge from the seeming chaos of local actions. Moving away from neoclassical models of economic equilibrium that focused on exchange and allocation, in Hayek's view the market is a coordinator of information between agents. Economic significance is tied to the value that individuals place on goods through the expression of their consumption needs. These are manifested through individual preferences and aggregated through a system where the market acts as a complex calculation device, where prices 'tell the individual how to best contribute to the pool from which we all draw in proportion to our contribution.'[8] The price system is therefore both the emergent result of economic practices and their precondition. According to the theory, when dealing with scarce resources, huge numbers of people will, without explicit knowledge of that scarcity, move 'to use the material or its products more sparingly; i.e., they move in the right direction'.[9]

This model didn't assume equilibrium like neoclassical economics, but foregrounded the dynamics between nature and human through local interactions and feedback loops. As Philip Mirowski puts it, classical liberal economists like Adam Smith 'imagined a night watchman state that would set the boundaries for the natural growth of the market, like a shepherd tending his flock'.[10] Core principles of good governance and liberty would then be set in place by the natural rights of citizens acting as they should in a liberal society. As such, markets require protection from state intervention as far as possible, whilst society would be protected from any potential disruptions of the market by natural rights and the principle of individual liberty. As described in Chapter 3, the 'natural order' comprised freedom for the parochial European as human, won through spatial and temporal differentiations, racialised segregation and violent extraction from the non-European other. This relied on a civilised form of the 'laws of nature', wielded against the unnatural order of those produced as other to it.

Working in this lineage, the preservation of regimes of private property and their inheritance was central to a neoliberal approach to the global commons. If classical liberalism understood laissez-faire markets as natural and benevolent entities, then neoliberalism as Foucault observed 'on the contrary, should be regarded as a call to vigilance, to activism, to perpetual interventions'.[11] Against the naturalisation of liberalism's genocidal freedoms, neoliberal markets were understood to be constructed, rather than natural, so requiring vigilance and work to build and maintain: '[i]n no system that could be rationally defended would the state just do nothing'.[12] The very idea of a free market is based on a false dichotomy between a state acting or not. Neoliberal markets have not required state roll-back so much as state-repurposing.

The major economic function of government lies in the organisation of markets to protect and promote competition by rules developed through spontaneous organisation. These rules must be implicit in individual's behaviour and abilities, rather than transparently accessible to the rational subject or made explicit in public fora. Herein lies Hayek's appeal to societal norms and the 'calming authority of tradition', together with the injunction that we '[t]rust the standards inherited from the past'.[13]

The idea is that social competition has determined the most advantageous norms for our society, selecting abstract social rules through our individual practices and interactions. These pre-existing norms and practices have supposedly been articulated and systematised into laws.[14] Even explicit laws and policies are both dependent upon a system of tacit rules, and productive of knowledge that is tacitly possessed. So it is paramount that such knowledge is not disrupted or distorted in such a way as to prevent the smooth functioning of the free market.

Generalised in Hayek's later work, this made way for a systems ecology that fosters the resilience 'of individuals and social, ecological and financial systems against unknowable, unpredictable and unmanageable catastrophe'.[15] Whilst nature would no longer provide an alibi for imperialist capitalism, this shift between liberalism and neoliberalism was motivated by the conditions under which the spatial and temporal freedoms of 'Western man' could be executed. In the period after the Second World War, the anxiety expressed on behalf of the neoliberal Mont Pelérin Society's (MPS) to wit that 'the central values of civilization are in danger' is explicable against the threat of a decolonising world.[16]

The tragedies of neoliberal development

Consistent with this approach to the global commons was its combination with the idea of natural limits. From the late 1960s, limits on the commons became popularised as a problem of scarcity of energy supplies and population excess.[17] Garrett Hardin's parable 'Tragedy of the Commons' (1968) drew on what he called the 'cybernetics of competition' to compute the consequences of population growth on ecological equilibria. He pictured herdsmen driven by the desire to maximise personal gain ultimately ruining common pastures for all.

Hardin's parable was written as a critique of Adam Smith's doctrine of laissez-faire, calling attention to the inevitable destruction of common resources by a rising population. He positioned his work as an ecological counterview to Smith, working in later papers to advocate for the close *management* of the commons through enclosure and privatisation. Echoing emergent neoliberal critiques of laissez-faire economies, Hardin argues that the tragedy of the commons could not be prevented by self-regulation, but required their mandatory enclosure and privatisation:

[...] the commons, if justifiable at all, is justifiable only under conditions of low-population density. As the human population has increased, the commons has had to be abandoned in one aspect after another.[18]

Whilst officially abjuring Hardin's talk of overpopulation and limits, as well as his insistence on state coercion as requisite solution, Hardin's parable provided neoliberal economists with the justification for interpreting scarce resources as common goods.

Together, the notions of 'global commons' and 'limits' underpinned a pragmatic approach to international markets and resources as a way of 'handling a range of things according to a procedure of abstraction in which laws, norms, or values are derived from [...] a common measure.'[19] Supposedly operating across networks that didn't recognise nation-state/market distinctions, this approach shifted attention from the local commons of newly sovereign, decolonised nations to a global commons and helped to justify interventionist forms of management as prophylactic measure against those pre-emptively judged to act against this common measure. What emerged was not a globalised system of free markets, but the development of neo-imperialist relations across borders.

Deemed authoritative by the IMF and the World Bank, Hardin's allegory can be read, speculatively, as a symbol of a neoliberal struggle to protect global resources against the backdrop of post-war instability, providing justification for neo-colonial development. Hardin's tragedy targeted the seemingly inevitable decisions of the global South, of 'impoverished communities in developed states and the people of the Third World.'[20] As with neoliberals more generally, Hardin relied on a characterisation of the human as *homo economicus* as the universal conditions of all social relations. However, as he made clear, there was a rift that lay within the concept of the human itself: between the rational liberal subject and the resource-grabbing other.

The era of structural adjustments, land grabs and militarised intervention was sedimented through these logics. As Rob Nixon argues, the figure of the herdsman in Hardin's essay provides this racialised splitting with its neo-colonial mythos. The herdsman is the symbol of a decolonising world. Following in the footsteps of Locke, the racialised herdsman is supposed incapable of the production of private property, now transmuted through the rational appropriation of market-based behaviour. In this way, Hardin 'helped vindicate a neoliberal rescue narrative, whereby privatization through enclosure, dispossession, and resource capture is deemed necessary for averting tragedy'.[21] Judged out of sync with the normative order of the global commons, coercion against people in the periphery was legitimised because they lacked the conscience necessary for its preservation.

On the latter, the corollary of interventionist economic coercion was the protectionism we have seen through the development of brutal migration controls, the proliferation of bordering practices and the hardening of nation-states as primary political container and agent. The virulent protection of Britain's property regimes required not just the expropriation of global resources, but also their fortification from possible incursion through the normalization and sanctification of 'the national exclusion of economic migrants and other nonnationals, whom they designate as political strangers'.[22] The theory of natural limits espoused by Hardin underpinned arguments for border controls, whilst discourses of the global commons legitimated international legal systems that governed the relative freedom of movement. For advocates of limits, the neo-Malthusian resurfacing of the population question was directed primarily at movements of populations across borders. Migration was an unnatural motor of population growth with poorer immigrants' infiltration of wealthier countries creating the conditions for the disastrous breakdown of the supposedly natural limits defined by territorial borders.[23]

'PROGRESSIVE' LEFT NATIONALISM

With this context in mind, let us consider how recent political movements have relied on the nation as their basic political unit as supposed protection against neoliberal globalism. In this section, I suggest that there has been a strong tendency within left state politics that implicitly relies on neo-Malthusian logics of natural limits and the naturalised nation-state. Not only a limit to the political imagination, the nation is reproduced as *horizon* for political thought and policy.

Economic nationalism

I am primarily interested in tendencies towards nationalism in the state-based movement within and around the Labour party that attempted to push it towards a specific form of socialist politics.[24] Its make-up can be characterised by the intersection of traditional left stalwarts of the Labour party (Jeremy Corbyn, John McDonnell, Diane Abbott, Seamus Milne) together with Len McCluskey of Unite union and Jon Lansman of Momentum, newer Members of Parliament such as Rebecca Long-Bailey, and popular approaches to post-capitalism influenced by Paul Mason, Novara Media, Owen Jones, and Alex Williams and Nick Srnicek. Not so much a doctrine, but a collection of loose affiliations and antagonisms, there are a number of strands to this new socialism, many of which are antagonistic to one another. Moreover, given the spectacular defeat of what has been termed 'Corbynism' in the 2019 general election, I want to avoid any simplistic autopsy of political failure. In what follows, then, I am concerned primarily with a particular set of political trajectories within the political left. For want of a better phrase, I shall refer to the alliance of these trajectories as the 'progressive left'. Their alignment certainly found focus in Corbynism, but has arguably been more evident since his resignation.

The political trajectory I have in mind turns on a characterisation of neoliberalism cohering with those presented and countered in the previous section. What emerges is an increasingly common-sense critique of neoliberal capitalism, focusing on disaggregating forms of governance such as those enacted through debt and austerity. This is to be rectified, so the thought goes, by aggregating forms of action and policy under the rubric of renationalising provision of health, education, childcare and income, and returning control of the economy to local and national scale. At the core of this position is, as Matt Bolton and Frederick Harry Pitts write,

>...a steadfast faith in the ability of the nation-state to eradicate inequality and poverty through a radical programme of intervention in the domestic economy.[25]

The guiding suggestion is that nation-states are the most viable vehicle for the protection of workers in resistance to capital.

The proposed form of this economic nationalism is such that the regulation of capitalism requires the strengthening of the state as ultimate arbiter of production, circulation and distribution. Such a project would therefore likely require some form of 'delinking from the global economy', in order to reclaim the national economy 'as a site of democratic politics'.[26] Under the weight of arguments against imposed austerity measures, increased state oversight over capital flows is promoted as means to decelerate capitalist speculation seen to be at the root of our current crises. As Jamie Marchant describes, this would involve 'subordinating financial institutions to the national state by withdrawing or sheltering them from the world market'.[27] The effects of this kind of project were made explicit by Paul Mason's discussion of a socialist economic strategy:

> Is this strategy designed to allow the populations of the developed world to capture more of the growth projected over the next 5–15 years, if necessary at the cost of China, India and Brazil having to find new ways to break out of the middle income trap? [...] For me the answer is yes. This is a programme to save democracy, democratic institutions and values in the developed world by reversing the 30-year policy of enriching the bottom 60% and the top 1% of the world's population. It is a programme to deliver growth and prosperity in Wigan, Newport and Kirkcaldy – if necessary at the price of not delivering them to Shenzhen, Bombay and Dubai.[28]

This is a protectionist programme to regulate capital inflows and outflows, which is consistent with a view of neoliberalism as unfettered corporate globalism that has undermined national welfare.

Inextricable from this programme, though not always explicitly conjoined with it, have been arguments for the end of the free movement of labour.[29] Subsequent to the Brexit referendum, the Labour party 2017 manifesto pledged to end free movement from the EU regardless of Brexit negotiations, with a policy more extreme than their Conservative opposition. These arguments for immigration controls found justification primarily in the suggestion that immigration drives up unemployment and depresses wages for 'ordinary' workers. When questioned about Labour's position on freedom of movement in 2017, Corbyn answered '[w]hat there wouldn't be is wholesale importation of underpaid workers from Central Europe in order to destroy [working] conditions, particularly in the construction industry'.[30] Len McCluskey of the union Unite has similarly argued that the needs of working people require greater controls over labour flows, and the stability of communities.[31]

Under these logics, freedom of movement is made synonymous with flows of capital and labour. In response, the left economic project has therefore emphasised controls over both. These controls are supposed to protect nationally produced wealth and to prevent jobs sliding away from localities.[32] The framework through which this is squeezed is that of a nation-state as a defined boundary that could protect against fluctuating financial systems and foreign capital investment. But this misunderstands the ways that a strengthened nation-state was already forged in the fire of neoliberalism, and not its antidote.

Borders, finance and risk

As described in Chapter 2, whilst financialisation operates as a disciplinary practice across national lines, it is neither reducible to abstract economies nor does it simply elide borders. Put simply, financialisation relies on a calculus of risk on anticipatory value. This is grounded in loans, often in the form of investments, and these require the proliferation of limits (including borders) to produce asymmetries along which risks are calculated and punitive measures exercised. For this reason, regimes of indebtedness in the decolonising world operated to open up newly sovereign nation-states to the influx of financial speculation and resource extraction *in the same moment* as border regimes were strengthened allowing that power to be wielded.

Capital inflows into Britain continue to rely upon globally distributed supply chains, transnational ownership and the financial relations between them. Maintaining all of these requires an operation that works with the affordances of borders and limits. These affordances rely upon the highly differentiated nature of borders and connections, as Doreen Massey writes:

> Different social groups and different individuals are placed in very distinct ways in relation to [...] flows and interconnections. This point concerns not merely the issue of who moves and who doesn't, although that is an important element of it; it is also about power in relation to the flows and the movement. Different social groups have distinct relationships to this anyway – differentiated mobility: some are more in charge of it than others; some initiate flows and movement, others don't; some are more on the receiving end of it than others; some are effectively imprisoned by it.[33]

The management of these relative flows relies upon a vast global machinery of transnational controls, differential laws and policies, and integrated technologies and information systems. The previous chapter also showed how the management of this machinery relies on regimes of fear, violence and surveillance.

As described above, neoliberal attempts to manifest a system of global commons involved international border policies that set out to manage resource, capital and labour movement. In part what these achieved were asymmetries across relationships and borders in order to produce surplus value. Allowing for the continuation of imperialism under the regime of neoliberalism, their aim was to appropriate value and resources from the global periphery. For example, we often see the periphery depicted as a hamstrung and damaged world that is in need of development. Against these standard narratives, which focus on aid from OECD to non-OECD countries, disparities are in part preserved by vast transfers of value in the opposite direction – via unequal exchange, transfer pricing, income and capital flows, and seigniorage – estimated at around £3.8tn each year. These are cross-border flows of profit, interest and rent that fundamentally rely on the relative fluidity and porosity of borders to differentially include and connect. Disparities in production costs and local workers' rights in the periphery are essential to the accumulation of capital in the imperial core. As Mark Graham and Mohammed Anwar describe in their analysis of the global gig economy:

> ...a planetary market doesn't do away with geography; it rather exists to take advantage of it [using] uneven geographies to facilitate labour arbitrage, cross-border competition.[34]

With bordering not spatially fixed but operational across our lives, these regimes sediment perverse hierarchies through the abstraction of risk into political and financial speculation. For instance, financial speculation drives inter-state agreements such as those between Britain and Africa as well as developing supply chains across borders. These work together with attempts to manage a migrant labour supply that can be stemmed and diverted by detention camps and border policies. Labour arbitrage is therefore made possible through regional and intra-state competition and capital flight that dismantles the possibility of localised labour power. The proliferation of comparative limits is part of the structure through which financial speculation has been made possible.

In shifting towards the fluidity and flexibility of spatial regimes, 'cross-border operations', as Angela Mitropoulos terms them, have become central to the coalition of capital and state.[35] The transfer of value from the periphery to Britain is primarily achieved through international trade under the tendency to equalise rates of profit. Global trade in goods and services has the appearance of equality of exchange. However, the equalisation of profit rates is set by competition in markets that are shaped by unequal development and border protections. As a result, on top of the surplus-value extracted in the periphery, an additional portion is extracted by the imperial core. This portion has steadily risen since the 1970s, with hyper-exploitation one of its major drivers – both inside and outside of British shores. The public–private partnerships that I have discussed throughout, but particularly in the context of bordering, similarly clarify the ways that borders are vital to transnational regimes in which spatio-temporal differences, legal relationships and affective regimes are capitalised upon both financially and politically.[36]

As Nadine El-Enany argues, Britain's immigration and nationality laws can be understood as an attempt to draw a border around the spoils of British colonial conquest as a final act of colonial theft.[37] The above analysis also shows that such 'theft' is ongoing – Britain's borders continue to ensure unequal exchange. Under the auspices of what many writers have termed neoliberalism, the twin logics of a global commons – as universalised common rule – and natural limits – as differentially prescribed – conspired to manage ongoing resource extraction and protectionist bordering. This has included the conditions through which currency variations, different laws and production costs, offshore manufacture and the making of hyper-exploitable groups of people are facilitated by borders, territorial limits and market segmentations by 'trading on ranked differences'.[38] In analysing how these operations involve both connections and boundaries, what emerges is a picture of neo-imperialism that has been grounded on the management and orientation of global movements of capital, goods and people. For this reason, the era has witnessed dominant states not just protecting but shaping and producing both markets and borders.

Lean exploitation

To put this succinctly: proliferating borders have been fundamental to the manifestation of neoliberal forms of capitalism, which are better understood in terms of neo-imperialist relationships of dependency. However, this characterisation has remained largely absent from the analysis of neoliberalism underpinning the progressive left. This is particularly apparent in arguments regarding the influx of immigrants depreciating the wages of 'native-born' workers. These replace analysis of power, finance and extraction across massive-scale circulations of extraction, accumulation and consumption 'with national aggregates of wage and employment rates that give the impression of a well-defined uniformity among workers within nation-states'.[39] With neo-Malthusianism barely left implicit, the production of 'surplus populations' is then considered in relation to the 'carrying capacity' of a mystificatory notion of national economy. Increases in population size are understood as a determining factor for wage and employment levels on the nation's interior rather than being considered one cog in the complex machinery of global capital relations.

This kind of argument has become practically chapter and verse across the political spectrum, where, supposedly, advocates from 'Karl Marx to Milton Friedman, have agreed that an over-supply of labour depresses wages'.[40] The apparently Marxist suggestion is that flows of capital tend towards the production of a reserve army of labour required as a condition for expanded production as discussed in Chapter 2. This surplus population is, therefore, intimately linked to the capitalist accumulation cycle, as surplus to capital's need to produce value at a specific time. However, as Mitropoulos argues, this fails to support the analysis that migrant people lower 'native' wages, in the main because it does not account for the relative nature of the surplus populations of workers. Any reserve army is, for Marx, always an artificial overpopulation that is endogenously indexed to the dynamics of capitalism at work in a particular context. These dynamics involve wage-setting through politically secured exploitation that has segmented labour markets and ensured that wages for white Britons are incrementally far higher than racially cheapened labour in Britain and across the periphery.[41]

A more nuanced account of surplus populations can be found in the stream of post-capitalist and post-work literature that has influenced the progressive left. There, the suggestion is that we ought to consider how neoliberal economies have increasingly expelled labour from the formal wage. The redistribution of wealth upwards since the 1980s has polarised income and led to rising levels of unemployment and precarious work. These result from the combination of automation of low-wage jobs and the outsourcing of median wage jobs to dominated nations together with the disaggregation of labour power – both by political force and by labour sector differentiation and working conditions.[42] It is these specific conditions rather than the shaky abstractions of population size, which have resulted in the increase of temporary and precarious work. Through the gig economy, or platform capitalism, as Nick Srnicek terms it, we are witnessing an increasingly precarious proletariat and increasingly informal economies.[43]

However, as discussed in Chapter 2, the mechanisms through which surplus-value is produced require us to also understand practices of the dehomogenisation of the proletariat – something which is often only alluded to in post-work discourse. Consider, for example, the make-up of precarious workers. In 2017, Black and Minority ethnic people in the UK were over twice as likely to be unemployed as white people.[44] At almost all qualification levels, white people were more likely to be employed in 2017 than people classed as Black and of Minority ethnicity.[45] To draw on the arguments of Chapter 2, any suggestion that automation and the neoliberal disaggregation of labour power has made for the production of a relative surplus population of potentially proletarianised wage-labourers necessarily requires taking into account the mechanisms establishing racialised groups as redundant and pathologised citizens from the outset. Far from automation smoothing out these discrepancies, it is much more likely that they will be exacerbated further.

Precarious workers have been continually funnelled into specific economies without workers' rights or access to welfare, hence underwriting unequal exchange within the territories of nations. This is not the case by necessity, rather it has been produced by the continuities and ruptures with empire to subsidise the metropole and create hyper-exploitable groups of people within and without of British shores. As argued in Chapter 2, far from driving down wages, the classification of migrants was a condition of the possibility for relatively stable wages and asset ownership by subsidising labour and capital for the largely white middle classes. Obscuring this, discussions of surplus populations tend to figure the differential exploitation of migrant people as only a collateral effect of capitalism, whose universal drive to accumulate goes unquestioned. However, these shifts relied on the sedimentation of people into a supposedly natural order of classification in which certain people have been deemed out of place: bodies that have become borders in regimes of modulation, precarity and hyper-exploitation.

As Srnicek points out, whilst the confluence of automation with platform capitalism creates a distinct set of affordances, the dynamics of lean platforms such as Uber and Amazon's Mechanical Turk are best understood as exacerbating techniques that are familiar to other forms of precarious labour.[46] By consolidating precarious contracts between labour and capital with workers figured as independent contractors, these platforms expand and centralise labour markets that have often been informal, filled by migrant populations, and characterised by poor working conditions and rights. As described throughout this book, the conditional entry and citizen-status of migrant workers coupled with their exclusion from workers' rights and welfare has been a consistent feature of post-war British economies. It is unsurprising, then, to find that jobs characterised by precarity and lack of rights are twice as likely to be filled by Black and Minority ethnic people than white workers. Of an estimated 1.1 million people on zero-hour contracts, a quarter are Black or Asian (who make up approximately 13% of the overall population).[47] Excluded from, or marginalised within, traditional labour markets, racialised groups continue to be pushed into forms of employment with fewer rights, less security, lower pay and less likelihood of career advancement.

Lean platforms do, however, afford the ability for employers to engage in labour arbitrage by outsourcing workers and offloading costs, with Uber, for example, requiring workers to provide vehicles, their maintenance and insurance. More importantly perhaps, these platforms enforce a degree of formality upon an informal economy. For example, they often require the use of tracking technologies and bank accounts, whilst continually allowing for the extraction of data across the platform with a 'layer of pervasive surveillance'.[48] For all of the promise that the future of work will be characterised by the gig economy, lean platforms have seen relatively small increases in labour force share in the UK, with only around 3.9 per cent of the labour force working through lean platforms at least once a week.[49] In other words, platform capitalism functions as adjunct to capitalism proper, continuing to take advantage of, and reproducing, the precarity and hyper-exploitability of disproportionately racialised groups of people.

Platform Keynesianism

Thinking about our current predicament as a struggle against globalised finance and the free movement of labour potentially reproduces the logics of neo-imperial forms of capitalism. The ongoing exploitation of migrant workers has been necessary to carve out the category of citizens who would benefit from the progressive political project:

> The strategies and technologies which define them (their containment within informal economies; the random policing which maintains them in a position of vulnerability) are also implicated in the constitution of insider-citizens, whose relative privilege now reflects the specific practices made possible in and through the spaces of the global political economy.[50]

The reliance on this deployment of colonial distinctions and practices to remake 'insider-citizens' is perhaps most evident in the rush to recentre a 'white working class'. Focusing on economic anxieties caused by austerity since 2008, the white working class have been consistently framed as those 'left behind' by global neoliberalism.[51]

According to Mason, the vote to leave the European Union was an expression of wider social attitudes that define this bloc of British voters:

> ...unsettled by high inward migration, turned-off by the cosmopolitan lifestyle of big cities, apt to call middle class people 'luvvies' – as the Sun does every day – proud of their industrial past and determinedly patriotic.[52]

Invoking this patriotic and nationalist group of people follows an emerging consensus that left politics needs to pay attention to 'legitimate concerns' regarding the protection of national sovereignty, opposition to immigration and British values. As a result, policies aimed at protecting the economy of the British nation-state have often focused on supporting this alleged social bloc. This was made clear by Labour's 2017 *Build it in Britain Again* campaign, which intended to galvanise British production against a reliance on cheap foreign labour and global capital.[53] These policies are inextricable from neo-Malthusian complaints regarding the population growth of migrant workers. As Mason put it, they are required to 'meet the objections of low-paid workers to wage suppression.'[54]

As Labour approached the 2019 general election, movements within the party fought to reverse the 2017 policy on ending free movement. This resulted in the passing of a conference motion to extend free movement, close detention centres and award equal voting rights to all

UK residents. However, the victory was short-lived in terms of affecting party policy. Lost in a storm of voter pragmatics and union wrangling, the position did not even make it to the election manifesto. The fallout of the election defeat looks incredibly likely to entrench this trajectory, as Labour under Corbyn is narrated as too far removed from the concerns of white working classes regarding immigration and multiculturalism. As Unite leader Len McCluskey put it, the party emphasised liberal values such as 'openness, tolerance, human rights' at the expense of the 'traditional' working class who 'have their own values of solidarity and community'.[55] In the wake of the defeat, prominent voices on the left such as Michael Walker and Thomas Fazi seized the opportunity to make the case that opposition to immigration should not be likened to racism, and that we should accept that national identity is the basis for any form of socialist politics. To win, apparently Labour should resolutely reject a 'woke-liberal' approach to borders, immigration and sovereignty, and focus on state security and civic nationalism.[56]

In this vision, migrant workers are bodies out of place, in a wholly distinct category to the white working class. The naturalisation of this distinction is prerequisite for arguments regarding the struggle for scarce resources to even get off the ground. For instance, every substantive proposal for Labour's 'radical' economic policies of a universal basic income or citizen dividend is in reality far from universal. Rather, they proscribe provision to recent migrant people until they have proved national allegiance through work or length of residence. The question of the global flows through which a surplus is produced so that it may be distributed to British people is not even mooted in these analyses, nor is the subsidising of British workers by empire, ongoing neo-colonial extraction, and migrant labour.

Politics under the horizon of the nation thus necessitates the erasure of hyper-exploitation and strategies of ongoing colonialism in order to frame a proletariat as both homogenised and delimited by territorial borders. Unlike Srnicek's more nuanced analysis, the production of relative surplus populations typically becomes another argument for the control and scapegoating of migrant workers in the context of supposedly dwindling resources. What results is a project that circumscribes equality and welfare within territorial borders, together with a secessionist fiscal policy underwritten by a moral economy of naturalised limits.

The strengthened 'socialist' state would therefore operate much like a state monopoly through which the state would extend its control over populations.[57] Leigh Phillips and Michal Rozworski have argued that this kind of socialist state has been made possible through shifts in increased automation and platform capitalism, readying large-scale monopolistic companies for state takeover.[58] In this vision, a strong state is required to nationalise services and industry, to promote alternative models of ownership, and to shift decarbonisation from private companies to solve climate change. Since practically all of Britain's problems are chalked up to globalised financialisation, the strong state is required for social stability, and contemporary socialism takes the form of a kind of platform Keynesianism. For example, the decision by Transport for London in 2017 to potentially suspend Uber's licence to operate in London was hailed as a necessary step towards socialist monopoly by Mason, who stated that:

> Transport for London finally gets tough with Uber. There are some good minicab firms that play fair by the rules. Let's have a single, free public minicab booking app for London.[59]

The safety of Uber users was cited as amongst the central reasons for the suspension. The platform allows unauthorised drivers to upload photographs to authorised drivers' accounts. Uber drivers had used the loophole allowing undocumented workers to share or rent accounts.[60] TfL's decision was exacerbated by the inability to monitor Uber due to its use of the encrypted software *Greyball* that could push different versions of the app to different users. The implications are clear: the layers of pervasive surveillance enabled by Uber should be transparent to state monitoring, and the systems through which undocumented workers have been able to attain access to lean platforms should be shut down.

The framework of the nation is the central imaginary of this approach to socialism. Focusing on a central antagonism between national capital and international capitalist competition, socialism is rewritten as national protectionism. Under these conditions, the political imaginary is limited to building social institutions and movements inextricably tied to the form of the nation, with their protection, preservation and reproduction made synonymous with national interest. Nonetheless, in even the most mundane operations of everyday life, British economy and politics are rooted in cross-border operations. Ultimately, progressive leftism would exacerbate the racial stratification and differential precarity of relative surplus populations. Without actively undermining a geopolitics productive of unequal exchange, a state monopoly over increasingly concentrated economic power would be inextricable from the protection of a highly differentiated surplus population, whilst ratcheting up bordering, securitisation, regimes of risk and violent exclusions.

EXTINCTION POLITICS

In this section, I trace the fault lines of the characterisation of struggles against globalised markets as productive of a strengthened state and the sedimented imaginary of the nation as the political horizon determining the boundaries of possibility. As described over the past chapters, these trajectories were forged through immigration policies and colonial practices since the middle of the twentieth century, but here they tend towards a politics of elimination that has become increasingly intense. The resurgence of the drive towards the restoration of the natural order makes explicit an underlying logic of people out of place.

Increasing surveillance, making temporary

Suggestions for policy after Brexit shifted over the moves between the tenure of Theresa May and Sajid Javid as prime minister and home secretary, respectively, to Boris Johnson and Priti Patel. However, Johnson continued May's insistence on a return to a 'one-nation' conservatism, which promotes a far more explicitly interventionist government than is familiar to those typically associated with the neoliberal state. Plans suggest not the ending of the movement of workers but an increasingly controlled and highly differentiated spatio-temporal regime brought under closer state management.

Changes in migration policy after Brexit have often been presented as simply expanding what is currently policy for non-EU migrant people to those from the EU. At present, Britain has a tiered point-based system for non-EU migrant people that assesses English language skills, company sponsorship and salary threshold. Under the euphemistically named 'skills based' immigration system, EU free movement would be ended whilst remaking migration under a single system that is grounded in the assessment of skilled workers and employer sponsorship. However, this is distinct from current policy for non-EU migrant people, which takes a decentralised approach that allows employers to decide whether or not somebody is qualified for a specific job.[61] Decision-making would be brought directly under the power of a branch of the state, whilst allowing an income threshold of £30,000 to decide migrant numbers. Under home secretary Priti Patel's proposals, this will be expanded to put in place a 'point based system' following that in use by the Australian government. This moves away from the kind of market-based allocation of the prior incumbent's skills-based approach to a more careful management system for different industries and different needs. As such, the state would have much more direct and unmediated control over those desiring to cross its borders and to work in Britain. Both approaches also allow for lower-skilled migrant workers under more stringent limitations to work on temporary visas of up to twelve months.

Motivated by calls to restore order to 'natural' increases in the size of the labour force over 'unnatural' shifts due to immigrant workers, Priti Patel in her speech at the 2019 party conference called to 'end freedom of movement once and for all'. However, this should not be misunderstood as the end of movement altogether. Instead, the call seeks to augment and quantify stratifications across the *migrant* workforce. The proposed shifts in policy afford an assemblage of power and interests across state(s) and (trans)national corporations to more tightly survey, orient and calibrate the movement of people across and inside territories. Proposals to control immigration for highly skilled, or points-scoring, migrant people allow the state to intervene in defining their parameters and demographics. Under a self-fulfilling set of purportedly neutral criteria regarding intelligence and appropriateness, this serves instead to reify racial analytics as 'data'. Shifts towards a state-controlled point-based system allow for the shaping of the race and religion of migrant people, whilst also offloading the costs of training higher-skilled migrant people to their countries of origin.

Supplementing these migration controls will be the increase of temporary and conditional statuses on migrant people, whilst operating under a much more closely guarded system of control and management. There will be an expansion of seasonal worker, overseas domestic worker and tied visas, the former two granting rights to stay in the country for a maximum of six months to a specific employer (though under certain controlled conditions this may be transferable), and the latter tying workers to a specific employer and location. Whilst some roles such as farm labour have been filled primarily by Eastern European workers, after Brexit it is likely that Britain will look further afield for these temporary roles. Two recruitment operators, Concordia and Pro-Force, were contracted by the Home Office to manage a pilot scheme for identifying migrant workers from outside of the EU for seasonal work on a Tier 5, six-month visa.

As they currently operate with very little oversight, the temporariness and precarity of these forms of migrant employment have often led to substantive physical and economic abuse with little supervision. Their precarity exacerbates the potential for exploitation by tying workers to specific employment conditions with little recourse against them, since workers face deportation at the termination of contract. These conditions are likely to worsen as the ability for these workers to access support and welfare diminishes or is more tightly controlled. For example, NHS Improvement which currently implements upfront charges in the NHS, are piloting a programme for assessing creditworthiness by sharing identifiable data with private company Experian. The immigration health surcharge already operates a form of double taxation by requiring migrant workers, whose taxes contribute to the NHS, to pay a premium for healthcare. Increasing temporary and conditional migrant employment thus prevents more people from accessing claims on the state or on corporations whilst maintaining regimes of fear and disposability through the sedimentation of citizenship hierarchies. This would produce a highly controlled and hyper-exploitable labour force that is precluded access to basic welfare or employment rights and who can be easily repatriated.

Repatriating citizens

The repatriation of migrant workers has become ever more possible through changes in policy, trans-agency collaboration and experimentation with legal and alegal procedures. One way this has been manifest is the more substantive targeting of homeless people and rough sleepers in collaboration with charities providing immigration support. Amongst others, the Home Office collaborated with the Salvation Army and St Mungo's charity for the homeless in central London, both of which are positioned as offering safe spaces for asylum seekers and homeless people. Whilst posing as charity support staff, state delegates ran sessions with both organisations that targeted precarious migrant people. ICE teams have also ramped up collaboration with private businesses, leading to coordinated raids on subcontracted workers across Amazon warehouses in the south of England, for instance. There are also trials to link street fingerprint scanning with immigration enforcement as part of the growing redeployment of police as internalised border control.

Whilst these practices more pervasively survey, target and single out migrant people, state powers to repatriate have been enhanced over a number of years. The 2014 Immigration Act provided the ability to make naturalised Britons stateless if the British state thinks it is possible that person can become a citizen elsewhere. By their design these powers are self-selecting for non-white citizens. They are enforced through infrastructures for massive-scale deportations: charter flights; private security firms; partnership schemes between Britain and countries via trade; the use of ICE raids to identify people without full evidence of nationality. Since removals on charter flights began in 2001, there have been around 28,283 removals on 798 flights.[62]

Light has recently been shed on these practices most visibly in the case of the Windrush scandal in 2018. This involved the wrongful detention and attempted repatriation via deportation of people who migrated from the Caribbean before 1973. Deprivation of citizenship is not uncommon and has been steadily rising, with 104 people deprived of British citizenship in 2017, up from 14 in the previous year. In 2013, then home secretary Theresa May announced the idea that 'citizenship is a privilege, not a right, and the Home Secretary will remove British citizenship from individuals where she feels it is conducive to the public good to do so'. This privilege of British citizenship has been enforced by the testing of state powers in what Nisha Kapoor has called 'experimental authoritarianism'.[63] It has led to the increased precarity of the status of certain kinds of British citizens, with cases such as the Windrush scandal, for Kapoor, functioning as an alibi for creeping totalitarianism. Executive powers are tested that have the potential to fulfil the anti-immigrant projects underlying British nationalism.

This is lent support by the previous chapter's analysis of Britain's national project as a form of COIN. Increasingly, this tends not towards purification through the end of immigration, but towards the restoration of a natural order both inside and outside of territorial boundaries. Policies of migrant control and repatriation on the one hand, and policies attempting to attract temporary workers on the other may appear to be contradictory, but they are better understood as a productive tension. We are seeing a series of moves towards the intensified temporariness, control and precarity of racialised people's ability to live and work in Britain. This trajectory was put in place decades ago: to reproduce people, not just as an undeserving poor under pressure of the production of surplus populations, but as a hyper-exploitable and expendable poor to be repatriated as deemed necessary. The ends of this surplus are not proletarianized exploitation, but elimination, exclusion and the deprivation of citizenship.

The horizon of extinction

At Heathrow a potential third runway has become a site of controversy after the British parliamentary declaration of the climate crisis as a state of emergency, a successful legal case against it, and a long appeals process. Heathrow is already the single biggest contributor to carbon emissions in the UK, with aviation set to contribute more than any other sector by 2050. In travelling to Harmondsworth on train and bus and foot, the region is littered with signs protesting the building of a third runway. Its stakeholders are not just owners of capital but also unions in thrall to the protection and production of British jobs. The expansion would mean the destruction of the detention centre, to see its re-emergence on recoded greenbelt land likely slightly further north.

The runway would increase Heathrow's carbon emissions by approximately 40 per cent, yet they will appear as zero on the balance sheet.[64] Tackling climate change has, for a long time, involved the acceptance of net-zero targets. These have incentivised creative carbon accounting, greenwashing and eco-sensitive fossil fuel companies. It is likely that, in part, Heathrow's future will look toward liquid natural gas (LNG) to cope with emissions targets. LNG is hailed by many in the global North as an ecological salve, becoming known as clean fossil fuel, whilst its CO_2 emissions are still 81 per cent of those of oil. The shift from fossil oil to LNG is set to be the new, greener, aeronautical fuel that will power charter flights to cleanse the British nation from the supposed destabilisation of migrant bodies.

Its extraction is an instance of the continuation of informal imperial intervention operating via coalition in places that Britain never formally colonised like Mozambique. As Idai struck in the north of the country, the capital Maputo saw financiers and executives from the oil industry meet to flesh out plans for a massive-scale project in the north of Mozambique to extract and export LNG in tandem with the Mozambique government. Whilst few LNG projects have been approved globally, for US company Andarko Petroleum, the Rovuma Basin is set to transform Mozambique into a leading global energy supplier. Central to the project is Andarko's building an LNG export facility on the coast in Cabo Delgado, expected to export up to 23 million metric tons of LNG per year. LNG won't just be used for our planes; we will cook with it and heat our homes as well. Centrica, whose headquarters are in Windsor, Berkshire, are the largest domestic energy supplier in the UK. A month or so before Idai, they confirmed the ongoing purchase of massive quantities of LNG from the project, in a 20-year-long contract. Operating under British Gas, the Centrica contract interweaves our homes with the fishing grounds being destroyed, with Quirimbas National Park (a UNESCO biosphere reserve of coral reefs, mangroves, seagrass beds) being threatened. With projects begun before environmental impact assessments were made, dredging, waste disposal and the immediate and after-effects of construction will destroy endangered plant and animal species.[65] Oil spills and chemical and waste leaching are likely, toxic compounds used in lubricating drilling machines will become intricated into the food web, and there will be a significant increase in methane emissions.

To offset emissions, these fossil fuel companies plan to plant forests in the region. Rather than protect ecosystems that already absorb emissions, offsetting incentivises quick-fix compensation schemes, with tree plantations that reduce biodiversity on expropriated land. These creeping acts of assault on land are coupled with the forced displacement of people. Geographies of historical colonialism give shape to these forces that divide and destroy land and lives once again. Some of the *machambas* (farmlands) onto which the project is moving people are not arable because they had been degraded by colonial cotton plantations.[66]

These interventions materially contribute to the conditions that lead to people's movements through Africa and towards Europe – their movement propelled and shaped by neo-imperialism. This meets the sharp edge of purposive extinction in the exacerbations of climate change and the offsetting of carbon emissions to dominated nations. For example, Britain is the largest net importer of emissions per capita in the G7 group of wealthy nations, mostly due to its importing of goods manufactured abroad. Between 1992 and 2007, this increased by 200 per cent.[67] Effectively offshoring the effects of climate change to the wastelands of the periphery, deaths are again brought to those whose land and livelihoods have been plundered time and time over.

Green nationalism

The most aggressive political movement against climate change in recent years has been Extinction Rebellion (XR). For them, nature becomes a powerful chaotic force from which we can no longer be cocooned. Their focus on imminent extinction folds apocalypse into the present, so making us all equal victims of a nature thrown off balance. In the process, nature out-of-sync becomes a common force that conceals the causes and effects of climate violence. As a consequence, their politics is grounded on the movement of a supposedly universal people against the crimes of humanity that have produced climate change. This populist undertaking is made out to be the condition of possibility for forcing the state to make the decisions necessary to see nature restored and our children's future secured.

In their declaration of rebellion, it becomes clear that this reproductive nationalism is core to their drive to protect 'all we hold dear: this nation, its peoples, our ecosystems and the future of generations to come'. Focusing on how the ecological crisis is impacting the nation, they declare it our duty to act on behalf of the 'security and well-being of our children'. The bounded nation and its perpetuation ground XR's demands for securing a future beyond the horizon of extinction. The apocalyptic register within which their manifesto sits reinforces a logic of progressive politics for 'us' that is complicit with a securitised approach to threat. Under these conditions, XR petitions the state apparatus to ensure 'adequate protection and security for its people's well-being and the nation's future – to secure the solutions needed to avert catastrophe and protect the future'. Behind this desire for securitisation is the threat of climate change driving mass migration as crisis:

> We are in the sixth mass extinction event and we will face catastrophe if we do not act swiftly and robustly [...] Flooding and desertification will render vast tracts of land uninhabitable and lead to mass migration.

This 'green nationalism' frames migrant and climate crises as intertwined threats.[68] The implicit logic of explicit calls for nation-based security is therefore the coupling of a universal commons with differential limits, whilst implicitly legitimating Britain's violent bordering under threat of climate catastrophe. Neo-Malthusianism is made explicit here, with incursions on the nation and climate catastrophe collapsed into one another, creating a vicious circle that is forged under the imaginary of nature itself.

In the process, what becomes clear is that the drive toward a nationalist political horizon in the age of global catastrophe is best understood as a cipher for geopolitical reconfigurations whose end is the lifeboat state. In the eschatological phase of Hardin's tragedy, wealthier countries are likened to lifeboats that must be economically and ecologically stabilised by protection from the global poor. Whilst calling to mind the literal analogues of migrant deaths in the Mediterranean, this is the broader, deterministic outworking of the tragedy of the commons as a 'theory of selective salvation propounded as a moral economy of "natural limits"'.[69] A revanchist program of expansive accumulation through neo-colonial property regimes is repackaged by borders around the naturalised limits of nations. This fixes certain people in place, and remakes value procured by imperial and neo-imperial theft into the natural inheritance of wealthy nations. Whilst eco-fascism makes explicit the violence at the heart of this position, its liberal variant is written off as a combination of natural disaster and incivility in the periphery together with austerity politics at home.

Both progressive politics and XR's environmentalism rely on an image of disorder which foregrounds a notion of the natural order of the nation and obligates its necessary restoration. Brexit has brought forth calls to end racial prejudice in the face of increased racial violence and reconsider the movements of migrations across British borders, as if violence began in 2016. But Britain's problems lie not just with discrimination and attitudes toward migration. Britain is built through hyper-exploitation, precarity, violent policing, surveillance and the ultimate expendability of largely migrants of colour and people deemed to fall outside of its matrix of whiteness. The staging of the battle between global finance and markets against the natural order of a native labour force dramatises an aesthetics of disordering and operates as an alibi for a politics in which increased protection against tragedy becomes imperative. National protectionism thus becomes essential and inextricable from securitisation and militarised expulsion.

6

The End of Britain

river, river, bath us from tear of trouble st-
eer us, stream us, trail us   aford
      to home's imperturbable current
            of peace, o

(Petero Kalulé, 'River')[1]

I'll tell you what Freedom is to me. No fear.

(Nina Simone)

ENTANGLEMENTS UNDER COVER OF DARKNESS

Britain's internal colonies were formed through the redeployment of logics of waste to underlie productive tensions of the liberal and the post-colonial other. They have been shaped by practices developed elsewhere, though still within Britain's imperial terrain.

Without trace, he's taken from Harmondsworth to Brook House, just beyond the wire fences of Gatwick's outer hangars. Just as quick, he's gone, released. Emphatic and overjoyed, case overturned, he's been turned out – not into Home Office care – but at the last minute 'allowed' to present an address – his cellmate's mother.

To segregate, to subsidise, to hyper-exploit, to extract; to make criminal, to subject people to the violent force of the law whilst being necessarily incapable of lawfulness, to make subject to surveillance and control, precarity and non-belonging; to launder race under culture, to reduce agency to integration, to pre-empt and neutralise struggle, to produce raced communities as suspect and raced bodies as spectral and threat, to shape Britain as a matrix of borders that sifts and shapes, to rely on the violence of unequal exchange, to deport, to make citizenship temporary and conditional, to closely monitor and guard; to sentence to death, to expedite extinction.

At 'mom house' sipping heavily sweetened tea, he's homed for a while. Until inter-family fractiousness and unexpected visitors mean he's turned out, again. Despite dutifully reporting to 'prob officer', he's forced to use his bag as pillow on a park bench.

This chapter asks what the tactics and strategies of violence that we've considered might have to tell us about a topography of struggles.

He can eat at temple, but he won't pray because he hasn't been able to shower. With some sustenance, he's sat in the park waiting for a charity line to speak to somebody in his mother tongue. The phone dies before he's put through.

If the productive force of the tensions at the core of the post-colonial cut have led to Britain as a COIN operation, its principal form is distributive apartheid – a systemic atmosphere whose segregations are produced as a terrain of affordances and interactions between bodies, laws, policies, capital, interpersonal relations, consumption, surveillance, force.

His 'prob officer' says that the council refuse that they have a duty of care. He should report to the job centre and sign up to universal credit. In the meantime, the park.

At the intersections of intimacy and dispersal, this has produced a tortuous and labyrinthine world – the viscosity and peril of passing through and within spaces felt by some is the condition of the relative ease for others.

They tell him there'll be an interpreter at the job centre, but there isn't. Agitated by the feeling of not being able to communicate, he's trapped in an office under suspicion, and before long they're on the phone to the Home Office – 'checking' his credentials. Unnerved, he runs.

Not only driven by existential crisis, this is rooted in the violent enclosures and exclusions required to reproduce differential wealth in an era of diminishing returns. A Britain reliant on subsidy, hyper-exploitation and expendability endures by weaponising hospitality, constituting belonging and non-belonging on distinctions manifesting lawlessness and lawfulness, enlisting its citizens as police, building a category of temporary citizens and illegalised people.

Having spent wet nights between bus depots and park benches, he manages to get enough money together for a night in a shared room in a hostel. It costs double to pay in cash what it would online.

In this movement of exterior violence inwards, the nation is excessively identified with its aporetic other – the spectral, the wastelands, the aliens, the insurgents. As its culmination, the fragility of Britain's refounding is woven into counter-insurgency writ large. Britain's neo-colonial structures are expansive across Africa and intensive across internal regimes in which all spaces are intersected by calculations of risk and threat.

Without a bank account, his passport not yet come through, somebody at temple offers him work above a shop. Cash in hand, a lifeline.

However, the threat of the real haunts Britain's formation. As Abdou-Maliq Simone writes, '[d]arkness is both condition and cover, and under cover of darkness emerge forms of "rogue care"'.[2] I am interested in how, from the undercover conditions of coloniality, living can be practised in a time concerned with the violent enforcement of limits.

We should be careful to foreground struggle and moments of gentle resistance, as well as imposition and composition through active and passive complicity. Even under watch of the shark, in desperation lies hope, overwhelming love and kinship. It is within this entangled politics of care that I want to situate this closing chapter, and to consider the question of how it might be possible to undo the harms of Britain itself.

TO DESTROY A COLONY

The shape that colonialism takes has ramifications for any project that seeks its end. But attempts to prefigure the ends of colonialism are fraught. For this reason, in the mid-1970s, Robert Blauner, who had been instrumental in constructing the concept of internal colonialism in the US, recanted the 'colonial analogy'. Whereas overseas colonisers might be repatriated to Europe, no such simple solution offered itself for

America's domestic colonies, which themselves resided within Indigenous land. Blauner could see little in the idea that offered revolutionary hope or practical solution, the disconnection between theory and practice seemingly providing evidence of conceptual flaw.[3] However, Blauner's reasoning is short-circuited by the premise that colonialism was sloughed off through the deportation of the white invader. This is undermined by arguments that we've made throughout: that the post-colonial cut was the condition of colonialism's continuation.

In this section, to address this knottiness more fully I consider three suggested forms of colonial struggle that might be pursued in the context of internal colonies: anticolonial nationalism, inclusive reform and anti-subordination.

Nation within a nation

Charles Pinderhughes disagrees with Blauner's decision to withdraw support from the theoretical framework of internal coloniality. His argument rests on an analogy between colonised nations and internal colonies in the US as geographically discontinuous, where 'each single internal colony exists within its own contiguous territory.'[4] This continues a longer US tradition, where the question of internal colonies came to circle around the idea of a 'nation within a nation.'[5] Given this characterisation, a strategy for anticolonial resistance became apparent: the Black nation should struggle for the right to self-determination and existence as a separate state. So in 1968 the Black Panther party produced a ten-point platform, in which it stated:

> We want land, bread, housing, education, clothing, justice and peace. And as our major political objective, a United Nations-supervised plebiscite to be held throughout the black colony in which only black colonial subjects will be allowed to participate for the purpose of determining the will of black people as to their national destiny.

The demand for separatism should not be confused with insularity. Rather, calls for political autonomy had long been intertwined with anti-colonial struggles across the world. In the tradition of Garveyism, Black nationalism was inextricable from Pan-Africanist internationalism. Whilst perhaps less blatant within British Black Power movements, the Black Unity and Freedom Party (BUFP) and Black Liberation Front

(BLF) had also formed in the early 1970s around the drive to self-determination and Black nationalism.[6] But similarly evident in both the Black Voice publication of the BUFP and the 1973 BLF Manifesto was that British Black Power struggles were inextricable from international struggles.

To a degree this emphasis coheres with Fanon's argument that 'national consciousness, which is not nationalism, is alone capable of giving us an international dimension'.[7] According to Fanon, national consciousness is required to produce the people as a political and social body of anticolonial struggle. Nonetheless, Fanon is clear that national consciousness is just a stage in a process through which 'a social and political consciousness' should be reached.[8] For Fanon, the goal of anticolonial struggle, as Sajed and Seidel write, 'is not simply the removal of the coloniser (thus ending the colonial occupation) and the establishment of an independent nation, but the overall transformation of state and society'.[9] Anticolonial nationalism thus becomes propaedeutic to struggles that could reach far beyond nation-building.

This weakens Blauner's concerns, but also expands the horizon of anticolonialism to consider broader geopolitical struggles and formations. Whilst this expansion is fruitful, it seems likely that a temporal and logical grounding in nation-based movements is inadequate to the shape of internal colonialism in Britain. Britain's geographical intimacies do not offer an easy analogy of nation with a nation, and its structures of coloniality are stretched across borders beyond the nation-state. Whilst any anticolonialism will necessarily be derived from the legacies of anti-colonial and anti-apartheid struggles, I have approached internal colonialism to think of quite different contexts. I have employed its conceptual tools not as a descriptive formalism that would freeze its object in contiguous space, but as highlighting the processual machinery of regimes that reverberate across colonial spaces and times. Doing so has also drawn attention to the ways that politically independent post-colonial nation-states were 'reincorporated into the Western world system'.[10]

Whilst trajectories towards the absolutisation of coloniality in spatio-temporal regimes have produced the territoriality of camps and detention centres, they have also produced dissociated forms of movement through everyday life. With borders 'transported into the middle of political space' as Balibar puts it,[11] the internal colony is better understood as the manifestation and sustenance of 'a thousand petty fortresses'.[12] The motile and diffuse nature of Britain's distributive apartheid within and beyond territorial limits seemingly evades characterisation under the auspices of a nation within a nation.

Reform the colony!

Calls to separatism are perhaps best understood as a response to the universalising structures of colonialism that so often deflate anticolonial struggles into movements for reform. The routes through which Black people have gained some right to self-determine have been fraught with co-opting reformism. Many writers have drawn attention to the exclusions produced under liberal humanism.[13] But their end-game is rarely anything approaching a significant terraforming of the power inequities upon which liberal democracy is founded, and, more often than not, is a matter of the inclusion of plural voices in liberal political spaces. There are well-worn arguments, for example, against the abstract universalism at work in liberal approaches to democratic deliberation. These tend to emphasise the exclusion of agents, viewpoints and specific interests, together with the subsequent masking of that exclusion. Appeals to impartiality, according to Iris Young, reduce a plurality of social positions to form a singular basis for subjectivity, and so ultimately assimilate the identity of the other to the identity of the 'one'.[14] Such universalisation has rightly been criticised, therefore, for the exclusion of gender, race, class, sexuality and so forth, from political discussion proper.

However, by emphasising the 'problem' of difference, the political theorist is allowed a wedge between ideals and practices making room for the idea that we may solve problems of power through increased inclusivity. The harms of coloniality are not due only to exclusions from access to political sovereignty – that exclusion is *produced* as the condition of possibility for political sovereignty. So rectifying these misrecognitions could only possibly fail within the constrictions of a nation-state whose sovereignty is arbiter of inclusions and recognitions. This is to offer minority groups a 'space within liberalism' as Elizabeth Povinelli put it, without accounting for the ways in which those spaces are constitutively bound up with racialised power.[15]

This is perhaps also why calls to decolonise Britain have often been drawn towards near synonymity with social justice. Power aligns, it diffuses resistance and opens up new corridors in which bureaucratic work transforms struggles into exhaustion. Arguably, decolonisation has been hollowed out and reframed as the work of diversity officers and curricula development in our institutions.[16] Eve Tuck and Wayne Yang's work reminds us that decolonisation should not be used as a metaphor for the resistance of oppression or improvements to society and education. Terminology has efficacy. Accentuating exclusion and inclusion requires us to have already given up on the terms of internal colonialism – it makes little sense to reform a colony or make it more inclusive. As discussed in Chapter 4, inclusivity lends itself to a normative standard against which differences may be measured and differential racisms produced. However, this is not just a matter of terminology but also of erasure and sublimation as well as of attempted containment of the realities of colonialism.

Writing from the context of settler colonialism, Tuck and Yang's analysis of decolonisation necessarily involves the repatriation of Indigenous lands and life. We risk falling into the trap of metaphor through simple extensions of their argument to the kinds of colonialism discussed in this book. But their analysis is limited to a historically specific and geographically particular form of colonialism, whose central form was dispossession and struggles over Indigenous sovereignty. In centring dispossession as the fundamental reality of colonialism, we would also risk eliding its other modalities whose form might also give shape to distinct approaches to struggle. As David Marriott writes in his discussion of Fanon, 'the nature of colonialism necessarily affects the nature of the resistance to it'.[17] Identifying the contours of internal colonialism then offers a language through which opposition to reformism can be strengthened. How could you reform a colony whose economy is rooted in extraction, hyper-exploitation and subsidy; whose police system is grounded in the reproduction of colonial control; whose integrity has become defined by a COIN operation driven toward extermination under pressure of ecological limits?

With the terms of inclusion and exclusion quantified and concretised as the regime of multiculturalism falters and returns to a sublimated ethno-nationalism, the gradualism of reforms increasingly confirms logics of extinction. Consider the contortions through which Kaufmann and Cantle's frameworks of white segregation and cohesion are supposed to support humanitarian reforms in the refugee system. Kaufmann's argument runs as follows. There is persistent political pressure and hostility towards the permanent settlement of migrant people and refugees in Britain. So-called liberal arguments for more open borders exacerbate this hostility, which is felt not only by economic and irregular migrants, but by 'genuine' refugees, because they are seen as a first step towards the right to remain. Political discourse around migration therefore turns on arguments for limitations, management and quotas. With these inexorably squeezed, a greater stringency is employed in the way that Britain deals with claims for refugee status. As a result, there are more unsuccessful claims, and refugees who fail to succeed are returned to countries where they are at risk of death or persecution. The solution, according to Kaufmann, is to build permanent refugee camps *inside* Britain, with refugees given the ability to move between these shadow zones globally, without entering the host country.

This would eliminate hostility towards the provision of refuge, according to Kaufmann, whose primary cause is not economic so much as fears that the ethnic composition of Britain is being dismantled by migrant and refugee influx. The confluence of arguments regarding incursions on the nation and demographic genocide thus find their apotheosis in this proposal for a humanitarian segregation at a global scale. Perhaps unsurprisingly, Hardin had anticipated these moves:

> [w]e are now in the process of destabilizing our own country through the unlimited acceptance of massive immigration [...]. In time the slowly reproducing population will be displaced by the fast one. This is passive genocide. It may be that no one is ever killed, but the genes of one group replace the genes of the other. That's genocide.[18]

Whilst finding an obvious home in the context of Hardin's eco-fascism, the idea that multiculturalism coupled with overpopulation is destroying the natural order of the nation is to be found in less vehement form in, for example, XR spokesperson Rupert Read's arguments against mass migration on the basis that it leads to the dissolution of social cohesion.[19]

Kaufmann's ghost-towns provide us with an image of spatially segregated zones that could become a simple target of the increasingly explicit discourse of fascism. We should be careful with our deployment of the spectre of fascism lest it erases a past and present colonialism, recouping the trajectories of violence underwriting liberalism's supposedly peaceful violence. Nonetheless, the point should be clear: reformism under pressure of ecological limits, COIN and demographic threat rapidly gives way to a politics of extinction.

Towards anti-subordination

For similar reasons citizenship does not offer an obvious category through which struggles against coloniality could be adequately fought. The protection of Britain's wealth is increasingly defined by the temporary and precarious inclusion of Britain's others and the machinery of unequal exchange. Appeals for entitlement to citizenship status or indefinite leave to remain within Britain thus prop up both its wealth and its legitimacy as the arbiter of who is able to access it. However, in a context where the notion of secure borders has become inextricable from national collective belonging, the agency of migrant people might be figured as a means through which *acts* of citizenship contest the existing political order:

> We can define acts of citizenship as those acts that transform forms (orientations, strategies, technologies) and modes (citizens, strangers, outsiders, aliens) of being political by bringing into being new actors as activist citizens (that is, claimants of rights) through creating or transforming sites and stretching scales.[20]

This works against making the movement of people synonymous with movements of capital resources, which fails to consider migrant people's experience and agency in practices of movement in relation to their attempted control or regulation. Even so, my concerns with the suggestion are twofold. First, responsibility is awarded to migrant people themselves, whose activities tend to be valorised as inherently productive of a capacity to unsettle and destabilise the foundations of Britain. Second, considerations of the political force of migration are misplaced, and so are underwhelming.

For example, Tendayi Achiume argues that migration can be understood as a form of decolonisation, formulated as an act of struggle by people currently subordinated under imperialism.[21] More equitable interconnection, rather than national independence, is figured as providing the grounds for decolonisation in this context. Whilst interdependence between imperial and dominated people remains, shifting power within the terms of that relationship is approached as a form of anti-subordination. So decolonisation would not require the severing of connections, but their renegotiation on terms of rebalancing the differential of power. The emphasis is on the enhancement of self-determination carried by individuals *within* neo-colonial empire – in which context migration is decolonisation.

Tendayi Achiume clarifies the position in terms of claims made on Britain by people originating from its prior colonies. In a study on Zimbabwean diaspora in Britain, Dominic Pasura writes of migrant people who feel a moral justification in their presence in Britain, claiming a right to be here because 'as you once ate in our house now it is our turn to eat in your house', as migrant Mthokhozisi put it.[22] Another Zimbabwean, Matthew, responded similarly:

This country takes responsibility why we are here. It's because of colonialism. The British people oppressed us; they took our land and made us live on infertile land. We were made captives in our own land [...] People grew up under oppression and it became even worse when we attained our independence as our economic situation deteriorated. It's our turn to come to this country. God is making an equation that somebody who used to gain might also, even though not suffering, serve somebody.[23]

The assertion of agency and moral rights is taken as evidence of the intent and ability to counteract colonialism and its legacy. In this regard, Tendayi Achiume suggests that migration should be understood as a technology for the reform and equalisation of Britain's global interrelations. However, as she remarks, even with the legal reformations required to support such migration, such decolonisation would only shift power within these relationships rather than beyond them.

The difficulty is that an emphasis on exclusion and subordination potentially leaves any route towards decolonisation left in moral terms that don't account for the real form that Britain takes, its modulated forms of inclusion, and its wounded attachment to colonialism. The other side of this coin is that the position also underestimates what such a movement might achieve. For example, arguments in support of border abolition have also called for the re-articulation of rights away from their association with membership in a national state. The general idea would be that rights are not to be granted by national sovereigns, but are carried by people themselves. This faces thorny issues, particularly regarding the way in which a system might be implemented such that it doesn't simply replicate a series of more insidious bordering practices at a global level. Nonetheless, importantly, a no borders politics refuses the amelioration of border reforms. For example, Bridget Anderson, Nandita Sharma and Cynthia Wright argue that in a world that is shaped through movement, its restrictions are synonymous with the production of inequalities that ground the nation-state in the imperial core.[24] For them, the end of border regimes would also involve a renegotiation of the global commons that would no longer be enforceable under the artifice of natural limits. In other words, if migration as decolonisation were envisaged through the dissolution of border regimes, it would call into question both the legitimacy of nation-states and the limits through which capital is accumulated and wealth is stored. More bluntly, decolonisation would then be better figured as anticolonialism – its results would not leave the world intact.

ANTICOLONIALISM AS ABOLITIONISM

Moving on from his rebuttal to Blauner, Pinderhughes argues that the theory of internal colonialism offers a central motif through which anticolonial movements can be forged. An internal colony can be ended in a project of its positive abolition. For Pinderhughes this is hamstrung by an insistence on geographical contiguity as definitional of the internal colony. So for all its radicalism, this leads to a remarkably detoothed form of abolitionism as the 'equality of result for the life-outcomes of internal colony residents relative to life-outcomes of the historically dominant population.'[25] Thinking of outcomes in terms of dominated and dominating populations presumes rather than dismantles the national territorial container. Instead, let us consider how, in the context of Britain, abolition offers an anticolonial politics neither through separatism, reform, nor more equitable interdependence.

Ghosts of empire

If Britain since the middle of the twentieth century was in the process of nation-building at the end of empire, the 1981 Nationality Act is its symbol. The act defined British nationality as whiteness, with citizenship and whiteness indelibly forged as a regime of property and belonging over the spoils of empire.[26] It categorised those who belong in Britain whilst making immigration law into a form of domestic control. Aliens were produced within the nation's borders by removing citizenship entitlements from British nationals in the former colonies from 1983 onwards. At the time of its passing, Powell marked the act as instituting the 'end of our brief imperial episode [...] and the laying of that ghost, the Commonwealth'.[27] This attempted cut was the frame through which the manifestation of ghosts could be warded off and territorialised.

Britain's whiteness is apophatic. It has been defined on the basis of its other – on whom it has been dependent for existential, political and economic integrity. The boundary lines drawn by whiteness are, therefore, fluid and flexing since the ability to hegemonically produce and control this other is always partial. From the magic mountains of northern India to white flight to British suburbs and the Muslim as terrorist, Britain's whiteness is riven with fear of the ghosts of empire.

So in this sense, we are not currently witnessing Britain's post-colonial reckoning, which had been staved off. Rather, Britain is necessarily stuck within the stuttering time-loops of the post-colonial cut. The supposed reckoning with attempts to recapture sovereignty that are highlighted by discourses around Brexit is better understood as an explicitation of the tensions underlying the colonial premise of Britain's attempted refounding as post-colonial nation. What results is a nation-state whose form increasingly tends towards extinction.

The end of the colony is the end of Britain.

Universalism and universalities

In *Theory*, Dionne Brand makes the following observation:

> How do you recover from a wound? I asked her. To recover isn't to betray or forget, I said. It's to resist the definition of the wound as the whole incident.[28]

Holding this thought, it is important to keep in mind that internal colonialism has not just been an incomplete and failing project, it is only possibly incomplete.

Reformist arguments against liberal humanism's exclusions have tended to settle on its universalisation as a process through which the other could be identified with the one.[29] The idea is that a universalised form of liberal humanism is imposed like a rubber stamp across all humanity and without respect for differences. The solution to this posing of the problem would be to expand the universal 'one' to include all people. The thought is that this might destabilise the initial universalisation through an openness to mutual recognition. I have argued, to the contrary, that the problems of liberal universalism lie not with exceptionalities whose wounds could be retroactively sutured into the one. Rather, they lie in the attempted totalisation through which the one could be considered *at all*.

Because Britain is refounded on a whiteness that is apophatic, it is also ever consuming – the coherence of the one is possible only through excessive identification with its other. This aporetic core is at the heart of the totalising drive of the liberal subject. Britain's juridical universalism is made possible only under the violent extermination and engulfment of its other. As David Roediger puts it, '[i]t is not merely that whiteness is oppressive and false; it is that whiteness is nothing but oppressive and false'.[30] With the universal one paradoxically written as a particularity that requires insulation from demographic incursion, Britain under the post-colonial cut has been beholden to an incessant tendency towards purification, containment and repression that is necessarily incomplete. The supposedly recent unravelling of a liberal consensus towards its fascistic and violent form is just the outworking of Britain's inner logics. Mass support for either platform Keynesianism or for ethno-nationalism is also support for neo-imperial extinction politics. Their divisions shed light on a web of tensions that point towards the same direction, where 'First World democracy finds its *sine qua non* in [...] national chauvinism increasingly embraced by capital in crisis'.[31]

But this also points us towards a terrain of struggle that has been forged under cover of darkness. Whilst the other is a necessary production for the totalisation of the one, it is far from containable under it. The mechanisms of stability that have held together Britain's coloniality have also provided the conditions for spaces of excess, resistance and rupture. As Fred Moten and Stefano Harney put it,

> The earth moves against the world. And today the response of the world is clear [...] The more the earth churns the more vicious the world's response. But the earth still moves [...] The earth's procession is not on the world's calendar.[32]

Calling into being the Earth's procession against the world resolutely refuses the terms of universalism under struggles for recognition. Universalism is juridical – it is grounded by a nation-state that maintains itself through coercive and productive regimes, private property and sovereign rights. Moreover, universalism's totalisation is not just exclusionary but it is vehemently apophatic – the contemporary threat of destabilisation drives more explicit and vehement forms of protection. Recalling the Copernican revolution in which the universe no longer turns around man, Moten and Harney evoke the decentring and destabilisation of the world-as-universality. That 'it still moves' articulates a universality that lies beyond and without the purported universalism of the totalising one. This Earth which acts against the world is not, therefore, just another universal that could be integrated or warded off. Rather, it might be understood as ungraspable possibility that undoes the universalising fundament of the world irrevocably. The closures required to produce universalisation also provide the conditions through which rupturing universalities can be born. This is because the world cannot comprehend the earth, which exists beyond the possibilities demarcated by its universalising form. Massimiliano Tomba offers an account of such universality – as always *insurgent*.[33] For Tomba, insurgent universality is grounded in the particularity of concrete acts that decentre the nation as horizon of political representation. Yet, such universalities are inevitably insurgent against the political and social order, and expressed through the ways that people act together beyond the legal order.

A rupture from within

According to Tomba, it is in particular and concrete forms of insurgency – to 'eat in your house' – through which universality is born:

> In insurgent universality, the human is the subject who, by acting as a citizen, albeit beyond one's legal status and the putative boundaries of citizenship, puts both the social and the political order into question.[34]

This shifts the ground on which struggles are understood to take place. For example, it is so often supposed that struggles are grounded by a desire to be counted as human: of bodies that could rely on recognition under the violence of state regimes; to be counted under law rather than rendered lawless; to be included in systems of labour and finance that demand their exploitation; to be citizens belonging to a state that has been made and remade as a world that is uninhabitable for the majority. Instead, anticolonial struggles are positioned at nodes of insurgency that could destabilise and abolish these universalisms, rather than count amongst them. As Simone puts it, this is a politics of:

> refusal to be subject to a law that refuses to recognize you [...] a politics defined not by opposition or necessarily resistance, but instead a refusal of the very premises that have [been] historically negated.[35]

Consider as example, Suhaiymah Manzoor-Khan's poem 'British Values'. This contains the powerful evocation that:

> Britain is bismillah
> Britain is basmati rice
> Britain is box braids and black barber's shops, Bollywood, and bhangra[36]

One can imagine this being read as a claim on behalf of a racialised minority to inclusion with Britain and British values. That is, to think of the so-called British values encapsulated in liberal humanism, of tolerance and openness, freedom of speech and so on. Their universalism then figured as a commitment to the commonality of humankind whose exceptions might be forgiven and exclusions reneged on. That reading is immediately ruined, however, by the claim that, since 'the sugar and tea had strings attached',

> Britain is the terror to be countered

Here, Britain names both existential horizon and the massive machinery that takes the form of a colonial present inscribed in security operations. This is not a security that could safeguard Britain, but a complex production of hyper-exploitation and subsidy under protection from the entitlements of others by the exercise of colonial sovereignty through surveillance and violent force.

Claiming that Britain *is* bismillah does work analogous to Matthew's statement that 'God is making an equation'. Both claim Britain in both partiality and particularity – as colonial machine – *and* through an insurgent universality that resists the definition of the wound as the whole incident. Manzoor-Khan goes on to say that,

> you'd be left with the fact that I am inside
> I am Britain now, cos

This insideness – this threat of the real – is the universality through which Britain has been forged by histories that are always already those of anticolonial struggle. It also clarifies the terms upon which struggles are made. Framing claims as issuing from the *outside*, for inclusion, access and entitlement is a figment that was produced under the post-colonial cut. Struggles of insurgent universality don't take the shape of external other or a Schmittian enemy to be included or separated-off. Instead they arise from internal ruptures – from the 'fact that I am inside'.[37]

Kinship at the end of the world

If the Earth moves against the world, what are the weapons that could engage the Earth in the end of the world that is totalised in the form of Britain?[38] As Moten and Harney write, '[t]he more the earth churns the more vicious the world's response'. The mechanisms through which a global ecology is held together in complexes of property, power and counter-insurgency – where these become weakened sanctions, punitive measures, dissonance and violence will be strengthened in favour of extant power. Public pressure against charter deportation flights has been knitted together, catalysed most prominently in the resistance of the Stansted 15 on the grounds of slow and patient work of SOAS Detainee Support (SDS), End Deportations, No Borders Network UK, Anti-Raids network, DocsNotCops and so many others. In response, however, the state reorganises and deploys new tactics across fluid regimes entangling military, corporation, criminal justice and immigration enforcement.

It is nonetheless in these practices through which the Earth still moves. The circuitous and frustrating bureaucracies of doing casework for people caged in detention centres brings into being an expansive relationship, operating within but also against the often semi-legalities with which those regimes are maintained. They offer distance and spaces through which communities coalesce and harms are abated. These are weapons whose form is a field of relations, affordances and materials to hand, but at whose core is kinship and solidarity.

Politicking tells us that nationalist horizons are merely pragmatic, that public 'common sense' is too wedded to the form of the nation. But the insistent and ongoing forces required to maintain the shape of the world are exhausting. We should ask who this public is – what are their interests, and how are they shored up? And, to whose common sense are these appeals made? The invocation of 'common sense' is, of course, defined by the very horizon that we would like to see unstitched. Common senses are made and remade constantly. They are built through complicity and co-option, and through passive consent and active iteration. Their glacial sedimentation and construction occur at the level, not of discursive rules, but of assumptions, habits and dispositions. Common sense is not the sort of thing that can be discursively elaborated, being composed of dispositions that are open-ended, differential responses to each other and to contexts, emotions and embodied actions. Nevertheless, since this social background shapes the meanings within which lives are formed, it is also the central site in which our local interactions and contexts are tied to broader structures, practices and sanctions.

As such, it is not correct to think that racisms are generated by the state as a means of control, nor that they arise simply through the passions of those from below. I have argued that race and racisms are technologies of colonialism whose underlying systems carve up the world and upon whose unequal terrain our interests are collected. So a reliance on the nation-state is not merely symbolic, it is required to maintain Britain – both as nation and economy as a white possession requiring protection from incursions from it. Whilst the common-sense structures of a nationalist horizon often look to be entrenched, natural and objective, they result from this matrix of processes and power relationships, and require ongoing maintenance through material and normative force.

What is currently common sense is a functional, usually invisible, means by which the present state of things is naturalised and masks the ability to consider the social world beyond its current form. But no social norms, nor the system of power in which they are embedded, is determined. Systems of common sense are never static – they require constant reinforcing and reforging. So there are dynamic tendencies for their modification in every situation, however sealed off they may appear. The conglomeration of these tendencies form resources that may be deployed to construct new forms of common sense.

Of course, as Sara Ahmed points out, common sense is so often figured as security:

> [m]aintaining public comfort requires that certain bodies 'go along with it'. To refuse to go along with it, to refuse the place in which

you are placed, is to be seen as causing trouble, as making others uncomfortable.[39]

Within this fabric of comfort, the force of internal rupture may be enacted in moments of insurgency. Actively unhoming from that which has become so common sense as to appear natural, insurgent universality provides the conditions for *actively* deracinating those systems from their contingent conditions. As Ahmed writes, '[b]y snapping you are saying: I will not reproduce a world I cannot bear, a world I do not think should be borne'.[40] The categories of common sense are fragile – of lawful and legal citizens, and those made illegal and lawless; those who deserve the right to life, and those who do not. Their preservation requisitions our complicity. Since common sense is looped in to its material practices and structures, we can move against its maintenance.

To establish a moratorium on Britain's coloniality would remove support from the institutions upholding it and the systems providing it with legitimacy. Many of the processes constitutive of Britain are reinforced by legal systems, institutions and policing. But as such, they are dependent on political legitimacy, and so also on the ways that everyday practices are involved in the production and reproduction of those structures – in part simply by acting according to the accepted norms of the communities in which we live, we reinforce Britain's coloniality.

To make a start – ending participation with regimes of expropriation, criminalisation, detention, incarceration and immigration, together with active sedition where necessary. Not calling to reform Prevent, but the abandonment of CONTEST and the collateral of counter-insurgency methods, increased state powers and special measures revoked. The dismantling of state-instituted violence requires the end of bordering regimes producing extreme wage differences, life prospects and disparate harms; immediate decriminalisation, decarceration and excarceration, closure of gang databases, repeal of joint enterprise, and the end of stop and search. Let us grasp wholeheartedly the revolutionary call unwittingly made by Conservative commentator Ollie Wright that 'a nation without borders is barely a nation'.[41]

As Tomba writes, universality is 'not given by spatial extent, but by a way of practicing politics'.[42] In this practising politics new publics are made: not in abstract solidarity, but in concrete relationships through which our position in the apparently natural order of the world could be put always in question. Kinships bring about a sense of dis-belonging to the horizon of the nation and belonging together under new imaginaries of freedoms. To provoke universality where many worlds fit.[43]

A sense in common; an Earth in common

As we've seen, colonialism's projects have always been expansionist, even under the supposed post-colonial cut. The world has been terraformed in planetary enterprise, its distributive apartheid has been instrumental in forming the contours and corridors of neo-imperialism. Current property regimes rely on enclosures that are structured by the exclusion and improvement of waste, extraction and hyper-exploitation through unequal exchange. This concentration of wealth and property in the hands of a largely white minority violates the freedoms and existence for the majority. In light of this, perhaps it might be possible not only to deracinate 'common sense' but also to forge new senses in common, and an Earth in common that might exist after the end of this world.

According to Mbembe this would bring with it 'a radical openness of and to the world, a deep breathing for the world as opposed to insulation'.[44] I wonder if we should be wary, however, of rushing towards a world in common that might be presented as a positive project. Undoing the proliferation of limits begins a process through which property regimes could also be dismantled. The dissipation of borders is also the de-formation of systems of risk, surveillance and arbitrage that currently sustain financial extraction and the accumulation of wealth. Interference in cross-border operations of profit, interest and rents would therefore decelerate the extraction of additional value subsidising the imperial core. This might also accelerate proscriptions from the hoarding of wealth through its reallocation and distribution. But would this necessarily constitute movement towards an Earth in common?

Answering this question would also require manoeuvring beyond the horizons under which recent socialist calls to redistribute wealth have been made. Invoking something like a wealth tax, these induce minor measures that could redistribute assets via the state. The reallocation of a small amount of wealth away from the minority elite would not prevent the extraction of rents nor the distribution of land ownership and housing through which their wealth continues to be created. Herein lies the problems with state monopoly over property in addition to those characterised in the previous chapter – leaning on the nationalisation of capital, state ownership relies on the contingencies of the state and its strategies for distribution to citizens. But to bring about the end of Britain's colonialism and neo-imperialism would necessitate infrastructures that are not dependent on the contingencies of the state – embedding more foundational shifts and the sequestering of property that could not be revoked without great upheaval. These would surely be otherwise derailed under pressures of the coalition between state and capital, which increasingly take the form of green nationalism. For decades, internal colonialism has stoked feelings of white possession as a natural right to dwindling resources, with any claim against them subject to discourses of management or revanchism depending upon which has better political efficacy. This trajectory will ramp up violent differentiations driven by rising economic inequality and increasing underemployment pushed towards ever diminishing returns.

If the annihilation of colonialism is required as a condition for an Earth in common, then it is also the condition for the end of the world. This is also why to live together demands the end of a Britain that could only be built on exploitation and elimination, and whose survival is dependent on the extinction of others. Otherwise we are left with the grim logics of lifeboat states propelled to excess – their threadbare façade unravelling under threat of climate destruction, territorial incursion and unequal exchange of the right to life.

Our continued subsistence demands the ends of this world to imagine another way of living with the Earth.[45]

> river, river, bath us from tear of trouble st-
> eer us, stream us, trail us   aford
>   to home's imperturbable current
>   of peace, o[46]

Notes

PREFACE

1   For a similar argument that places Brexit in the longer history of post-colonial crisis, see Nisancioglu, K. (2019) Racial sovereignty. European Journal of International Relations.

2   Dahlgren, W. (2014) The British Empire is 'something to be proud of'. Available at: https://yougov.co.uk/topics/politics/articles-reports/2014/07/26/britain-proud-its-empire (accessed 24 December 2019).

3   Hartman, S (2020). *Wayward Lives, Beautiful Experiments: Intimate histories of social upheaval.* New York: W.W. Norton & Company.

CHAPTER 1

1. Shire, W. (2015) Home. Available at www.care.org/sites/default/files/lesson_1_-_home-poem-by-warsan-shire.pdf (accessed 20 March 2020) © 2015, Warsan Shire. My thanks to Hannah Boast for reminding me of this poem in connection with the shark at Harmondsworth.

2. Anzaldúa, G. (1987) *La frontera/Borderlands: The New Mestiza.* San Francisco, CA: Aunt Lute.

3. Plimmer, G. (2016) Mitie criticised for 'insanitary' immigration centre. *Financial Times,* 1 March. Available at: www.ft.com/content/a6d3dd74-df03-11e5-b67f-a61732c1d025 (accessed 26 December 2019).

4. These are fragments of accounts of people who have been detained in Harmondsworth. Available at: http://detainedvoices.com (accessed 26 December 2019).

5. Bhambra, G. (2016) Brexit, class, and British national identity. *Discover Society,* 5 July. Available at: https://discoversociety.org/2016/07/05/viewpoint-brexit-class-and-british-national-identity/ (accessed 26 December 2019).

6. Karatani, R. (2003) *Defining British Citizenship: Empire, Commonwealth and Modern Britain.* London: Frank Cass; Getachew, A. (2019) *Worldmaking after Empire: The Rise and Fall of Self-Determination.* Princeton, NJ: Princeton University Press.

7. Chaudhary, V. (2018) How London's Southall became 'Little Punjab'. *The Guardian,* 4 April. Available at: www.theguardian.com/cities/2018/apr/04/how-london-southall-became-little-punjab- (accessed 26 December 2019).

8. There were, of course, substantive racial tensions and political ramifications of empire within the metropole prior to the post-war period. I am limiting the narrative to that time, in part for the sake of necessary restrictions on an

already unwieldy subject, and in part because I am interested in Britain's self-image under the auspices of a post-colonial nation, whilst problematising that notion in the process.

9. On the following, see Shilliam, R. (2018) *Race and the Undeserving Poor: From Abolition to Brexit.* Bristol: Agenda Books.
10. Shilliam, *Race and the Undeserving Poor,* p. 74.
11. Shilliam, *Race and the Undeserving Poor,* p. 75.
12. Vickers, T. (n.d.) Racism and politics in British state welfare. Unpublished manuscript.
13. Hall, H. (1946) The British Commonwealth and Trusteeship. *International Affairs (Royal Institute of International Affairs 1944),* 22(2), 199–213.
14. Paul, K. (1997) *Whitewashing Britain: Race and Citizenship in the Postwar Era.* Ithaca, NY: Cornell University Press.
15. Virdee, S. (2014) *Racism, Class and the Racialized Outsider.* Basingstoke: Palgrave Macmillan (p. 98).
16. Fanon, F. (1963) *Wretched of the Earth.* New York: Grove Weidenfeld (p. 52).
17. See Barkawi, T. (2016) Decolonising war. *European Journal of International Security,* 1(2), 199–214; Jabri, V. (2012) *The Postcolonial Subject: Claiming Politics/Governing Others in Late Modernity.* Abingdon: Routledge.
18. Turner, J. (2018) Internal colonisation: the intimate circulations of empire, race and liberal government. *European Journal of International Relations,* 24(4), 765–90.
19. Rodney, W. (2018) *How Europe Underdeveloped Africa.* London and New York: Verso (p. 149).
20. Robinson, C.J. (2005) *Black Marxism: The Making of the Black Radical Tradition.* Chapel Hill, NC: University of North Carolina Press.
21. Jubilee Debt Campaign (2013) Whose development is it? Available at: https://jubileedebt.org.uk/report/whose-development-is-it (accessed 1 January 2020).
22. Li, T. (2010) To make live or let die? Rural dispossession and the protection of surplus populations. *Antipode,* 41, 66–93.
23. Rabaka, R. (2007) *W.E.B. Du Bois and the Problems of the Twenty-First Century: An Essay on Africana Critical Theory.* Lanham, MD: Lexington Books.
24. Cited in Adi, H. and Sherwood, M. (1995) *The 1945 Manchester Pan-African Congress Revisited.* London: New Beacon Books (p. 44).
25. Tuck, E. and Yang, W. (2012) Decolonization is not a metaphor. *Decolonization: Indigeneity, Education & Society,* 1(1), 1–40 (p. 4).
26. Pinderhughes, C. (2011) Toward a new theory of internal colonialism. *Socialism and Democracy,* 25(1), 235–56; Allen, R. (1970) *Black Awakening in Capitalist America; An Analytic History.* Garden City, NY: Doubleday; Calderón-Zaks, M. (2010) Domestic colonialism: the overlooked significance of Robert L. Allen's contributions. *The Black Scholar,* 40(2), 39–48; Harris, D. (1972) The black ghetto as colony: a theoretical critique and alternative formulation. *The Review of Black Political Economy,* 2(4), 3–33; Blauner, R. (1969) Internal colonialism and ghetto revolt. *Social*

Problems, 16(4), 393–408; Allen, R.L. (2005) Reassessing the internal (neo) colonialism theory. *The Black Scholar*, 35(1), 2–11; Blaut, J. (1974) The ghetto as an internal neo-colony. *Antipode*, 6(1), 37–41.

27. Blauner, R. (1972) *Racial Oppression in America*. New York: Harper & Row.
28. Gutiérrez, R. (2004) Internal colonialism: an American theory of race. *Du Bois Review Social Science Research on Race*, 1(2), 281–95.
29. Zureik, E. (1979) *The Palestinians in Israel: A Study in Internal Colonialism*. London: Routledge & Kegan Paul; Smith, A. and Ng, A. (2002) Papua: moving beyond internal colonialism? *New Zealand Journal of Asian Studies*, 4(2), 90–114. Sivaram, D. (2003) Tokyo & the cost of the unitary state's internal colonialism. *Northeastern Herald*, 13–19 June. Available at: www. tamilnation.org/conflictresolution/tamileelam/norway/030613taraki.htm (accessed 27 December 2019).
30. Barder, A. (2015) *Empire Within: International Hierarchy and its Imperial Laboratories of Governance*. New York: Routledge; Bhambra, G.K. (2016) Comparative historical sociology and the state: problems of method. *Cultural Sociology*, 10(3), 335–51; Gregory, D. (2004) *The Colonial Present: Afghanistan, Palestine, Iraq*. Oxford: Blackwell; Shilliam, R. (2016) The aims and methods of liberal education: notes from a nineteenth century Pan-Africanist. *International Journal of Politics, Culture and Society*, 29(3), 251–67; Stoler, A.L. (2016) *Imperial Durabilities in Modern Times*. Durham, NC: Duke University Press; Turner, J. (2018) Internal colonisation: the intimate circulations of empire, race and liberal government. *European Journal of International Relations*, 24(4), 765–90; Wynter, S. (2003) Unsettling the coloniality of being/power/truth/freedom: towards the human, after man, its overrepresentation – an argument. *CR: The New Centennial Review*, 3(3), 257–33.
31. Byrd, J.A., Goldstein, A., Melamed, J. and Reddy, C. (2018) Predatory value: economies of dispossession and disturbed relationalities. *Social Text*, 135, 1–18.
32. Harvey, D. (2007) *A Brief History of Neoliberalism*. New York: Oxford University Press (p. 15). See also Brown, W. (2017) *Undoing the Demos: Neoliberalism's Stealth Revolution*. New York: Zone Books; Davies, W. (2014) *The Limits of Neoliberalism: Authority, Sovereignty and the Logic of Competition*. Los Angeles, CA: SAGE; Wood, E.M. (2016) *Democracy Against Capitalism*. London: Verso.
33. Tilley, L. and Shilliam, R. (2018) Raced markets: an introduction. *New Political Economy*, 23(5), 534–43 (p. 5).
34. Quijano, A. (2007) Coloniality and modernity/rationality. *Cultural Studies*, 21(2–3), 168–78. See also Maldonado-Torres, N. (2007) On the coloniality of being: contributions to the development of a concept. *Cultural Studies*, 21(2–3), 240–70.
35. Maldano-Torres, *On the Coloniality of Being*, p. 243.
36. Omi, M. and Winant, H. (2014) *Racial Formation in the United States*. London and New York: Routledge (p. 55).

37. Bonilla, S.E. (2001) *White Supremacy and Racism in the Post-Civil Rights Era*. Boulder, CO: Lynne Rienner (pp. 31; 51–54).

38. Silva, D.F. (2007) *Toward a Global Idea of Race*. Minneapolis, MN: University of Minnesota Press (p. xxvi). The approach here broadly follows that of Weheliye G. A. (2014) *Habeas Viscus*: Racializing assemblages, biopolitics, and black feminist theories of the human. Durham, NC: Duke University Press.

39. Hartman, S. (2008) *Lose Your Mother: A Journey Along the Atlantic Slave Route*. London: Macmillan (p. 8).

40. See Bhattacharyya, G. (2018) *Rethinking Racial Capitalism: Questions of Reproduction and Survival*. Lanham, MD: Rowman & Littlefield International; Chen, C. (2013) The limit point of capitalist equality: notes towards an abolitionist anti-racism. *Endnotes*, 3, 202–23; Robinson, *Black Marxism*; Virdee, S. (2019) Racialized capitalism: an account of its contested origins and consolidation. *The Sociological Review*, 67(1), 3–27.

41. Bhattacharyya, *Rethinking*, p. 21.

42. Anzaldúa, *La frontera/Borderlands*. See also Lugones, M. (2003) *Peregrinajes/ Pilgrimages: Theorizing Coalition Against Multiple Oppressions*. New York: Rowman & Littlefield Press.

43. Anzaldua, *La frontera*, p. 3.

44. Keenan, S. (2017) A border in every street. *The Disorder of Things*, 29 June. Available at: https://thedisorderofthings.com/2017/06/29/a-border-in-every-street/ (accessed 28 December 2019). See also Keenan, S. (2014) *Subversive Property: Law and the Production of Spaces of Belonging*. Abingdon: Routledge.

45. Massey, D. (1993) Politics and space/time. In *Place and the Politics of Identity*, ed. M. Keith and S. Pile. London: Routledge, pp. 141–60.

46. Simone, A. (2018) *Improvised Lives: Rhythms of Endurance in an Urban South*. London: John Wiley & Sons (p. 10).

47. Coulthard, G.S. (2014) *Red Skin, White Masks: Rejecting the Colonial Politics of Recognition*. Minneapolis, MN: Minnesota University Press.

48. Nixon, R. (2011) *Slow Violence and the Environmentalism of the Poor*. Cambridge, MA: Harvard University Press (p. 7).

49. Glissant, E. (1992) *Caribbean Discourse: Selected Essays*. Charlottesville, VA: University of Virginia Press (p. 2).

50. Urion, C. (1999) Recording first nations traditional knowledge. Unpublished paper, U'mista Cultural Society, 11.

51. Allen, T.W. (1994) *The Invention of the White Race* (Vols 1 & 2). London: Verso; Roediger, D.R. (1999) *The Wages of Whiteness: Race and the Making of the American Working Class*. London: Verso; Goldberg, D.T. (2016) *Racial Subjects: Writing on Race in America*. London: Routledge; Lentin, A. and Titley, G. (2011) *The Crises of Multiculturalism: Racism in a Neoliberal Age*. London: Zed Books.

52. Tuck and Yang, Decolonisation is not a metaphor, p. 5 n. 3.

53. Feagin, J. and Elias, S. (2013) Rethinking racial formation theory: a systemic racism critique. *Ethnic and Racial Studies*, 36(6), 931–60 (p. 942).

54. Mbembe, A. (2017) *Future Knowledges and the Dilemmas of Decolonization.* Durham, NC: Duke University Franklin Humanities Institute (pp. 45–46).
55. Roediger, D.R. (1994) *Toward the Abolition of Whiteness: Essays on Race, Politics, and Working Class History.* New York: Verso (p. 13).
56. Kinouani, G. (2019) On bodies that don't belong. *Race Reflections,* 3 August. Available at: https://racereflections.co.uk/2019/08/03/on-bodies-that-dont-belong/ (accessed 28 December 2019).
57. Anzaldúa, *La frontera,* p. 39.
58. Nixon, *Slow Violence,* p. 2.
59. Bhambra, G. (2017) Why are the white working classes still being held responsible for Brexit and Trump? LSE Blog. Available at: https://blogs.lse.ac.uk/brexit/2017/11/10/why-are-the-white-working-classes-still-being-held-responsible-for-brexit-and-trump/ (accessed 28 December 2019).

CHAPTER 2

1. Ponsot, M. (2011) *Easy.* New York: Knopf Doubleday Publishing Group (pp. 73–74). © 2011, Knopf Doubleday.
2. BBC Caribbean Service (1959) *Going to Britain?* London: British Broadcasting Corporation.
3. Howe, D. (1978) Enter Mrs Thatcher. In *Here to Stay, Here to Fight: A Race Today Anthology,* ed. P. Field, R. Bunce, L. Hassan and M. Peacock. London: Pluto Press, pp. 22–30 (pp. 27–28).
4. Brace, L. (2004) *The Politics of Property: Labor, Freedom, and Belonging.* New York: Palgrave Macmillan.
5. McAuslan, P. (2015) Property and empire. *Social & Legal Studies,* 24(3), 339–57 (pp. 341–42). See also McIntyre, M. and Nast, H.J. (2011) Bio(necro)polis: Marx, surplus populations, and the spatial dialectics of reproduction and 'race'. *Antipode,* 43(5), 1465–88; Robinson, *Black Marxism.*
6. Locke, J. (1689) *Two Treatises*: II §34. An excellent analysis of Locke's treatise relevant to this context is in Wood, E.M. (2003) *Empire of Capital.* London: Verso. The relationship with waste is elucidated most clearly in Gidwani, V. and Reddy, R.N. (2011) The afterlives of 'waste': notes from India for a minor history of capitalist surplus. *Antipode,* 43(5), 1625–58.
7. Fanon, F. (2018) Why we use violence. In *Alienation and Freedom,* ed. R. Young and J. Khalfa. London: Bloomsbury, pp. 653–60 (p. 654).
8. See Bhandar, B. (2018) *Colonial Lives of Property: Law, Land, and Racial Regimes of Ownership.* Durham, NC: Duke University Press; Harris, C.I. (1993) Whiteness as property. *Harvard Law Review,* 106, 1707–91.
9. On the racialisation of the Irish, see Ignatiev, N. (2012) *How the Irish Became White.* London: Routledge; Mackey, E. (2016) *Unsettled Expectations: Uncertainty, Land and Settler Decolonization.* Winnipeg: Fernwood; Moreton-Robinson, A. (2015) *The White Possessive: Property, Power, and Indigenous Sovereignty.* Minneapolis, MN: University of Minnesota Press.
10. On this conception, see Douglas, M. (2003) *Purity and Danger: An Analysis of Concepts of Pollution and Taboo.* London: Routledge.

11. Seed, P. (1995) *Ceremonies of Possession in Europe's Conquest of the New World, 1492–1640*. Cambridge: Cambridge University Press.

12. Nightingale, C. (2006) The transnational contexts of early twentieth-century American urban segregation. *Journal of Social History*, 39(3), 667–702. More generally, see Jones, B.G. (2012) Civilising African cities: international housing and urban policy from colonial to neoliberal times. *Journal of Intervention and Statebuilding*, 6(1), 23–40; King, A.D. (2015) *Urbanism, Colonialism, and the World-Economy*. London: Routledge; Legg, S. (2008) *Spaces of Colonialism: Delhi's Urban Governmentalities*. London: John Wiley & Sons; Nightingale, C.H. (2012) *Segregation: A Global History of Divided Cities*. Chicago, IL: University of Chicago Press. On the influence of colonial segregation on Victorian city planning, see Rich, P. (1985) Doctrines of racial segregation in Britain: 1800–1914. *New Community*, 12, 75–88.

13. Fanon, *Wretched of the Earth*, pp. 37–38.

14. Razack, S. (2002) Gendered racial violence and spatialized justice: the murder of Pamela George. In *Race, Space and the Law: Unmapping a White Settler Society*, ed. S. Razack. Toronto: Between the Lines, p. 129.

15. For example, by the 1960s, Moss Side in Manchester was depicted as a marginalised ghetto to parallel those of Watts or Harlem; see Brown, L. and Cunningham, N. (2016) The inner geographies of a migrant gateway: mapping the built environment and the dynamics of Caribbean mobility in Manchester, 1951–2011. *Social Science History*, 40(1), 93–120. See also Wacquant, L.J.D. (2008) *Urban Outcasts: A Comparative Sociology of Advanced Marginality*. Cambridge: Polity Press.

16. See Karn, V.A. and Phillips, D.A. (1998) Race and ethnicity in housing: a diversity of experience. In *Race Relations in Britain: A Developing Agenda*, ed. T. Blackstone, B. Parekh and P. Sanders. London: Routledge, pp. 128–57; Smith, D. and Whalley, A. (1975) *Racial Minorities and Public Housing*. London: PEP.

17. Freeson, cited in Smith, S.J. (1987) Residential segregation: a geography of English racism? In *Race and Racism: Essays in Social Geography*, ed. Peter Jackson. London: Routledge, pp. 22–41 (p. 26).

18. Selvon, cited in Ingrams, E. (2001) The Lonely Londoners: Sam Selvon and the literary heritage. *Wasafiri*, 16(33), 33–36.

19. Goldberg, D.T. (1993) *Racist Culture*. Cambridge, MA: Blackwell (p. 48). See also Nightingale, The transnational contexts, p. 677; Curtin, P.D. (1985) Medical knowledge and urban planning in tropical Africa. *American Historical Review*, 90(3), 594–613; Hogarth, R.A. (2017) *Medicalizing Blackness: Making Racial Difference in the Atlantic World, 1780–1840*. Chapel Hill, NC: University of North Carolina Press.

20. Nightingale, The transnational contexts, p. 677. See Arnold, D. and Muraleedharan, V.R. (1995) Colonising the body: state medicine and epidemic disease in nineteenth-century India. *The Indian Economic and Social History Review*, 32(3), 399–401; Prashad, V. (1994) Native dirt/ imperial ordure: the cholera of 1832 and the morbid resolutions of modernity. *Journal of Historical Sociology*, 7(3), 243–60; Baldwin, P. (1999)

Contagion and the State in Europe, 1830–1930. Cambridge: Cambridge University Press; Spitzer, L. (1968) The mosquito and segregation in Sierra Leone. *Canadian Journal of African Studies*, 2, 49–61; Frenkel, S. and Western, J. (1988) Pretext or policy? Racial segregation and malarial mosquitoes in a British tropical colony: Sierra Leone. *Annals of the Association of American Geographers*, 78, 211–28; Gale, T. (1951) Segregation in British West Africa. *Cahiers d'Etudes Africaines*, 20, 495–507.

21. Chopra, P. (2012) Free to move, forced to flee: the formation and dissolution of suburbs in colonial Bombay, 1750–1918. *Urban History*, 39(1), 83–107. Nightingale, The transnational contexts, p. 670; Kennedy, D.K. (1996) *The Magic Mountains: Hill Stations and the British Raj*. Berkeley, CA: University of California Press.

22. Jones, Civilising African cities, p. 26. See also Home, R.K. (1997) *Of Planting and Planning: The Making of British Colonial Cities*. London: Routledge.

23. Sivanandan, A. (1981) From resistance to rebellion: Asian and Afro-Caribbean struggles in Britain. *Race & Class*, 23, 111–52.

24. Lukes, S., de Noronha, N. and Finney, N. (2018) Slippery discrimination: a review of the drivers of migrant and minority housing disadvantage. *Journal of Ethnic and Migration Studies*, 1–19.

25. Scrutiny of child-raising was familiar, and particularly evident in analyses of the fostering of African children by white families in the 1950s and 1960s. A widespread practice for West African student parents temporarily residing in London, private fostering played the role of extended familial care and removing children from harms caused by living in London shared accommodation. These children were uniquely placed as object of sociological study whose relative health or pathology might provide insight into integration and migration. Under pressure from reports on poor conditions of foster homes, with 18 African children having died in them between 1961 and 1964, in 1966 the London Council of Social Service argued for reforms that would build better relationships between biological and foster families. The continued justification for their use was that fostering would help lead towards the creation of a non-racial society. See Bailkin, J. (2009) The postcolonial family? West African children, private fostering, and the British state. *The Journal of Modern History*, 81(1), 87–121.

26. Pollack, M. (1972) *Today's Three Year Olds in London*. London: Heinemann; Pollack, M. (1979) *Nine Years Old*. London: Heinemann. See also Hampshire, J. (2005) *Citizenship and Belonging: Immigration and the Politics of Demographic Governance in Postwar Britain*. Basingstoke: Macmillan.

27. In the face of this failing education system, Black Supplementary Schools were created from the mid-1960s. These would provide additional teaching in core subjects, but also community history, pan-Africanism and culture. See Andrews, K. (2013) *Resisting Racism: Race, Inequality, and the Black Supplementary School Movement*. London: Institute of Education Press.

28. Dahrendorf, R. (1987) The underclass and the future of Britain. Tenth annual lecture, delivered in St George's Chapel, Windsor Castle, Friday 27

April to a gathering of the associates of St George's House and distinguished guests. See Goldberg, *Racist Culture*, p. 172; Shilliam, R., *Race and the Undeserving Poor*; Boss, P. and Homeshaw, J. (1975) Britain's black citizens. *Social Work Today*, 18 September, pp. 334–37.

29. Pearce, J. (2013) *Who Lives in the Private Rented Sector?* Coalville, Leicestershire: Building and Social Housing Foundation.

30. Ward, R. (1982) Race housing and wealth. *Journal of Ethnic and Migration Studies*, 10(1), 3–15.

31. Williams, P. (1978) Building societies and the inner city. *Transactions of the Institute of British Geographers*, 3(1), 23–34.

32. Smith, Residential segregation, p. 27.

33. Brown, C. (1984) *Black and White Britain*. London: Heinemann.

34. McKay, D.H. (1977) *Housing and Race in Industrial Society. Civil Rights and Urban Policy in Britain and the United States*. London: Croom Helm (p. 16).

35. Johnson, M.R. (2003) Ethnic minorities and racism in welfare provision. In *Race and Racism: Essays in Social Geography*, ed. P. Jackson. London: Allen & Unwin, pp. 206–18.

36. Parrenas, R.S. (2001) *Servants of Globalization: Women, Migration, and Domestic Work*. Stanford, CA: Stanford University Press.

37. McKittrick, K. (2013) Plantation futures. *Small Axe: A Caribbean Journal of Criticism*, 17(3), 1–15 (p. 3).

38. See note 30. The following roughly follows that given in Harvey, *A Brief History*.

39. Virdee, *Racism, Class and the Racialized Outsider*, p. 102ff.

40. Cited in Paul, *Whitewashing Britain*, p. 134.

41. Roediger, *Wages of Whiteness*. For Harvey, the logic justifying welfare retrenchment was as follows: individual freedom in the workplace meant that unemployment was seen as voluntary; labour simply prefers not to work below a certain reserve price; unemployment rises when this reserve price is set too high; the reserve price is partly set by welfare payments; so, welfare retrenchment is inextricable from reducing unemployment. Harvey, *A Brief History*, pp. 53–54.

42. Da Silva, *Towards a Global Idea of Race*, p. xxvii.

43. United Coloured People's Association, cited in Narayan, J. (2019). British Black Power: the anti-imperialism of political blackness and the problem of nativist socialism. *The Sociological Review*, 67(5), 945–67 (p. 957).

44. Sivanandan, From resistance to rebellion; Harris, C. (1993) Post-war migration and the industrial reserve army. In *Inside Babylon: The Caribbean Diaspora in Britain*, ed. W. James and C. Harris. London: Verso, pp. 7–54.

45. Arghiri, E. (1972) *Unequal Exchange*. New York: Monthly Review Press; Beckford, G.L. (1999) *Persistent Poverty: Underdevelopment in Plantation Economies of the Third World*. Kingston, Jamaica: University of West Indies Press; Best, L. (1968) Outlines of a model of the pure plantation economy. *Social and Economic Studies*, 17(3), 283–323; Best, L. and Levitt, K. (2014) *Essays on the Theory of Plantation Economy: A Historical and Institutional Approach to Caribbean Economic Development*. Kingston, Jamaica:

University of the West Indies Press; Escobar, A. (2011) *Encountering Development: The Making and Unmaking of the Third World*. Princeton, NJ: Princeton University Press; Girvan, N. (1971) Making the rules of the game: country-company agreements in the bauxite industry. *Social and Economic Studies*, 20(4), 378–419; Harris, D.J. (1972) The black ghetto as colony: a theoretical critique and alternative formulation. *Review of Black Political Economy*, 2(4), 3–33; Lordon, F. (2014) *Willing Slaves of Capital: Spinoza and Marx on Desire*. London: Verso.

46. Smith, J. (2016) *Imperialism in the Twenty-First Century: Globalization, Super-Exploitation, and Capitalism's Final Crisis*. New York: Monthly Review Press.

47. Race Today Collective, cited in Richmond, M. and Charnley, A. (2018) Race, class and borders. Available at: http://www.basepublication.org/?p=665 (accessed 29 December 2019).

48. Cope, Z. (2019) *Wealth of (Some) Nations: Imperialism and the Mechanics of Value Transfer*. London: Pluto Press (p. 161ff.).

49. McIntyre and Nast, Bio(necro)polis; Merrill, H. (2011) Migration and surplus populations: race and deindustrialization in northern Italy. *Antipode*, 43(5), 1542–72.

50. Lowe, L. (2007) *Immigrant Acts: On Asian American Cultural Politics*. Durham, NC: Duke University Press (p. 28). See also Roediger, D.R. and Esch, E.D. (2012) *The Production of Difference: Race and the Management of Labor in US History*. Oxford: Oxford University Press.

51. Wolfe, P. (2006) Settler colonialism and the elimination of the native. *Journal of Genocide Research*, 8(4), 387–409. On the persistence of labour segmentations, see Kapadia, D., Nazroo, J. and Clark, K. (2015) Have ethnic inequalities in the labour market persisted? In *Ethnic Identity and Inequalities in Britain: The Dynamics of Diversity*, ed. S. Jivraj and L. Simpson. Bristol: Policy Press.

52. McKittrick, Plantation futures, p. 7.

53. Lapavitsas, C. (2011) Theorizing financialization. *Work, Employment and Society*, 25(4), 611–26. See also Federici, S. (2014) From commoning to debt: financialization, microcredit, and the changing architecture of capital accumulation. *South Atlantic Quarterly*, 113(2), 231–44.

54. Goldstein, A. (2014) Finance and foreclosure in the colonial present. *Radical History Review*, 118, 42–63.

55. Perera, J. (2019) *The London Clearances: Race, Housing and Policing*. London: The Institute of Race Relations. This was combined with the Housing Corporation's BME Housing Strategy in 1986, which founded BME-specific housing associations as a means to allocate some response to racialized housing with minimal support and housing stock.

56. Leyshon, A. and Thrift, N. (1995) Geographies of financial exclusion: financial abandonment in Britain and the United States. *Transactions of the Institute of British Geographers*, 20(3), 312–41.

57. See Perera, *The London Clearances*.

58. Burton, D. (2012) *Credit and Consumer Society*. London: Routledge.

59. Leyshon and Thrift, Geographies of financial exclusion, p. 316. See also Walters, W. (2004) Secure borders, safe haven, domopolitics. *Citizenship Studies*, 8(3), 237–60; Robinson, D. and Reeve, K. (2006) *Neighbourhood Experiences of New Immigration*. York: Joseph Rowntree Foundation.

60. Gulliver, K. (2017) *Forty Years of Struggle: A Window on Race and Housing, Disadvantage and Exclusion*. London: Human City Institute.

61. Garrett, H., Piddington, J. and Nicol, S. (2014) The housing conditions of minority ethnic households in England. Better Housing briefing paper, 24. I will use the category Black and Minority Ethnic (BAME) only to report the statistical data and the way it was collected. However, I hope that it is clear that the arguments regarding demographic analytics and ethnicity made in Chapter 4, together with the argument throughout that such demographics should always be understood as a colonial construction, problematise the category at root. For one, we should question what work the characterisation as a minority racialised people who undoubtedly form the global majority is doing.

62. Dorling, D. (2011) *So You Think You Know About Britain?* London: Hachette.

63. Gulliver, *Forty Years of Struggle*.

64. Shelter (2001) Far from home: ethnicity and housing. Available at: www.shelter.orguk/housing/factsheets/ethnicity_and_housing.asp (accessed 22 July 2019). See also Runnymede Trust (2013) No dogs, no blacks: new findings show that minority ethnic groups are still discriminated against when trying to rent private housing. Available at: www.runnymedetrust.org/news/525/272/No-Dogs-No-Blacks-new-findings-show-that-minority-ethnic-groups-are-still-discriminated-against-when-trying-to-rent-private-housing.html (accessed 29 December 2019).

65. Emejulu, A. and Bassel, L. (2018) Austerity and the politics of becoming. *Journal of Common Market Studies*, 56, 109–19; Datta, K. (2011) Last hired and first fired? The impact of the economic downturn on low-paid Bulgarian migrant workers in London. *Journal of International Development*, 23, 565–82.

66. Hall, S. et al. (2017) *Intersecting Inequalities: The Impact of Austerity on Black and Minority Ethnic Women in the UK*. London: Runnymede and Women's Budget Group.

67. Runnymede Trust (2018) Runnymede submission to the UN Special Rapporteur. Available at: www.runnymedetrust.org/uploads/policyResponses/Runnymede%20submission%20-%20UN%20Special%20Rappoteur.pdf (accessed 29 December 2019). This is calculated after housing costs, and the measure used by the Child Poverty Act 2010, as household income below 60 per cent of median income.

68. Gulliver, *Forty Years of Struggle*.

69. Roughly, a corporation takes over responsibility for the development, not upkeeping maintenance and improvements so allowing its value as property to decline. This reaches the point where it is claimed that the sunk costs of improvement as is far outweigh those of regeneration through rebuilding.

70. Desmond, M. (2012) Eviction and the reproduction of urban poverty. *American Journal of Sociology*, 118, 88–133; Brickell, K., Arrigoitia, M.F. and Vasudevan, A (2017) Geographies of forced eviction: dispossession, violence, resistance. In *Geographies of Forced Eviction*, ed. K. Brickell, M.F. Arrigoitia and A. Vasudevan. London: Palgrave Macmillan; Atkinson, R. (2015) Losing one's place: narratives of neighbourhood change, market injustice and symbolic displacement. *Housing, Theory and Society*, 32, 373–88; Kern, L. (2016) Rhythms of gentrification: eventfulness and slow violence in a happening neighbourhood. *Cultural Geographies*, 23, 441–57.

71. Elmer, S. and Dening, G. (2016) The London clearances. *City*, 20(2), 271–77. On the violence of unhoming, see Elliott-Cooper, A., Hubbard, P. and Lees, L. (2019) Moving beyond Marcuse: gentrification, displacement and the violence of un-homing. *Progress in Human Geography*.

72. See also Beckford, *Persistent Poverty*.

73. Cited in Gutiérrez, Internal colonialism.

74. Cited in *The Guardian* (2005) Britain sleepwalking to segregation. *The Guardian*, 19 September. Available at: www.theguardian.com/world/2005/sep/19/race.socialexclusion (accessed 29 December 2019).

75. Andrews, K. (2016) The psychosis of whiteness: the celluloid hallucinations of Amazing Graze and Belle. *Journal of Black Studies*, 47(5), 435–53.

76. Pinderhughes, Toward a new theory, p. 236; Allen, *Black Awakening*. Similar problems with the co-option of internal colonialism as a political position were identified by Gloria Anzaldúa; see Gutiérrez, Internal colonialism.

77. To an extent, this coheres with Etienne Balibar's analysis of European apartheid involving the 'stigmatisation and repression of populations whose presence within European societies is nonetheless increasingly massive and legitimate': Balibar, E. (2009) *We, the People of Europe? Reflections on Transnational Citizenship*. Princeton, NJ: Princeton University Press (p. x).

78. El-Enany, N. (2017) The colonial logic of Grenfell. *Verso Blog*. Available at: www.versobooks.com/blogs/3306-the-colonial-logic-of-grenfell (accessed 29 December 2019). See also Danewid, I. (2019) The fire this time: Grenfell, racial capitalism and the urbanisation of empire. *European Journal of International Relations*.

79. Anzaldúa, *La frontera*, p. 3.

80. Razack, S. (2015) *Dying from Improvement: Inquests and Inquiries into Indigenous Deaths in Custody*. Toronto: University of Toronto Press.

81. Fanon, *Wretched of the Earth*, p. 37.

CHAPTER 3

1. Manzoor-Khan, S. (2019) *Postcolonial Banter*. Kenilworth: Verve. © 2019, Verve Press.

2. Simons, J. (2016) 35th anniversary of the Black People's Day of Action. Revolutionary Communist Group. Available at: www.revolutionarycommunist.org/britain/fight-racism/4337-a0200516 (accessed 30 December 2019).

3. Slogan of the New Cross Massacre Action Group on an unused poster titled *New Cross Massacre: 12 Dead 27 Injured. Support Black Peoples Day of Action.*

4. Kwesi-Johnson, L. (2006) Di Great Insohreckshan. In *Selected Poems.* London: Penguin.

5. Clayton, A. and Killingray, D. (1989) *Khaki and Blue: Military and Police in British Colonial Africa.* Athens, OH: Ohio University Center for International Studies (p. 52).

6. Moore, J. (2014) Is the empire coming home? Liberalism, exclusion and the punitiveness of the British state. In *Papers from the British Criminology Conference,* vol. 14, pp. 31–48.

7. Moritz, E. (1958) Winston Churchill – prison reformer. *The Historian,* 20(4), 428–40; Howard League for Penal Reform & Commission on English Prisons Today (2007) *The Principles and Limits of the Penal System: Initiating a Conversation.* London: Howard League for Penal Reform. Available at: https://howardleague.org/wp-content/uploads/2016/04/The-Principles-and-Limits-of-the-Penal-System.pdf (accessed 30 December 2019); Godfrey, B.S. (2014) *Crime in England 1880–1945: The Rough and the Criminal, the Policed and the Incarcerated.* London: Routledge; Bailey, V. (1997) English prisons, penal culture, and the abatement of imprisonment, 1895–1922. *Journal of British Studies,* 36(3), 285–324; Scott, D. (2018) *Against Imprisonment: An Anthology of Abolitionist Essays.* Sherfield, Hants: Waterside Press.

8. Moore, Is the empire coming home?, p. 35. See also Wagner, K.A. (2018) Savage warfare: violence and the rule of colonial difference in early British counterinsurgency. *History Workshop Journal,* 85, 217–37; Kolsky, E. (2005) Codification and the rule of colonial difference: criminal procedure in British India. *Law and History Review,* 23(3), 631–83.

9. Cited in Mahmud, T. (1999) Colonialism and modern constructions of race: a preliminary inquiry. *University of Miami Law Review,* 53, 1219–999 (p. 1222).

10. Wynter, Unsettling the coloniality of being.

11. The following is drawn in part from Tully, J. (2008) *Public Philosophy in a New Key: Imperialism and Civic Freedom.* Cambridge: Cambridge University Press (p. 145ff). See also Bhambra, G.K. (2009) *Rethinking Modernity: Postcolonialism and the Sociological Imagination.* Basingstoke: Palgrave Macmillan; Krug, J.A. (2018) *Fugitive Modernities: Kisama and the Politics of Freedom.* Durham, NC: Duke University Press.

12. Belsey, C. (2014) *The Subject of Tragedy (Routledge Revivals): Identity and Difference in Renaissance Drama.* London: Routledge (p. 8).

13. Raedler, S. (2015) *Kant and the Interests of Reason.* Berlin: Walter de Gruyter (p. 41). See also Korsgaard, C.M. and O'Neill, O. (2014) *The Sources of Normativity.* Cambridge: Cambridge University Press.

14. Wittgenstein, L. (2009) *Philosophical Investigations,* 4th edition, trans. Hacker and Schulte. London: Wiley-Blackwell. See Trafford, J. (2017)

Reconstructing intersubjective norms. *Phenomenology and Mind*, 13, 176–82.

15. Kant, I. (2010) Idea for a universal history with a cosmopolitan purpose. In *Kant: Political Writings*, ed. H.S. Reiss. Cambridge: Cambridge University Press (p. 47).

16. Kant, I. (2010) Metaphysics of morals. In *Kant: Political Writings*, ed. H.S. Reiss. Cambridge: Cambridge University Press (p. 143).

17. Tully, *Public Philosophy in a New Key*, p. 148.

18. Da Silva, *A Global Idea of Race*, p. 436. See also Mahmud, Colonialism and modern constructions of race, p. 1223. See also Hartman, S.V. (2010) *Scenes of Subjection: Terror, Slavery, and Self-Making in Nineteenth-Century America*. New York: Oxford University Press; Brown, M. (2005) That heavy machine: the colonial apparatus in 21st century social control. *Social Justice*, 32, 41–52.

19. Goldberg, *Racist Culture*, pp. 4–5.

20. For example, Christie, N. (2016) *Crime Control as Industry: Towards Gulags, Western Style*. London: Routledge; Pratt, J. (2002) *Punishment and Civilization: Penal Tolerance and Intolerance in Modern Society*. Los Angeles, CA: SAGE.

21. Pinney, C. (1990) Colonial anthropology in the 'laboratory of mankind'. *The Raj: India and the British*, 1600(1947), 252–63; Nijjar, J.S. (2018) Echoes of empire: excavating the colonial roots of Britain's war on gangs. *Social Justice*, 45(2/3), 147–201 (p. 149).

22. Mahmud, Colonialism and modern constructions of race.

23. Brown, M. (2014) *Penal Power and Colonial Rule*. Abingdon: Routledge; Bayly, C.A. (1999) *Empire and Information: Intelligence Gathering and Social Communication in India, 1780-1870* (Vol. 1). Cambridge: Cambridge University Press; Henderson, C.R. (1913) Control of crime in India. *Journal of the American Institute of Criminal Law and Criminology*, 4(3), 378–401.

24. In Raghaviah, V. (1968) *Nomadism: Its Cause and Cure*. Hyderabad, India: Tribal Cultural Research & Training Institute (p. 189). See also Arnold, D. (1985) Bureaucratic recruitment and subordination in colonial India: the Madras Constabulary, 1859-1947. *Subaltern Studies*, IV, 1–53.

25. Peplow, S. (2019) *Race and Riots in Thatcher's Britain*. Manchester: Manchester University Press.

26. Brabazon, T. (1998) 'Brixton's aflame': television history workshop and the battle for Britain. *Limina*, 4, 49–58 (p. 49).

27. Northam, G. (1989) *Shooting in the Dark: Riot Police in Britain*. London: Faber & Faber (pp. 89–89).

28. Barker, M. and Beezer, A. (1983) The language of racism – an examination of Lord Scarman's report and the Brixton riots. *International Socialism*, 2(18), 108.

29. Gutzmore, C. (1983) Capital, 'black youth' and crime. *Race & Class*, 25(2), 13–30 (p. 17). See also Gilroy, P. (1982) The myth of black criminality. *Socialist Register*, 19, 47–56; Centre for Contemporary Cultural Studies.

(2004) *Empire Strikes Back: Race and Racism In 70's Britain*. London: Routledge.

30. Jackson, N.M. (2016) Imperial suspect: policing colonies within 'post'-imperial England. *Callaloo*, 39(1), 203–15 (p. 203).

31. In Moore, Is the empire coming home?, p. 38.

32. Gutzmore, C. (1982) The Notting Hill Carnival. *Marxism Today*, 26(8), 31–33. This was particularly transparent in targeting members of the Rastafari movement, whose resistance to internal colonialism was hugely significant. See www.rastafari-in-motion.org (accessed 30 December 2019).

33. T.V. Stephens, a Law Member of the Executive Council, 1871. In D'Souza, D. (2001) Declared criminal at birth: India's denotified tribes. *Manushi*, 123, 22–26.

34. Hall, S., Critcher, C., Jefferson, T., Clarke, J. and Roberts, B. (2013) *Policing the Crisis: Mugging, the State and Law and Order*. London: Macmillan International Higher Education.

35. Select Committee on Race Relations and Immigration, cited in Gutzmore, Capital, 'black youth' and crime.

36. Gilroy, The myth of black criminality, p. 48. See also Alexander, C. (2010) *The Asian Gang: Ethnicity, Identity, Masculinity*. Oxford: Berg.

37. See McCulloch, J. and Pickering, S. (2009) Pre-crime and counter-terrorism. *British Journal of Criminology*, 49(5), 628–45.

38. Gilroy, P. (2013) *There Ain't No Black in the Union Jack*. London: Routledge (p. 74).

39. Ferreira da Silva, D. (2009) No-bodies: law, raciality and violence. *Griffith Law Review*, 18(2), 212–36.

40. Rushdie, S. (1982) The new empire within Britain. *New Society*, 9, 417–21.

41. See Sivanandan, A. (1978) *Race, Class and the State: The Black Experience in Britain*. London: Institute of Race Relations.

42. Karatani, *Defining British Citizenship*.

43. Jackson, Imperial suspect, p. 213.

44. See Kennison, P. and Squires, P. (2013) *Shooting to Kill: Policing, Firearms and Armed Response*. Hoboken, NJ: Wiley.

45. See Sinclair, G. and Williams, C.A. (2007) 'Home and away': the cross-fertilisation between 'colonial' and 'British' policing, 1921–85. *Journal of Imperial and Commonwealth History*, 35(2), 221–38; Northam, *Shooting in the Dark*; Brogden, M. (1987) The emergence of the police – the colonial dimension. *The British Journal of Criminology*, 27(1), 4–14; Reith, C. (1943) *British Police and the Democratic Ideal*. Oxford: Oxford University Press.

46. In Northam, *Shooting in the Dark*, p. 133.

47. Foucault, M. (2003) *Society Must Be Defended: Lectures at the Collège de France, 1975–1976*. London: Macmillan (p. 103).

48. Brogden, The emergence of the police. Anderson, D.M. and Killingray, D. (eds) (1991) *Policing the Empire: Government, Authority, and Control, 1830–1940*. Manchester: Manchester University Press.

49. Bell, E. (2013) Normalising the exceptional: British colonial policing cultures come home. *Mémoire(s), identité(s), marginalité(s) dans le monde*

occidental contemporain. *Cahiers du MIMMOC*, 10, 3. See also Hall, C. (2009) *At Home with the Empire: Metropolitan Culture and the Imperial World*. New York: Cambridge University Press.

50. Elkins, C. (2005) *Imperial Reckoning: The Untold Story of Britain's Gulag in Kenya*. London: Macmillan; Elkins, C. (2005) *Britain's Gulag: The Brutal End of Empire in Kenya*. London: Random House.

51. Elkins, *Britain's Gulag*, pp. xv–xvi.

52. Cole, B. (1999) Post-colonial systems. In *Policing across the World: Issues for the Twenty-First Century*, ed. R. Mawby. London: UCL Press, pp. 88–108 (p. 94). See also Emsley, C. (1992) The English bobby: an indulgent tradition. In *Myths of the English*, ed. R. Porter. Oxford: Polity Press, pp. 114–35.

53. Much of the following relies on Northam, *Shooting in the Dark*; Sinclair and Williams, Home and away.

54. Northam, *Shooting in the Dark*, p. 135.

55. Cited in Institute of Race Relations (1987) *Policing against Black People*. London: The Institute of Race Relations.

56. Northam, *Shooting in the Dark*, p. 138.

57. Williams, P. (2015) Criminalising the other: challenging the race–gang nexus. *Race & Class*, 56(3), 18–35 (p. 25).

58. As Williams writes, 'this is vividly illustrated through the front page of the Manchester Evening News (16 August 2007) which presented the predominantly black and brown faces of people who had been killed by guns since 1999 under the banner 'How many more?'.' Criminalising the other, p. 24.

59. Wintour, P. and Dodd, V. (2007) Blair blames spate of murders on black culture. *The Guardian*, 12 April. Available at: www.theguardian.com/politics/2007/apr/12/ukcrime.race (accessed 30 December 2019).

60. For example, Dodd, V. and Davies, C. (2011) London riots escalate as police battle for control. *The Guardian*, 9 August. Available at: www.theguardian.com/uk/2011/aug/08/london-riots-escalate-police-battle (accessed 30 December 2019); Riddell, M. (2011) London riots: the underclass lashes out. *The Daily Telegraph*, 8 August. Available at: www.telegraph.co.uk/news/uknews/law-and-order/8630533/Riots-the-underclass-lashes-out.html (accessed 30 December 2019).

61. In Newburn, T., Diski, R., Cooper, K., Deacon, R., Burch, A. and Grant, M. (2018) 'The biggest gang'? Police and people in the 2011 England riots. *Policing and Society*, 28(2), 205–22.

62. Campbell, C. (2014) *Race and Empire: Eugenics in Colonial Kenya*. Manchester: Manchester University Press; Tilley, H. (2011) *Africa as a Living Laboratory: Empire, Development, and the Problem of Scientific Knowledge, 1870–1950*. Chicago, IL: University of Chicago Press.

63. For example, *The Guardian* (2005) Constable suspended after racist tirade caught on mobile. *The Guardian*, 19 May. Available at: www.theguardian.com/uk/2005/may/19/ukcrime.race (accessed 30 December 2019).

64. In Newburn et al., The biggest gang?

65. Williams, Z. and Fishwick, C. (2016) Conditions that caused English riots even worse now, says leading expert. *The Guardian*, 5 August. Available at: www.theguardian.com/uk-news/2016/aug/05/conditions-that-caused-english-riots-even-worse-now-says-leading-expert (accessed 30 December 2019).

66. Toscano, A. (2017) *Fanaticism: On the Uses of an Idea*. London: Verso.

67. O'Carroll, L. (2011) David Starkey Newsnight race remarks: hundreds complain to BBC. *The Guardian*, 15 August. Available at: www.theguardian.com/media/2011/aug/15/david-starkey-newsinght-race-remarks (accessed 30 December 2019).

68. Dikötter, F. and Brown, I. (eds) (2018) *Cultures of Confinement: A History of the Prison in Africa, Asia, and Latin America*. Ithaca, NY: Cornell University Press; Bernault, F. (ed.) (2003) *A History of Prison and Confinement in Africa*. Portsmouth, NH: Heinemann; Browne, S. (2015) *Dark Matters: On the Surveillance of Blackness*. Durham, NC: Duke University Press; Bernault, *History of Prison and Confinement in Africa*.

69. Brown, M. (2002) The politics of penal excess and the echo of colonial penality. *Punishment & Society*, 4(4), 403–23.

70. Williams, P. and Clarke, B. (2016) *Dangerous Associations: Joint Enterprise, Gangs and Racism*. London: Centre for Crime and Justice Studies. See also Katz, J. and Jackson-Jacobs, C. (2004) *The Criminologists' Gang. The Blackwell Companion to Criminology*. Oxford: Blackwell, pp. 91–124.

71. Amnesty International (2018) Trapped in the matrix: secrecy, stigma, and bias in the Met's gang database. Available at: www.amnesty.org.uk/files/reports/Trapped%20in%20the%20Matrix%20Amnesty%20report.pdf (accessed 25 March 2020), p. 43.

72. Gunnell, D., Hillier, J. and Blakeborough, L. (2016) Social network analysis of an urban street gang using police intelligence data. Home Office, p. 12.

73. Samota, N. (2008) Foreword. In C. Alexander, *(Re)thinking Gangs*. London: Runnymede Perspectives. See Nijjar, Echoes of empire, p. 150.

74. London Assembly Police and Crime Committee (2016) Serious youth violence. Available at: www.london.gov.uk/sites/default/files/serious_youth_violence_report_-_london_assembly.pdf (accessed 30 December 2019).

75. Williams, P. and Clarke, B. (2018) The black criminal Other as an object of social control. *Social Sciences*, 7(11), 10.

76. Cited in Amnesty International, Trapped in the matrix.

77. Nijjar, Echoes of empire, p. 152.

78. Amnesty International, Trapped in the matrix.

79. On this argument, see Field, S., Britain, G. and Unit, P. (1990) *Trends in Crime and Their Interpretation: A Study of Recorded Crime in Post War England and Wales*. London: Home Office. The study found that violent crime increases during periods of increased consumption and declines during periods of economic downturn.

80. Bridges, L. (2015) The Met Gangs Matrix – institutional racism in practice. *IRR News*, 9 April. Available at: www.irr.org.uk/news/the-met-gangs-matrix-institutional-racism-in-action/ (accessed 30 December 2019).

81. Mayor of London's Office (2017) The London knife crime strategy. Available at: www.london.gov.uk/sites/default/files/mopac_knife_crime_strategy_june_2017.pdf (accessed 30 December 2019).

82. Rawlinson, K. (2018) 'Gangs' families should lose council homes' – Home Office minister. *The Guardian*, 22 June. Available at: www.theguardian.com/society/2018/jun/23/gangs-families-should-lose-council-homes-urges-minister (accessed 30 December 2019).

83. Koram, K. (2019) *War on Drugs and the Global Colour Line*. London: Pluto Press.

84. Scott, S. (2018) *The War on Gangs or a Racialised War on Working Class Black Youths*. London: The Monitoring Group (p. 26).

85. Marsh, S. and Siddique, H. (2018) Met Police's use of force jumps 79% in one year. *The Guardian*, 8 October. Available at: www.theguardian.com/uk-news/2018/oct/08/met-polices-use-of-force-jumps-79-in-one-year (accessed 30 December 2019).

86. Sturge, G. (2019) House of Commons Briefing Paper Number CBP-04334, 23 July, Home Office, London.

87. Lammy, D. (2017) The Lammy review: an independent review into the treatment of, and outcomes for, Black, Asian and Minority Ethnic individuals in the Criminal Justice System. HM Government.

88. Sveinsson, K.P. (ed.) (2013) *Criminal Justice v. Racial Justice: Minority Ethnic Overrepresentation in the Criminal Justice System*. London: Runnymede Trust.

89. Uhrig, N. (2016) Black, Asian and minority ethnic disproportionality in the criminal justice system in England and Wales. Ministry of Justice, London.

90. Ministry of Justice (2017) Justice Secretary Elizabeth Truss unveils landmark Prisons and Courts Bill. Available at: www.gov.uk/government/news/justice-secretary-elizabeth-truss-unveils-landmark-prisons-and-courts-bill (accessed 30 December 2019).

91. Davis, A. (2011) *Are Prisons Obsolete?* New York: Seven Stories Press.

92. See https://offenderemployment.campaign.gov.uk.

93. Elgot, J. (2018) Thousands of ex-prisoners likely to be sleeping rough. *The Guardian*, 13 August. Available at: www.theguardian.com/society/2018/aug/13/thousands-of-ex-prisoners-likely-to-be-sleeping-rough (accessed 30 December 2019); Goddard, E. (2018) The scandal of ex-prisoners released into a new life – on the streets. *The Guardian*, 28 November. Available at: www.theguardian.com/society/2018/nov/28/ex-prisoners-streets-rough-sleeping-short-sentences (accessed 2 January 2020).

94. Grierson, J. (2019) Freed prisoners killing themselves at a rate of one every two days. *The Guardian*, 18 November. Available at: www.theguardian.com/society/2019/nov/18/freed-prisoners-killing-themselves-at-a-rate-of-one-every-two-days (accessed 30 December 2019).

95. Moore, Is the empire coming home?, p. 36.

96. Abourahme, N. (2018) Of monsters and boomerangs: colonial returns in the late liberal city. *City*, 22(1), 106–15 (p. 107).

97. Rancière, J. (1999) *Disagreement: Politics and Philosophy*. Minneapolis, MN: University of Minnesota Press.

CHAPTER 4

1. Wadud, A. (2018) *Crosslight for Youngbird*. New York: Nightboat Books. © 2018, Nightboat Books.

2. Kerbaj, R. and Griffiths, S. (2014) Islamist plot to take over schools. *The Times*, 2 March. Available at: www.thetimes.co.uk/article/islamist-plot-to-take-over-schools-655mhbwovtc (accessed 31 December 2019).

3. Razwan Faraz – one of the teachers singled out by press and politicians – cited in Shackle, S. (2017) Trojan Horse: the real story behind the fake Islamic plot to take over schools. *The Guardian*, 1 September. Available at: www.theguardian.com/world/2017/sep/01/trojan-horse-the-real-story-behind-the-fake-islamic-plot-to-take-over-schools (accessed 31 December 2019).

4. Education Funding Agency (2014) Review of Park View Educational Trust. Available at: https://assets.publishing.service.gov.uk/government/uploads/system/uploads/attachment_data/file/318392/Review_of_Park_View_Educational_Trust.pdf (accessed 31 December 2019).

5. Ofsted (2014) Inspection report: Park View School Academy of Mathematics and Science. Available at: https://files.ofsted.gov.uk/v1/file/2391877 (accessed 31 December 2019).

6. BBC (2014) May and Gove in row over extremism in schools. *BBC*, 4 June. Available at: www.bbc.co.uk/news/education-27691901 (accessed 31 December 2019).

7. To an extent my discussion follows Schwarz, B. (2000) Actually existing postcolonialism. *Radical Philosophy*, 104, 16–24. But also see Schofield, C. (2015) *Enoch Powell and the Making of Postcolonial Britain*. Cambridge: Cambridge University Press; Hirsch, S. (2018) *In the Shadow of Enoch Powell: Race, Locality and Resistance*. Manchester: Manchester University Press. Schwartz, B. (1999) Reveries of race: the closing of the imperial moment. In *Moments of Modernity: Reconstructing Britain, 1945–1964*, ed. B. Conekin, F. Mort and C. Waters. London: Rivers Oram Press, pp. 189–207.

8. On the relationship between citizenship and settlement, see Lawrence, S. (2003) *Archaeologies of the British: Explorations of Identity in the United Kingdom and Its Colonies, 1600–1945*. London: Routledge; Young, R. (2008) *The Idea of English Ethnicity*. Maiden, MA: Blackwell; Gorman, D. (2006) *Imperial Citizenship: Empire and the Question of Belonging*. Manchester: Manchester University Press. Paul, *Whitewashing Britain*.

9. Powell, E. (1970) The enemy within. Speech made to the Turves Green Girls School, Northfield, Birmingham, 13 June.

10. See Heffer, S. (1998) *Like the Roman: The Life of Enoch Powell*. London: Weidenfeld & Nicolson; Smith, A.M. (1994) *New Right Discourse on Race*

and Sexuality: Britain 1968–1990. Cambridge: Cambridge University Press; Valluvan, S. (2019) *The Clamour of Nationalism: Race and Nation in Twenty-First-Century Britain.* Manchester: Manchester University Press; Shilliam, R. (2018) Populism and the spectre of Enoch Powell. *Discover Society,* 4 December. Available at: https://discoversociety.org/2018/12/04/viewpoint-populism-and-the-spectre-of-enoch-powell/ (accessed 31 December 2019).

11. Schwarz, Actually existing postcolonialism.

12. This complements, but also differs from, Valluvan's recent analysis of contemporary nationalism: 'today's nationalism might be best understood as the set of discourses by which primary culpability for significant sociopolitical problems, whether real or imagined, is attributed to various ethno-racial communities who are understood as not belonging', Valluvan, *The Clamour of Nationalism,* p. 1.

13. Niang, A. (2018) Rehistoricizing the sovereignty principle: stature, decline, and anxieties about a foundational norm. In *Recentering Africa in International Relations,* ed. M. Iñiguez de Heredia and Z. Wai. London: Palgrave Macmillan. See also Anghie, A. (2007) *Imperialism, Sovereignty and the Making of International Law.* Cambridge: Cambridge University Press.

14. Schwarz, Actually existing postcolonialism. See also Mercer, K. (1994) *Welcome to the Jungle: New Positions in Black Cultural Studies.* London: Routledge. The rise in concern over 'British values' was an attempt to remake Britishness in the intimate presence of its other. Using Google's Ngram Viewer over Books between 1900 and 2008 to search for British values, incidences remain low until the mid-1940s, from which point they rise by 2,329 per cent. This was brought to my attention by Charlotte Lydia Riley.

15. Shilliam, Populism and the spectre.

16. Powell, The enemy within.

17. Mills, C.W. (2007) Multiculturalism as/and/or anti-racism? In *Multiculturalism and Political Theory,* ed. A.S. Laden and D. Owen. New York: Cambridge University Press, pp. 89–114.

18. In Rose, E.J.B. et al. (1969) *Colour and Citizenship: A Report on British Race Relations.* Oxford: Oxford University Press (p. 25).

19. Melamed, J. (2006) The spirit of neoliberalism: from racial liberalism to neoliberal multiculturalism. *Social Text,* 24(4), 1–24.

20. Gilroy, *Ain't No Black.*

21. Kundnani, A. (2002) The death of multiculturalism. *Race & Class,* 43(4), 67–72.

22. Kundnani, The death of multiculturalism. That this can be understood as 'parallel' is well evidenced by the fact that disparities in pay, academic success, criminalisation and wealth remain when class is controlled for. See also Meghji, A. (2019) *Black Middle-Class Britannia: Identities, Repertoires, Cultural Consumption.* Manchester: Manchester University Press.

23. Allen, R.L. (2005) Reassessing the internal (neo) colonialism theory. *The Black Scholar,* 35(1), 2–11. Sartre, in his preface to *The Wretched of the Earth*

writes that Fanon's analysis illuminates how through: 'dividing and ruling she [*the colonial ruler*] has created a native bourgeoisie [...] Europe has multiplied divisions and opposing groups, has fashioned classes and sometimes even racial prejudices, and has endeavoured by every means to bring about and intensify the stratification of colonized societies.'

24. Pitcher, B. (2016) Race, debt and the welfare state. *New Formations*, 87, 47–63. See also Baumann, G. (1999) *The Multicultural Riddle: Rethinking National, Ethnic and Religious Identities*. London: Routledge. For some critics, it is precisely these shifts that render frameworks of internal colonisation unworkable because they centre racial affinity rather than material class experience. Cedric Johnson argues this because it is complexified by an expanding black middle class, the class fissures being ignored by the thesis. Not only are the production of new forms of social stratification traceable to forms of colonial control, they are not reducible to class stratifications – for all of the reasons discussed in previous chapters. Johnson, C. (2017) The Panthers can't save us now. *Catalyst*, 1(1), 57–87.

25. Lentin, A. (2014) Post-race, post politics: the paradoxical rise of culture after multiculturalism. *Ethnic and Racial Studies*, 37(8), 1268–85. See also Spence, L.K. (2012) The neoliberal turn in black politics. *Souls: A Critical Journal of Black Politics, Culture and Society*, 14(3–4), 139–59.

26. Kapoor, N. (2013) The advancement of racial neoliberalism in Britain. *Ethnic and Racial Studies*, 36(6), 1028–46 (p. 1031). See also Modood, T. (2005) *Multicultural Politics: Racism, Ethnicity and Muslims in Britain*. Edinburgh: Edinburgh University Press.

27. Melamed, J. (2006) The spirit of neoliberalism: from racial liberalism to neoliberal multiculturalism. *Social Text*, 24(489), 1–24.

28. Meghji, A. and Saini, R. (2018) Rationalising racial inequality: ideology, hegemony and post-racialism among the Black and South Asian middle-classes. *Sociology*, 52, 671–87. See also Lentin, A. (2004) *Racism and Anti-Racism in Europe*. London: Pluto Press.

29. Hall, S. (1996) Race, articulation, and societies structured in dominance. In *Black British Cultural Studies: A Reader*, ed. H.A. Baker, Jr, M. Diawara and R.H. Lindeborg. Chicago, IL: University of Chicago Press, pp. 16–60. See also Moreton-Robinson, A.M. (2014) Imagining the good Indigenous citizen: race war and the pathology of patriarchal white sovereignty. In *History, Power, Text: Cultural Studies and Indigenous Studies*, ed. T. Neale, C. McKinnon and E. Vincent. Sydney: UTS Press, pp. 310–30.

30. Brah, A. (1996) *Cartographies of Diaspora: Contesting Identities*. New York: Routledge.

31. Cantle, T. (2001) *Community Cohesion: A Report of the Independent Review Team*. London: Home Office.

32. Lentin and Titley, *The Crises of Multiculturalism*.

33. Alexander, C. (2018) Breaking black: the death of ethnic and racial studies in Britain. *Ethnic and Racial Studies*, 41(6), 1034–54 (p. 1044). See also Meer, N. and Nayak, A. (2015) Race ends where? Race, racism and contemporary sociology. *Sociology*, 49(6), 3–20.

34. Kapoor, N. (2018) *Deport, Deprive, Extradite: 21st Century State Extremism.* London: Verso Books; Kapoor, N. and Narkowicz, K. (2019) Characterising citizenship: race, criminalisation and the extension of internal borders. *Sociology,* 53(4), 652–70.

35. Several elements of the following draw upon Miller, D. and Sabir, R. (2012) Counter-terrorism as counterinsurgency in the UK 'war on terror'. In *Counter-terrorism and State Political Violence,* ed. D. Whyte and S. Poynting. London: Routledge, pp. 12–32.

36. Wagner, Savage warfare; Newsinger, J. (2015) *British Counterinsurgency.* Basingstoke: Palgrave Macmillan; French, D. (2011) *The British Way in Counterinsurgency, 1945–1967.* Oxford: Oxford University Press; Bennett, H. (2013) *Fighting the Mau Mau: The British Army and Counter-insurgency in the Kenya Emergency.* Cambridge: Cambridge University Press; Thompson, R. (1978) *Defeating Communist Insurgency: Experiences from Malaya and Vietnam.* London: Palgrave Macmillan.

37. Gwynn, C.W. (1934) *Imperial Policing.* London: Macmillan. See also Guha, R. (1999) *Elementary Aspects of Peasant Insurgency in Colonial India.* Durham, NC: Duke University Press; Callwell, C.E. (1903) *Small Wars: Their Principles and Practice.* London: HM Stationery Office.

38. Natarajan, R. (2013) Ties of blood: how Thatcher altered British. *Open Democracy.* Available at: www.opendemocracy.net/en/opendemocracyuk/ties-of-blood-how-thatcher-altered-british/ (accessed 31 December 2019).

39. Kilcullen, D.J. (2005) Countering global insurgency. *Journal of Strategic Studies,* 28(4), 597–617.

40. Sharma, S. and Nijjar, J. (2018) The racialized surveillant assemblage: Islam and the fear of terrorism. *Popular Communication,* 16(1), 72–85 (p. 74).

41. Kundnani, A. (2012) Radicalisation: the journey of a concept. *Race & Class,* 54(2), 3–25. See also Manzoor-Khan, S. (2019) Notes on Shamima. *The Brown Hijabi,* 18 February. Available at: https://thebrownhijabi.com/2019/02/18/notes-on-shamima/ (accessed 31 December 2019).

42. Qureshi, A. (2017) Blacklisted: the secretive Home Office unit silencing voices of dissent. *CAGE.* Available at: www.cage.ngo/product/blacklisted-report (accessed 31 December 2019); Qurashi, F. (2018) The Prevent strategy and the UK 'war on terror': embedding infrastructures of surveillance in Muslim communities. *Palgrave Communications,* 4, 17.

43. Miller and Sabir, Counter-terrorism as counterinsurgency, p. 16. On their colonial roots, see Linstrum, E. (2016) *Ruling Minds: Psychology in the British Empire.* Cambridge, MA: Harvard University Press.

44. Miller and Sabir, Counter-terrorism as counterinsurgency, p. 25.

45. Miller, D. and Sabir, R. (2012) Propaganda and terrorism. In *Media and Terrorism: Global Perspectives,* ed. D. Freedman and D.K. Thussu. London: SAGE, pp. 77–94.

46. Hayes, B. and Qureshi, A. (2016) 'We are completely independent': The Home Office, Breakthrough Media and the PREVENT counter narrative industry. CAGE, London.

47. Home Office (2016) *Building a Stronger Britain Together Guidance*. London: Home Office. Available at: www.gov.uk/guidance/building-a-stronger-britain-together (accessed 31 December 2019).

48. Manzoor-Khan, S. (2019) Statement on building a stronger Britain together counter-extremism fund and withdrawal from Bradford Literature Festival. *The Brown Hijabi*, 7 July. Available at: https://thebrownhijabi.com/2019/07/01/statement-on-building-a-stronger-britain-together-counter-extremism-fund-and-withdrawal-from-bradford-literature-festival-full-text/ (accessed 31 December 2019).

49. Grierson, J. (2019) Counter-terror police running secret Prevent database. *The Guardian*, 6 October. Available at: www.theguardian.com/uk-news/2019/oct/06/counter-terror-police-are-running-secret-prevent-database (accessed 31 December 2019). See also Smithson, R. and White, C. (2017) Birmingham City Council Prevent duty: Early help and children's social care extremism guidance and assessment support.

50. Perra, A. (2018) UK Statutory Prevent Duty. *Global Security Review*, 3 August. Available at: https://globalsecurityreview.com/uk-statutory-prevent-duty-creation-consequences-police-state/ (accessed 31 December 2019).

51. Sharma, N. (2015) Racism. In *Citizenship and Its Others*, ed. B. Anderson and V. Hughes. Basingstoke: Palgrave Macmillan, pp. 98–118 (pp. 109–10). See also Papadopoulos, D., Stephenson, N. and Tsianos, V. (2008) *Escape Routes: Control and Subversion in the Twenty-First Century*. London: Pluto Press; Goldberg, D.T. (2009) *The Threat of Race*. Oxford: Blackwell.

52. McCulloch, J. and Pickering, S. (2009) Pre-crime and counter-terrorism. *British Journal of Criminology*, 49(5), 628–45.

53. Kundnani, Radicalisation, p. 4.

54. In McCulloch and Pickering, Pre-crime and counter-terrorism.

55. Zedner, L. (2007) Pre-crime and post-criminology? *Theoretical Criminology*, 11, 261–81 (pp. 261–62). See also Sageman, M. (2004) *Understanding Terror Networks*. Philadelphia, PA: University of Pennsylvania Press; Sageman, M. (2011) *Leaderless Jihad: Terror Networks in the Twenty-First Century*. Philadelphia, PA: University of Pennsylvania Press.

56. NHS (2017) Prevent training and competencies framework. Available at: www.england.nhs.uk/publication/prevent-training-and-competencies-framework/ (accessed 31 December 2019), p. 5.

57. HM Government (2010) *Channel: Supporting Individuals Vulnerable to Recruitment by Violent Extremists – A Guide for Local Partnerships*. London: Home Office (pp. 9–10).

58. Townsend, M. (2019) Brain scans show social exclusion creates jihadists, say researchers. *The Guardian*, 6 January. Available at: www.theguardian.com/uk-news/2019/jan/06/social-exclusion-radicalisation-brain-scans (accessed 31 December 2019).

59. Munk, T.B. (2017) 100,000 false positives for every real terrorist: why anti-terror algorithms don't work. *First Monday*, 22(9). See also Sharma and Nijjar, The racialized surveillant assemblage, p. 81; Qureshi, A. (2016) The 'science' of pre-crime: the secret radicalisation study underpinning prevent.

CAGE. Available at: https://cage.ngo/wp-content/uploads/2016/09/CAGE-Science-Pre-Crime-Report.pdf (accessed 31 December 2019).

60. Mbembe, A. (2019) Thoughts on the planetary: an interview with Achille Mbembe. *New Frame,* 5 September. Available at: www.newframe.com/thoughts-on-the-planetary-an-interview-with-achille-mbembe/ (accessed 31 December 2019).

61. Foucault, M. (1982) The subject and power. *Critical Inquiry,* 8(4), 777–95 (p. 789).

62. Ahmed, S. (2017) *Living a Feminist Life.* Durham, NC: Duke University Press (p. 43).

63. McCulloch and Pickering, Pre-crime and counter-terrorism.

64. NATO (2016) Allied joint doctrine for counter-insurgency (COIN), 1 July. Available at: https://assets.publishing.service.gov.uk/government/uploads/system/uploads/attachment_data/file/625810/doctrine_nato_coin_ajp_3_4_4.pdf (accessed 31 December 2019).

65. Hall, S., Hobson, D., Lowe, A. and Willis, P. (eds) (2003) *Culture, Media, Language: Working Papers in Cultural Studies, 1972–79.* London: Routledge (p. 36).

66. Miller and Sabir, Counter-terrorism as counterinsurgency, p. 12.

67. Ahmed, S. (2004) Affective economies. *Social Text,* 22(2), 117–39 (p. 126).

68. Bourke, J. (2006) *Fear: A Cultural History.* Berkeley, CA: Counterpoint Press (p. x).

69. Puar, J.K. (2017) *Terrorist Assemblages: Homonationalism in Queer Times.* Durham, NC: Duke University Press (p. 160).

70. Puar, *Terrorist Assemblages,* p. 185. See also Sharma and Nijjar, The racialized surveillant assemblage.

71. On bordering in the British university system as making the 'student identity is now contingent on non-academic criteria, that of physical presence at checkpoints', see Jenkins, M. (2014) Commentary. *The Geographical Journal,* 180, 265–70.

72. Pawlak, P. (2012) The unintentional development of the EU's security governance beyond borders. *European Foreign Affairs Review,* 2(1), 87–107.

73. De Genova, N. (2016) The 'crisis' of the European border regime: towards a Marxist theory of borders. *International Socialism,* 150, 31–54.

74. Hyndman, J. (2000) *Managing Displacement: Refugees and the Politics of Humanitarianism.* Minneapolis, MN: University of Minnesota Press.

75. Balibar, *We, the People of Europe?*

76. Mbembe, A. (2019) Bodies as borders. *European South,* 4. Available at: http://europeansouth.postcolonialitalia.it (accessed 31 December 2019).

77. Walia, H. (2013) *Undoing border imperialism.* Chicago, IL: AK Press (p. 38).

78. Cazeneuve, B. and May, T. (2014) Joint declaration by M. Bernard Cazeneuve, Minister of the Interior, and Mrs Theresa May, Home Secretary of the United Kingdom. Available at: www.statewatch.org/news/2014/sep/uk-fr-2014-09-20-joint-statement-calais-en.pdf (accessed 31 December 2019).

79. De Genova, N. (2005) *Working the Boundaries: Race, Space, and 'Illegality' in Mexican Chicago*. Durham, NC: Duke University Press (p. 234).
80. For detailed history of New Labour's role in these policies, see Consterdine, E. (2018) *Labour's Immigration Policy: The Making of the Migration State*. Dordrecht: Springer.
81. Bosworth, M. (2014) *Inside Immigration Detention*. Oxford: Oxford University Press.
82. CorporateWatch (2018) UK Border regime immigration raids briefing. *Corporate Watch*. Available at: https://corporatewatch.org/uk-border-regime-immigration-raids-briefing-2018/ (accessed 31 December 2019).
83. McNevin, A. (2006) Political belonging in a neoliberal era: the struggle of the sans-papiers. *Citizenship Studies*, 10(2), 135–51 (p. 141).
84. Lefebvre, H. (1991) *The Production of Space*. Oxford: Blackwell.
85. Mbembe, Bodies as borders. See also Parizot, C. (2018) Viscous spatialities: the spaces of the Israeli permit regime of access and movement. *South Atlantic Quarterly*, 117(1), 21–42; Bhattacharyya, *Rethinking Racial Capitalism*; Goldberg, D., Jadhav, S. and Younis, T. (2017) Prevent: what is pre-criminal space? *BJPsych Bulletin*, 41(4), 208–11; Peteet, J. (2018) Closure's temporality: the cultural politics of time and waiting. *The South Atlantic Quarterly*, 117(1), 43–64.
86. Sharma and Nijjar, The racialized surveillant assemblage, p. 79.
87. Miller and Sabir, Counter-terrorism as counterinsurgency, p. 19.
88. Mbembe, Thoughts on the planetary.
89. United Against Refugees (2019) List of 36570 documented deaths of refugees and migrants due to the restrictive policies of Fortress Europe. Available at: http://unitedagainstrefugeedeaths.eu/wp-content/uploads/2014/06/ListofDeathsActual.pdf (accessed 31 December 2019).
90. Gordon, A.F. (2008) *Ghostly Matters: Haunting and the Sociological Imagination*. Minneapolis, MN: University of Minnesota Press (p. 115).
91. Anderson, W.C. and Samudzi, Z. (2018) *As Black as Resistance: Finding the Conditions for Liberation*. Chicago, IL: AK Press (p. 47).
92. Husain, N. (2010) Counterinsurgency's comeback: can a colonialist strategy be reinvented? *Boston Review*, 1 September. Available at: http://bostonreview.net/world/counterinsurgency's-comeback (accessed 31 December 2019).
93. Parizot, Viscous spatialities, p. 38. See also Gilroy, P. (2004) *Postcolonial Melancholia*. New York: Columbia University Press (p. 51).
94. Ciccariello-Maher, G. (2017) *Decolonizing Dialectics*. Durham, NC: Duke University Press (p. 81).
95. Fanon, *The Wretched of the Earth*, p. 44.
96. In Fanon, *The Wretched of the Earth*, p. 44.
97. Gordon, A. (2011) Some thoughts on haunting and futurity. *Borderlands*, 10(2), 2.

CHAPTER 5

1. Energy, S. (2019) *Galaxy Walk*. Bristol: Burning Eye Books. © 2019, Burning Eye Books.

2. Davies, *The Limits of Neoliberalism*, p. xiv.

3. Harvey, *A Brief History*, p. 20.

4. Brown, *Undoing the Demos*.

5. Davies, *The Limits of Neoliberalism*, p. xii.

6. Slobodian, Q. (2018) *Globalists: The End of Empire and the Birth of Neoliberalism*. Cambridge, MA: Harvard University Press.

7. Cooper, M. (2008) *Life as Surplus: Biotechnology and Capitalism in the Neoliberal Era*. Seattle, WA: University of Washington Press; Elichirigoity, F. (1999) *Planet Management: Limits to Growth, Computer Simulation, and the Emergence of Global Spaces*. Evanston, IL: Northwestern University Press; Locher, F. (2013) Cold war pastures: Garrett Hardin and the 'tragedy of the commons'. *Revue d'histoire moderne et contemporaine*, 1, 7–36.

8. Hayek, F. (1988) *The Fatal Conceit: The Errors of Socialism*. London: Routledge (p. 59).

9. Hayek, F. (1949) *Individualism and Economic Order*. London: Routledge (p. 88).

10. Mirowski, P. (2014) The political movement that dared not speak its own name: the neoliberal thought collective under erasure. *Institute for New Economic Thinking Working Papers*, 23, 1–34 (p. 12).

11. In Mirowski, P. (2013) *Never Let a Serious Crisis Go to Waste: How Neoliberalism Survived the Financial Meltdown*. London: Verso (p. 53).

12. Hayek, F. (1944/2001) *The Road to Serfdom*. Hove: Psychology Press (p. 40).

13. Lynch, M. (2012) Democracy as a space of reasons. In *Truth in Politics*, ed. J. Elkins and A. Norris. Philadelphia, PA: University of Pennsylvania Press, pp. 114–29 (p. 117).

14. Hayek, F. (1973) *Rules and Order*. Vol. 1 of *Law, Legislation and Liberty*. London: Routledge & Kegan Paul.

15. Dean, M. (2014) Rethinking neoliberalism. *Journal of Sociology*, 50(2), 150–63 (p. 159).

16. See the discussion in Slobodian, *Globalists*.

17. Bashford, A. (2014) *Global Population: History, Geopolitics, and Life on Earth*. New York: Columbia University Press; Ranganathan, S. (2016) Global commons. *European Journal of International Law*, 27(3), 693–717.

18. Hardin, G. (1968) The tragedy of the commons. *Science*, 162(3859), 1243–48.

19. Mitropoulos, A. (2016) The commons. In *Gender: Nature* (MacMillan Interdisciplinary Handbooks), ed. I.V.D. Tuin. Farmington Hills, MI: Macmillan Reference USA, pp. 165–81 (p. 176).

20. Ranganathan, Global commons, p. 699. See also Nelson, S.H. (2014) Beyond the limits to growth: ecology and the neoliberal counterrevolution. *Antipode*, 47, 461–80.

21. Nixon, R. (2012) Neoliberalism, genre, and 'the tragedy of the commons'. *PMLA*, 127(3), 593–99 (pp. 595–96).

22. Tendayi Achiume, E (2019) Migration as decolonisation. *Stanford Law Review*, 71(6), 1509–73. Available at: www.stanfordlawreview.org/print/article/migration-as-decolonization/ (accessed 24 October 2019).

23. Hardin, G. (1974) Lifeboat ethics: the case against helping the poor. *Psychology Today*, 8(4), 38–43.

24. The publication *New Socialist* is an excellent example of the diversity of positions and antagonisms at work within this project, and is particularly emblematic of a critical stance towards the trajectories that I am interested in here.

25. Bolton, M. and Pitts, F.H. (2018) Corbynism and Blue Labour: post-liberalism and national populism in the British Labour party. *British Politics*, 1–22 (p. 4).

26. Mason, J.W. (2017) A cautious case for economic nationalism. *Dissent Magazine*. Available at: www.dissentmagazine.org/article/cautious-case-economic-nationalism-global-capitalism (accessed 31 December 2019).

27. Merchant, J. (2018) Fantasies of secession: a critique of left economic nationalism. *Brooklyn Rail*. Available at: https://brooklynrail.org/2018/02/field-notes/Fantasies-of-Secession-A-Critique-of-Left-Economic-Nationalism (accessed 31 December 2019).

28. Mason, P. (2018) What kind of capitalism is it possible for the left to build? *Open Democracy*, 20 June. Available at: https://neweconomics. opendemocracy.net/kind-capitalism-possible-left-build/ (accessed 25 March 2020).

29. For analysis of how media discourses and political narrativisation of immigration has given credence to this view, see Jones, H. et al. (2018) Go home? The politics of immigration controversies. *Refuge: Canada's Journal on Refugees*, 34(1), 76–78.

30. Corbyn, J. (2017) Interview with Andrew Marr. BBC, 23 July.

31. For similar views, see also Streeck, W. (2019) Wolfgang Streeck: a second referendum could tear society apart more than the first. *New Statesman*, 20 March; Žižek, S. (2016) *Against the Double Blackmail: Refugees, Terror and Other Troubles with the Neighbours*. London: Penguin; Streeck, W. (2018) Between charity and justice: remarks on the social construction of immigration policy in rich democracies. *Culture, Practice & Europeanization*, 3(2), 3–22.

32. Labour Party (2017) Alternative models of ownership. Report to Shadow Chancellor of the Exchequer. Available at: www.labour.org.uk/page/-/PDFs/9472_Alternative%20Models%20of%20Ownership%20all_v4.pdf (accessed 20 July 2019).

33. Massey, D. (1993) Power geometry and a progressive sense of place. In *Mapping the Futures: Local Cultures, Global Change*, ed. J. Bird, B. Curtis, T. Putnam and L. Tickner. London: Routledge, pp. 59–69 (p. 61).

34. Graham, M. and Anwar, M.A. (2019) The global gig economy: towards a planetary labour market? *First Monday*, 24(4). See also Peck, J. (2017) *Offshore: Exploring the Worlds of Global Outsourcing*. Oxford: Oxford University Press (p. 42).

35. Mitropoulos, A. and Kiem, M. (2015) Cross-border operations. *The New Inquiry*, 18.

36. Mitropoulos, A. (2015) Archipelago of risk: uncertainty, borders and migration detention systems. *New Formations* 84–85, 163–83.
37. El-Enany, N. (2020) *Bordering Britain: Law, Race and Empire*. Manchester: Manchester University Press.
38. Mitropoulos, A. (2019) Workers of the world unite. *New Socialist*. Available at: https://newsocialist.org.uk/workers-world-unite/ (accessed 31 December 2019).
39. Mitropoulos, Workers of the world unite.
40. Embery, P. (2018) Labour's conspiracy of silence on immigration. *Unherd*. Available at: https://unherd.com/2018/09/labours-conspiracy-silence-immigration/ (accessed 31 December 2019).
41. Mitropoulos, Workers of the world unite. See also Cope, *Wealth of (Some) Nations*, p. 161.
42. Srnicek, N. and Williams, A. (2015) *Inventing the Future: Postcapitalism and a World Without Work*. London: Verso. See also Graham, M., Hjorth, I. and Lehdonvirta, V. (2017) Digital labour and development: impacts of global digital labour platforms and the gig economy on worker livelihoods. *Transfer: European Review of Labour and Research*, 23(2), 135–62.
43. Srnicek, N. (2018) *Platform Capitalism*. Cambridge: Polity.
44. Department for Work and Pensions (2018) Employment by Ethnicity, Data source: Annual Population Survey 2004–2017. Available at: www.ethnicity-facts-figures.service. gov.uk/work-pay-and-benefits/employment/employment/latest (accessed 21 October 2019).
45. Equality and Human Rights Commission (2016) Healing a divided Britain: the need for a comprehensive race equality strategy. Available at: www.equalityhumanrights.com/sites/default/files/healing_a_divided_britain_-_the_need_for_a_comprehensive_race_equality_strategy_final.pdf (accessed 21 October 2019). See also Zwysen, W. and Longhi, S. (2016) Labour market disadvantage of ethnic minority British graduates: university choice, parental background or neighbourhood? ISER Working Paper Series. Available at: www.iser.essex.ac.uk/research/publications/working-papers/iser/2016-02 (accessed 21 October 2019).
46. Srnicek, *Platform Capitalism*, ch. 2.
47. TUC (2017) Insecure work and ethnicity. Available at: www.tuc.org.uk/sites/default/files/Insecure%20work%20and%20ethnicity_0.pdf (accessed 21 October 2018).
48. Srnicek, *Platform Capitalism*, p. 78. See also Benanav, A. (2019) Automation and the future of work. *New Left Review*, 119, 5–38.
49. Huws, U. and Joyce, S. (2016) Size of the UK's 'gig economy' revealed for the first time. Crowd Working Survey, Foundation for European Progressive Studies (FEPS) and UNI Europa, February.
50. McNevin, Political belonging in the neoliberal era.
51. Shilliam, *Race and the Undeserving Poor*.
52. Mason, P. (2018) To beat the Tories, Labour needs to win in areas where UKIP has faded away. *iNews*, 20 May. Available at: https://inews.co.uk/

opinion/comment/paul-mason-ukip-general-election-511204 (accessed 31 December 2019).

53. Corbyn, J. (2018) Build it in Britain again. *LabourList*, 24 July.

54. Mason, P. (2017) We can escape Brexit doom with one small tweak to free movement. *The Guardian*, 16 January. Available at: www.theguardian.com/commentisfree/2017/jan/16/we-can-escape-brexit-doom-with-one-small-tweak-to-free-movement (accessed 31 December 2019).

55. Honeycombe-Foster, M. (2019) Len McCluskey blames Jeremy Corbyn's 'London' mindset and 'incontinent' policies for Labour defeat. *PoliticsHome*, 13 December. Available at: www.politicshome.com/news/uk/political-parties/labour-party/jeremy-corbyn/news/108558/len-mccluskey-blames-jeremy-corbyns (accessed 4 January 2020).

56. Fazi, T. (2020) Twitter, 8 January. Available at: https://twitter.com/battleforeurope/status/1214823325022720000 (accessed 9 January 2020).

57. See Federici, S. (2012) *Revolution at Point Zero: Housework, Reproduction, and Feminist Struggle*. San Francisco, CA: PM Press (p. 21).

58. Phillips, L. and Rozworski, M. (2019) *The People's Republic of Wal-Mart: How the World's Biggest Corporations Are Laying the Foundation for Socialism*. New York: Verso.

59. Mason, P. (2019) Twitter, 25 November. Available at: https://twitter.com/paulmasonnews/status/1198909556430163968 (accessed 31 December 2019).

60. Bridge, M. (2019) Deliveroo and Uber were told of illegal workers months ago. *The Times*, 7 January. Available at: www.thetimes.co.uk/article/deliveroo-and-uber-were-told-of-illegal-workers-months-ago-85wtn2b20 (accessed 31 December 2019).

61. Secretary of State for the Home Department (2018) The UK's future skills-based immigration system. Available at: https://assets.publishing.service.gov.uk/government/uploads/system/uploads/attachment_data/file/766465/The-UKs-future-skills-based-immigration-system-print-ready.pdf (accessed 31 December 2019).

62. Freedom of Information (FOI) request 30574.

63. Kapoor, N. (2019) Citizenship deprivation at the nexus of race, gender and geopolitics. *Verso Blog*, 22 February. Available at: www.versobooks.com/blogs/4250-citizenship-deprivation-at-the-nexus-of-race-gender-and-geopolitics (accessed 31 December 2019).

64. Murray, L. (2019) Why a third runway at Heathrow fails the litmus test for environmental breakdown. *New Statesman*. Available at: www.newstatesman.com/politics/uk/2019/06/why-third-runway-heathrow-litmus-test-environmental-breakdown (accessed 31 December 2019).

65. Rawoot, I. (2014) Mozambique fishermen decry gas drilling. *Al Jazeera*. Available at: www.aljazeera.com/indepth/features/2014/01/mozambique-fishermen-decry-gas-drilling-201411414032481195.html (accessed 31 December 2019); JA4Change (2019) Climate criminals ENI and Shell. JA4Change, 13 May. Available at: https://ja4change.wordpress.com/2019/05/13/climate-criminals-eni-and-shell/13/15 (accessed 31 December 2019).

66. JA4Change (2019) JA visit finds confusion and distrust in Cabo Delgado gas region. *JA4Change*, 27 June. Available at: https://ja4change.org/2019/06/27/ja-visit-finds-confusion-and-distrust-in-cabo-delgado-gas-region/ (accessed 31 December 2019).

67. Partington, R. (2019) Britain now G7's biggest net importer of CO_2 emissions per capita, says ONS. *The Guardian*, 21 October. Available at: www.theguardian.com/uk-news/2019/oct/21/britain-is-g7s-biggest-net-importer-of-co2-emissions-per-capita-says-ons (accessed 31 December 2019).

68. Trafford, J. (2019) Against green nationalism. *Open Democracy*, 29 March. Available at: www.opendemocracy.net/en/opendemocracyuk/against-green-nationalism (accessed 25 October 2019).

69. Mitropoulos, A. (2018) Lifeboat capitalism, catastrophism, borders. *Dispatches Journal*, 1 [online], 19 November. Available at: http://dispatches journal.org/articles/162/ (accessed 25 October 2019).

CHAPTER 6

1. Kalulé, P. (2019) *Kalimba*. Cornwall, UK: Guillemot Press. © 2019, Guillemot Press.

2. Simone, *Improvised Lives*, p. 90.

3. See Pinderhughes, Toward a new theory.

4. Pinderghughes, Toward a new theory, p. 251.

5. Woodard, K. (1999) *A Nation within a Nation: Amiri Baraka (LeRoi Jones) and Black Power Politics*. Chapel Hill, NC: University of North Carolina Press. Singh, N.P. (2004) *Black Is a Country: Race and the Unfinished Struggle for Democracy*. Cambridge, MA: Harvard University Press.

6. Angelo, A.M. (2009) The Black Panthers in London, 1967–1972: a diasporic struggle navigates the Black Atlantic. *Radical History Review*, 103, 17–35; Waters, R. (2018) *Thinking Black: Britain, 1964-1985*. Oakland, CA: University of California Press; Narayan, J. (2019) British Black Power: the anti-imperialism of political blackness and the problem of nativist socialism. *The Sociological Review*, 22.

7. Fanon, *Wretched of the Earth*, p. 179. See Sajed, A. (2019) Re-remembering Third Worldism: an affirmative critique of national liberation in Algeria. *Middle East Critique*, 28(3), 243–60; Sajed, A. and Seidel, T. (2019) Introduction: escaping the nation? National consciousness and the horizons of decolonization. *Interventions*, 21(5), 583–91.

8. Fanon, *Wretched of the Earth*, p. 142.

9. Sajed and Seidel, Introduction: escaping the nation, p. 585.

10. Wynter, S. and McKittrick, K. (2014) Unparalleled catastrophe for our species? Or, to give humanness a different future. *Conversations*, 8 December, pp. 9–89. See also Nyers, P. (2010) No one is illegal between city and nation. *Studies in Social Justice*, 4(2), 127–43.

11. Balibar, *We, the People of Europe?*, p. 109.

12. Walzer, M. (1989) The distribution of membership. In *Boundaries: National Autonomy and Its Limits*, ed. Peter G. Brown and Henry Shue. Lanham, MD: Rowman & Littlefield, p. 39.

13. Benhabib, S. (1992) *Situating the Self: Gender, Community, and Post modernism in Contemporary Ethics.* London: Routledge; Habermas, J. (1996) *Between Facts and Norms.* Cambridge: Polity Press; Mouffe, C. (1999) Deliberative democracy or agonistic pluralism? *Social Research,* 66(3), 745–58; Young, I.M. (1990) *Justice and the Politics of Difference.* Princeton, NJ: Princeton University Press.

14. Young, *Justice and the Politics of Difference,* p. 101.

15. Povinelli, E.A. (2013) *Economies of Abandonment: Social Belonging and Endurance in Late Liberalism.* Durham, NC: Duke University Press. See also Goldberg, *The Threat of Race.*

16. On the complications arising with the decolonisation project in the context of universities, see Bhambra, G.K., Nisancioglu, K. and Gebrial, D. (2018) *Decolonizing the University.* London: Pluto Press.

17. Marriott, D. (2011) Inventions of existence: Sylvia Wynter, Frantz Fanon, sociogeny, and the damned. *CR: The New Centennial Review,* 11(3), 45–89 (p. 54).

18. Hardin, G. (1991) Conspicuous benevolence and the population bomb. *Chronicles,* 15, 20–22.

19. Read, R. (2014) Love immigrants, rather than large-scale immigration. *The Ecologist* [online], 19 June. Available at: https://theecologist.org/2014/jun/19/love-immigrants-rather-large-scale-immigration (accessed 25 October 2019).

20. Isin, E.F. (2009) Citizenship in flux: the figure of the activist citizen. *Subjectivity,* 29(1), 367–88 (p. 383).

21. Tendayi Achiume, Migration as decolonisation, p. 1522. See also Wilder, G. (2015) *Freedom Time: Negritude, Decolonization, and the Future of the World.* Durham, NC: Duke University Press.

22. Pasura, D. (2010) Competing meanings of the diaspora: the case of Zimbabweans in Britain. *Journal of Ethnic and Migration Studies,* 36(9), 1445–61 (p. 1448–49). This echoes Sivanandan's infamous quip that 'we are here because you were there'.

23. Pasura, Competing meanings of the diaspora, pp. 1448–49.

24. Anderson, B., Sharma, N. and Wright, C. (2009) Why no borders? *Refuge: Canada's Journal on Refugees,* 26(2), 5–18.

25. Pinderhughes, Toward a new theory, p. 252.

26. El-Enany, *Bordering Britain.*

27. In Tyler, I. (2010) Designed to fail: a biopolitics of British citizenship. *Citizenship Studies,* 14(1), 61–74 (p. 64).

28. Brand, D. (2019) *Theory.* Toronto: Vintage Books.

29. See also Wynter and McKittrick, Unparalleled catastrophe.

30. Roediger, *Toward the Abolition of Whiteness.*

31. Cope, *The Wealth of (Some) Nations,* p. 163.

32. Harney, S. and Moten, F. (2017) Base faith. *E-Flux Journal*, 86, 1–7. Available at: www.e-flux.com/journal/86/162888/base-faith/ (accessed 31 December 2019).

33. Tomba, M. (2019) *Insurgent Universality: An Alternative Legacy of Modernity*. New York: Oxford University Press.

34. Tomba, M. (2015) 1793: the neglected legacy of insurgent universality. *History of the Present*, 5(2), 109–36 (p. 122).

35. Simone, *Improvised Lives*, p. 22.

36. Manzoor-Khan, *Postcolonial Banter*. © 2019, Verve Press.

37. Ciccariello-Maher, *Decolonizing Dialectics*, pp. 130–32.

38. See Cabral, A. (1979) The weapon of theory: presuppositions and objectives of national liberation in relation to social structure. In *Unity and Struggle: Speeches and Writings of Amilcar Cabral*, ed. PAIGC. New York and London: Monthly Review Press, pp. 119–37.

39. Ahmed, S. (2012) Feminist killjoys (and other willful subjects). *Cahiers du Genre*, 2, 77–98.

40. Ahmed, *Living a Feminist Life*, p. 199.

41. Wright, O. (2019) Labour's no-borders policy would take a wrecking ball to Britain. *Conservative Woman*. Available at: www.conservativewoman.co.uk/labours-no-borders-policy-would-take-a-wrecking-ball-to-britain/ (accessed 31 December 2019).

42. Tomba, M. (2018) Insurgent university. *Krisis*, 2. Available at: https://krisis.eu/insurgent-universality/ (accessed 31 December 2019).

43. As the Zapatistas wrote in their 1996 Fourth Declaration.

44. Mbembe, Thoughts on the planetary.

45. With thanks to Petero Kalulé for this phrasing, against the overdetermination of the eschatological form 'to save the world'. See also Sharpe, C. (2016) *In the Wake: On Blackness and Being*. Durham: Duke University Press; Wilderson, F. (2013). *Red, White & Black: Cinema and the structure of U.S. antagonisms*. Durham: Duke University Press.

46. Kalulé, *Kalimba*. © 2019, Guillemot Press.

Indicative Bibliography

Ahmed, S. (2004) Affective economies. *Social Text*, 22(2), 117–39.

Ahmed, S. (2017) *Living a Feminist Life*. Durham, NC: Duke University Press.

Alexander, C. (2010) *The Asian Gang: Ethnicity, Identity, Masculinity*. Oxford: Berg.

Anderson, W.C. and Samudzi, Z. (2018) *As Black as Resistance: Finding the Conditions for Liberation*. Chicago, IL: AK Press.

Anzaldúa, G. (1987) *La frontera/Borderlands: The New Mestiza*. San Francisco, CA: Aunt Lute.

Arghiri, E. (1972) *Unequal Exchange*. New York: Monthly Review Press.

Balibar, E. (2009) *We, the People of Europe? Reflections on Transnational Citizenship*. Princeton, NJ: Princeton University Press.

Bhambra, G.K. (2009) *Rethinking Modernity: Postcolonialism and the Sociological Imagination*. Basingstoke: Palgrave Macmillan.

Bhandar, B. (2018) *Colonial Lives of Property: Law, Land, and Racial Regimes of Ownership*. Durham, NC: Duke University Press.

Bhattacharyya, G. (2018) *Rethinking Racial Capitalism: Questions of Reproduction and Survival*. Lanham, MD: Rowman & Littlefield International.

Byrd, J.A., Goldstein, A., Melamed, J. and Reddy, C. (2018) Predatory value: economies of dispossession and disturbed relationalities. *Social Text*, 135, 1–18.

Cope, Z. (2019) *Wealth of (Some) Nations: Imperialism and the Mechanics of Value Transfer*. London: Pluto Press.

Coulthard, G.S. (2014) *Red Skin, White Masks: Rejecting the Colonial Politics of Recognition*. Minneapolis, MN: Minnesota University Press.

Davis, A. (2011) *Are Prisons Obsolete?* New York: Seven Stories Press.

De Genova, N. (2016) The 'crisis' of the European border regime: towards a Marxist theory of borders. *International Socialism*, 150, 31–54.

El-Enany, N. (2020) *Bordering Britain: Law, Race and Empire*. Manchester: Manchester University Press.

Elkins, C. (2005) *Imperial Reckoning: The Untold Story of Britain's Gulag in Kenya*. London: Macmillan.

Energy, S. (2019) *Galaxy Walk*. Bristol: Burning Eye Books.

Fanon, F. (1963) *Wretched of the Earth*. New York: Grove Weidenfeld.

Fanon, F. (2018) Why we use violence. In *Alienation and Freedom*, ed. R. Young and J. Khalfa. London: Bloomsbury, pp. 653–60.

Ferreira da Silva, D. (2007) *Toward a Global Idea of Race*. Minneapolis, MN: University of Minnesota Press.

Ferreira da Silva, D. (2009) No-bodies: law, raciality and violence. *Griffith Law Review*, 18(2), 212–36.

Field, P., Bunce, R., Hassan, L. and Peacock, M. (eds) (2019) *Here to Stay, Here to Fight: A Race Today Anthology*. London: Pluto Press.

Getachew, A. (2019) *Worldmaking after Empire: The Rise and Fall of Self-Determination*. Princeton, NJ: Princeton University Press.

Gilroy, P. (1982) The myth of black criminality. *Socialist Register*, 19, 47–56.

Gilroy, P. (2013) *There Ain't No Black in the Union Jack*. London: Routledge.

Glissant, E. (1992) *Caribbean Discourse: Selected Essays*. Charlottesville, VA: University of Virginia Press.

Goldberg, D.T. (1993) *Racist Culture*. Cambridge, MA: Blackwell.

Goldberg, D.T. (2009) *The Threat of Race*. Oxford: Blackwell.

Goldstein, A. (2014) Finance and foreclosure in the colonial present. *Radical History Review*, 118, 42–63.

Gutzmore, C. (1983) Capital, 'black youth' and crime. *Race & Class*, 25(2), 13–30.

Hall, S., Critcher, C., Jefferson, T., Clarke, J. and Roberts, B. (2013) *Policing the Crisis: Mugging, the State and Law and Order*. London: Macmillan International Higher Education.

Harney, S. and Moten, F. (2017) Base faith. *E-Flux Journal*, 86, 1–7. Available at: www.e-flux.com/journal/86/162888/base-faith/ (accessed 31 December 2019).

Harris, C.I. (1993) Whiteness as property. *Harvard Law Review*, 106, 1707–91.

Hartman, S. (2008) *Lose Your Mother: A Journey Along the Atlantic Slave Route*. London: Macmillan.

Hartman, S.V. (2010) *Scenes of Subjection: Terror, Slavery, and Self-Making in Nineteenth-Century America*. New York: Oxford University Press.

Jackson, N.M. (2016) Imperial suspect: policing colonies within 'post'-imperial England.

Callaloo, 39(1), 203-215.

Kalulé, P. (2019) *Kalimba*. Cornwall, UK: Guillemot Press.

Kapoor, N. (2013) The advancement of racial neoliberalism in Britain. *Ethnic and Racial Studies*, 36(6), 1028–46.

Kapoor, N. (2018) *Deport, Deprive, Extradite: 21st Century State Extremism*. London: Verso Books.

Karatani, R. (2003) *Defining British Citizenship: Empire, Commonwealth and Modern Britain*. London: Frank Cass.

King, A.D. (2015) *Urbanism, Colonialism, and the World-Economy*. London: Routledge.

Kinouani, G. (2019) On bodies that don't belong. *Race Reflections*, 3 August. Available at: https://racereflections.co.uk/2019/08/03/on-bodies-that-dont-belong/ (accessed 28 December 2019).

Kundnani, A. (2002) The death of multiculturalism. *Race & Class*, 43(4), 67–72.

Kundnani, A. (2012) Radicalisation: the journey of a concept. *Race & Class*, 54(2), 3–25.

Lefebvre, H. (1991) *The Production of Space*. Oxford: Blackwell.

Lentin, A. (2004) *Racism and Anti-Racism in Europe*. London: Pluto Press.

Lentin, A. and Titley, G. (2011) *The Crises of Multiculturalism: Racism in a Neoliberal Age*. London: Zed Books.

Leyshon, A. and Thrift, N. (1995) Geographies of financial exclusion: financial abandonment in Britain and the United States. *Transactions of the Institute of British Geographers*, 20(3), 312–41.

Li, T. (2010) To make live or let die? Rural dispossession and the protection of surplus populations. *Antipode*, 41, 66–93.

Mahmud, T. (1999) Colonialism and modern constructions of race: a preliminary inquiry. *University of Miami Law Review*, 53, 1219–999.

Manzoor-Khan, S. (2019) *Postcolonial Banter*. Kenilworth: Verve.

Mbembe, A. (2019) *Necropolitics*. Johannesburg: Wits University Press.

McCulloch, J. and Pickering, S. (2009) Pre-crime and counter-terrorism. *British Journal of Criminology*, 49(5), 628–45.

McIntyre, M. and Nast, H.J. (2011) Bio(necro)polis: Marx, surplus populations, and the spatial dialectics of reproduction and 'race'. *Antipode*, 43(5), 1465–88.

McKittrick, K. (2013) Plantation futures. *Small Axe: A Caribbean Journal of Criticism*, 17(3), 1–15.

Melamed, J. (2006) The spirit of neoliberalism: from racial liberalism to neoliberal multiculturalism. *Social Text*, 24(4), 1–24.

Miller, D. and Sabir, R. (2012) Counter-terrorism as counterinsurgency in the UK 'war on terror'. In *Counter-terrorism and State Political Violence*, ed. D. Whyte and S. Poynting. London: Routledge, pp. 12–32.

Mitropoulos, A. (2018) Lifeboat capitalism, catastrophism, borders. *Dispatches Journal*, 1 [online], 19 November. Available at: http://dispatchesjournal.org/articles/162/ (accessed 25 October 2019).

Mitropoulos, A. (2019) Workers of the world unite. *New Socialist*. Available at: https://newsocialist.org.uk/workers-world-unite/ (accessed 31 December 2019).

Modood, T. (2005) *Multicultural Politics: Racism, Ethnicity and Muslims in Britain*. Edinburgh: Edinburgh University Press.

Moore, J. (2014) Is the empire coming home? Liberalism, exclusion and the punitiveness of the British state. In *Papers from the British Criminology Conference*, vol. 14, pp. 31–48.

Moreton-Robinson, A. (2015) *The White Possessive: Property, Power, and Indigenous Sovereignty*. Minneapolis, MN: University of Minnesota Press.

Nightingale, C.H. (2012) *Segregation: A Global History of Divided Cities*. Chicago, IL: University of Chicago Press.

Nijjar, J.S. (2018) Echoes of empire: excavating the colonial roots of Britain's war on gangs. *Social Justice*, 45(2/3), 147–201.

Nixon, R. (2011) *Slow Violence and the Environmentalism of the Poor*. Cambridge, MA: Harvard University Press.

Nixon, R (2012) Neoliberalism, genre, and 'the tragedy of the commons'. *PMLA*, 127(3), 593–99.

Northam, G. (1989) *Shooting in the Dark: Riot Police in Britain*. London: Faber & Faber.

Parizot, C. (2018) Viscous spatialities: the spaces of the Israeli permit regime of access and movement. *South Atlantic Quarterly*, 117(1), 21–42.

Paul, K. (1997) *Whitewashing Britain: Race and Citizenship in the Postwar Era*. Ithaca, NY: Cornell University Press.

Pitcher, B. (2016) Race, debt and the welfare state. *New Formations*, 87, 47–63.

Ponsot, M. (2011) *Easy*. New York: Alfred A. Knopf.

Puar, J.K. (2017) *Terrorist Assemblages: Homonationalism in Queer Times*. Durham, NC: Duke University Press.

Quijano, A. (2007) Coloniality and modernity/rationality. *Cultural Studies*, 21(2–3), 168–78.

Razack, S. (2015) *Dying from Improvement: Inquests and Inquiries into Indigenous Deaths in Custody*. Toronto: University of Toronto Press.

Robinson, C.J. (2005) *Black Marxism: The Making of the Black Radical Tradition*. Chapel Hill, NC: University of North Carolina Press.

Rodney, W. (2018) *How Europe Underdeveloped Africa*. London and New York: Verso.

Roediger, D.R. (1994) *Toward the Abolition of Whiteness: Essays on Race, Politics, and Working Class History*. New York: Verso.

Schwarz, B. (2000) Actually existing postcolonialism. *Radical Philosophy*, 104, 16–24.

Sharma, S. and Nijjar, J. (2018) The racialized surveillant assemblage: Islam and the fear of terrorism. *Popular Communication*, 16(1), 72–85.

Shilliam, R. (2018) *Race and the Undeserving Poor: From Abolition to Brexit*. Bristol: Agenda Books.

Shire, W. (2011) *Teaching My Mother How to Give Birth*. London: Mouthmark.

Simone, A. (2018) *Improvised Lives: Rhythms of Endurance in an Urban South*. London: John Wiley & Sons.

Sivanandan, A. (1981) From resistance to rebellion: Asian and Afro-Caribbean struggles in Britain. *Race & Class*, 23, 111–52.

Slobodian, Q. (2018) *Globalists: The End of Empire and the Birth of Neoliberalism*. Cambridge, MA: Harvard University Press.

Srnicek, N. (2018) *Platform Capitalism*. Cambridge: Polity.

Tendayi Achiume, E. (2019) Migration as decolonisation. *Stanford Law Review*, 71(6), 1509–73.

Tomba, M. (2019) *Insurgent Universality: An Alternative Legacy of Modernity*. New York: Oxford University Press.

Tuck, E. and Yang, W. (2012) Decolonization is not a metaphor. *Decolonization: Indigeneity, Education & Society*, 1(1), 1–40.

Turner, J. (2018) Internal colonisation: the intimate circulations of empire, race and liberal government. *European Journal of International Relations*, 24(4), 765–90.

Virdee, S. (2014) *Racism, Class and the Racialized Outsider*. Basingstoke: Palgrave Macmillan.

Wadud, A. (2018) *Crosslight for Youngbird*. New York: Nightboat Books.

Wagner, K.A. (2018) Savage warfare: violence and the rule of colonial difference in early British counterinsurgency. *History Workshop Journal*, 85, 217–37.

Walia, H. (2013) *Undoing Border Imperialism*. Chicago, IL: AK Press.

Williams, P. (2015) Criminalising the other: challenging the race-gang nexus. *Race & Class*, 56(3), 18–35.

Wolfe, P. (2006) Settler colonialism and the elimination of the native. *Journal of Genocide Research*, 8(4), 387–409.

Wynter, S. (2003) Unsettling the coloniality of being/power/truth/freedom: towards the human, after man, its overrepresentation – An argument. *CR: The New Centennial Review*, 3(3), 257–33.

Wynter, S. and McKittrick, K. (2014) Unparalleled catastrophe for our species? Or, to give humanness a different future. *Conversations*, 8 December, pp. 9–89.

Index

The Pluto Press Newsletter

Hello friend of Pluto!

Want to stay on top of the best radical books
we publish?

Then sign up to be the first to hear about our
new books, as well as special events,
podcasts and videos.

You'll also get 50% off your first order with us
when you sign up.

Come and join us!

Go to bit.ly/PlutoNewsletter

Thanks to our Patreon Subscribers:

Abdul Alkalimat
Andrew Perry

Who have shown their generosity and comradeship in difficult times.

Check out the other perks you get by subscribing to our Patreon – visit patreon.com/plutopress.

Subscriptions start from £3 a month.